Georgian Faces: Portrait of a County

Gwen Yarker

Dorset County Museum
15 January–30 April 2011

The exhibition has been sponsored by

The Anthony du Boulay Charitable Trust.
Axa Art Insurance Limited.
Duke's of Dorchester, Fine Art Auctioneers.
Farrow & Ball.
R. K. Harrison Group Limited.
Henry Ling Limited.
The Mansel-Pleydell Trust.
Henry Moss-Blundell, in memory of Mrs Moss-Blundell.
The Heritage Lottery Fund, South West.
Humphries Kirk L.L.P.
NADFAS: Wessex Region and Dorset County.
The Anthony Pitt-Rivers Trust.

The catalogue has been published with the support of
The Paul Mellon Centre for British Art

Designed, Typeset & Printed by Henry Ling Ltd, at the Dorset Press, Dorchester, DT1 1HD

Frontispiece: *George Pitt, First Lord Rivers surveying Dorset Militia,* Thomas Gooch, 1782, private collection.
Inside front and inside back covers: *Detail from map of Dorset showing Dorchester,* Isaac Taylor, 1765
Back Cover: *Rebecca Steward,* 1783, Thomas Beach, DNH&AS.

ISBN 978-0-900341-05-2

Printed in Dorset 2010

Contents

On a visit to the Dorset County Museum in 2008 I saw the portrait of twelve-year old *Thomas Rackett* and his parents by George Romney. It had recently been purchased following a successful fundraising campaign supported by the Heritage Lottery Fund South West, Art Fund and considerable local effort.

The curators outlined some of the projects that would result from the acquisition. This included the exhibition, *Georgian Faces: Portrait of a County,* for which this catalogue, supported by the Paul Mellon Centre for Studies in British Art, provides the ideal companion.

It is particularly gratifying that the relevance of several portraits included in both the catalogue and the exhibition has resulted from the recent work of the Public Catalogue Foundation in the county – a charity which I am delighted to support as Patron.

I wish the exhibition every success and know that the accompanying catalogue will be a source of interest and pleasure for years to come.

Camilla

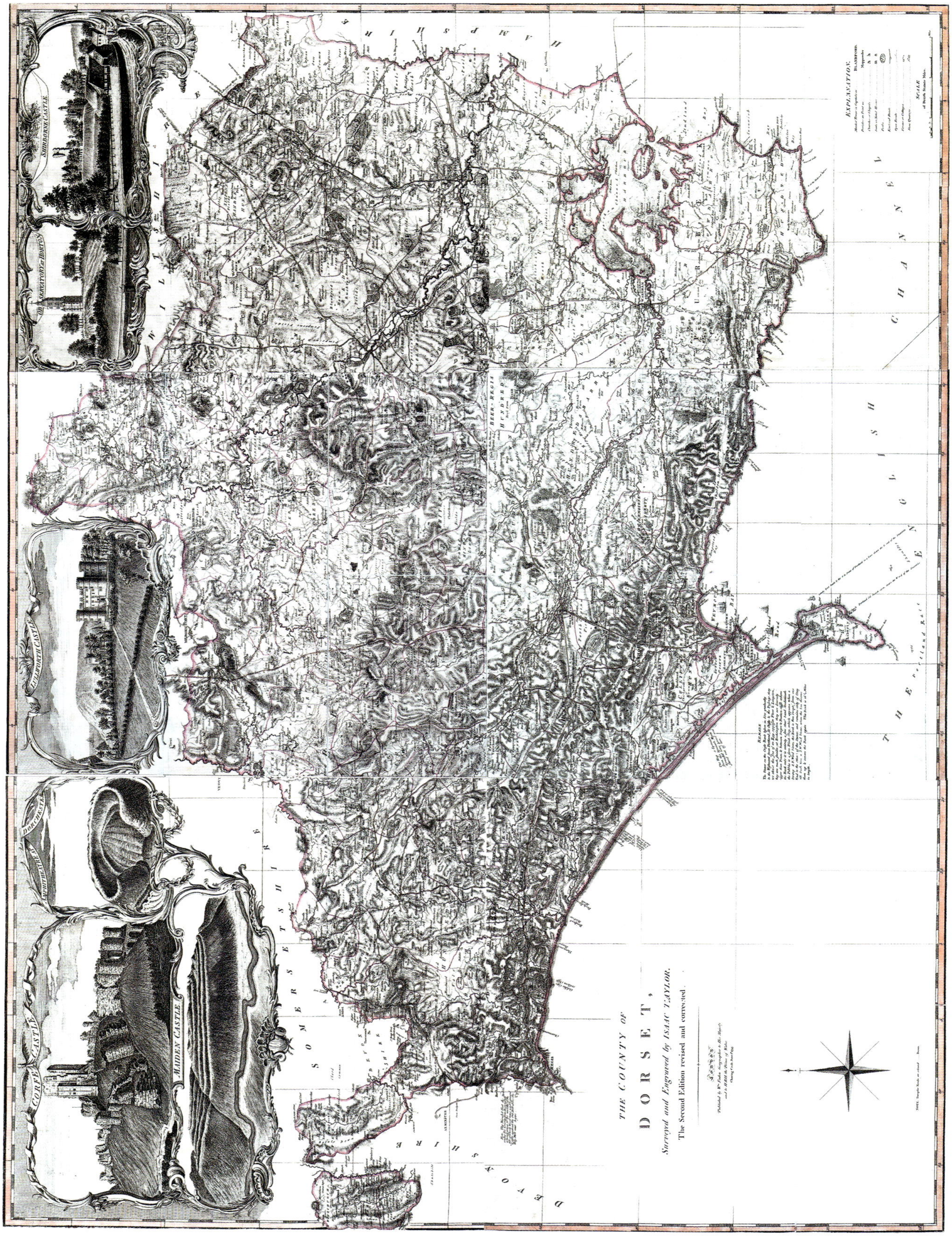

The County of Dorset, map surveyed and engraved by Isaac Taylor, 1795.

Director's Foreword

When I first arrived at the Dorset County Museum in April 2009 I was delighted to discover that preparations were well underway for a major exhibition examining the county in the eighteenth century. A project that began with the acquisition of the Rackett family portraits by George Romney – demonstrating once again that additions to a collection can so often prove to be the starting point for great exhibitions and new museum developments – it was the ambition of *Georgian Faces: Portrait of a County* that so captured my imagination, especially because I also knew how little funding would be available to deliver it from our own resources.

Yet working closely with the curator, Gwen Yarker, it was also clear how *Georgian Faces* would not only be delivered, but would be a triumph. Gwen's research and scholarship had inspired a wide range of local people, institutions, sponsors and donors to get behind the exhibition, graphically demonstrating the continued relevance, sense of belonging and community support for the Dorset Natural History and Archaeological Society – a state of affairs that dates right back to Thomas Rackett himself. Indeed, it is marvellous that so many private lenders have been sufficiently enthused by the concept of the exhibition to allow us to include their paintings within it. Their faith, trust and support for the Society and its Museum has been unwavering and without them the exhibition simply would not have been possible. Equally important has been the continued backing of the President, Vice Presidents, Chairman, Board of Trustees, Members, Volunteers and Staff of the Dorset Natural History and Archaeological Society. Without their input and encouragement the project could not possibly have come to fruition in the successful manner that it has.

The Society is indebted to the Duchess of Cornwall for her interest and support. Our thanks must go to the Anthony du Boulay Charitable Trust; Axa Art Insurance Limited; RK Harrison Insurance Services; Duke's of Dorchester, Fine Art Auctioneers; Farrow & Ball; Henry Ling Limited; the Mansel-Pleydell Trust; Henry Moss-Blundell in memory of Mrs Moss-Blundell; the Heritage Lottery Fund South West; Humphries Kirk LLP; Wessex NADFAS; Dorset DFAS and the Anthony Pitt-Rivers Trust for their generous sponsorship. We also extend our deepest gratitude to the Paul Mellon Centre for British Art for its support of this catalogue.

Recognition must also go to George Wickham and Dave Penman for their photographic work, and all of the institutional lenders who have been so supportive: Blandford Town Council; Holburne Museum; the Keep Military Museum, Dorchester; the Linnean Society; the National Portrait Gallery; the National Trust; Poole Museum Service and the Russell-Cotes Art Gallery and Museum.

Above all though I want to thank Gwen Yarker for everything she has done to make every aspect of *Georgian Faces: Portrait of a County* a success. She has voluntarily worked countless hours to make it all possible, and I'm sure I speak for all of us involved when I say that the Society and its Museum are deeply grateful for her knowledge, curatorial skill, enthusiasm, effort and commitment. She should be warmly congratulated both on the exhibition and on this wonderful catalogue, which will provide lasting testimony to her work.

Dr Jon Murden
July 2010

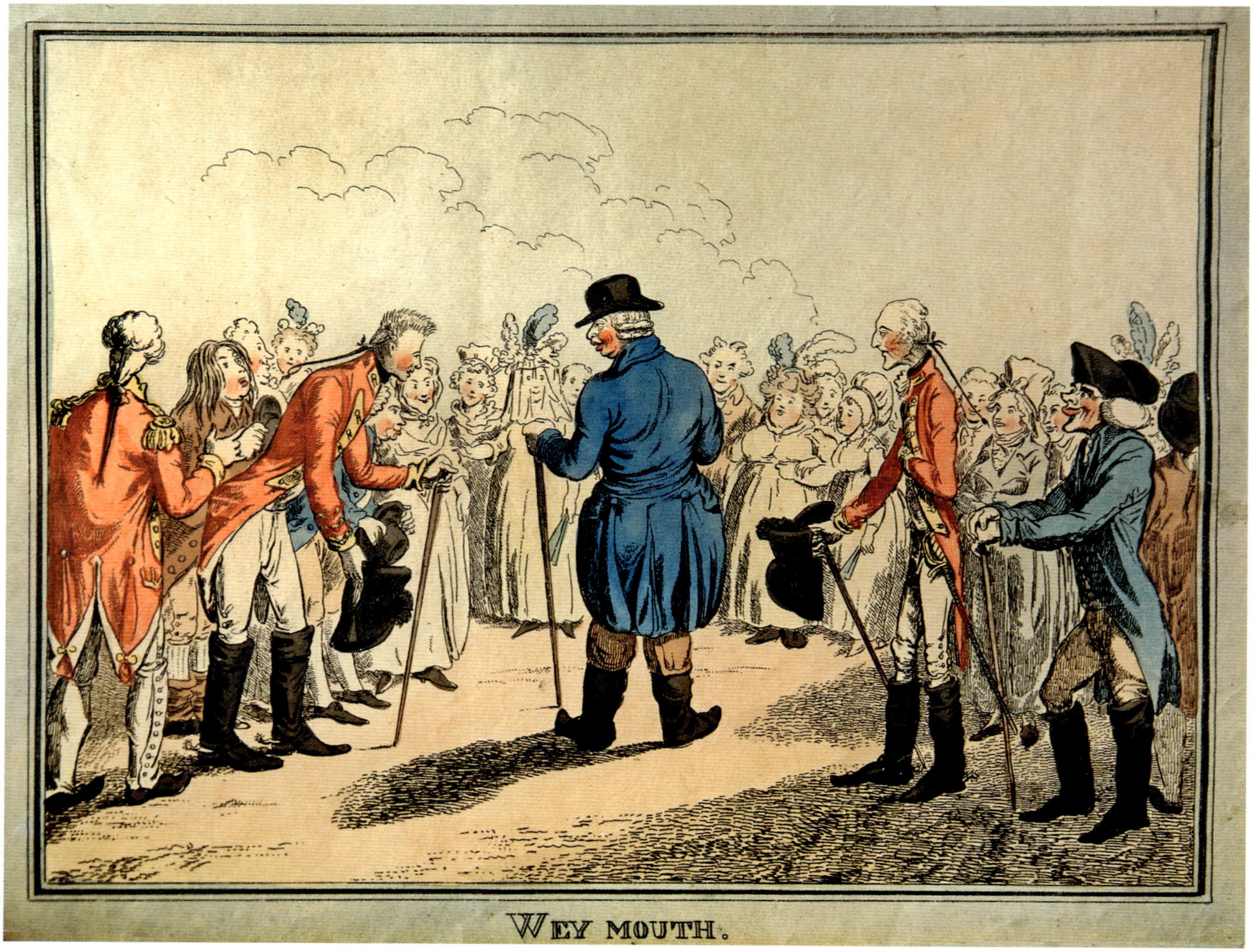

Wey Mouth, James Gillray, 1797.

Curator's Preface

Defining Dorset in the Eighteenth Century

The idea for this exhibition resulted from the successful purchase of George Romney's portraits of the Rackett family in 2008. I became aware, whilst researching the life of the Reverend Thomas Rackett and his extensive circle of friends and acquaintances, of just how formative the century was in shaping the county and its institutions, not least the Dorset County Museum itself. More than that, it was clear that many of the people whose portraits are included in this exhibition were of national, as well as local significance.

Many of the sitters contributed to the first comprehensive account of an English county written during the eighteenth century, the Reverend John Hutchins's *History and Antiquities of the County of Dorset*. First published in 1774, Hutchins surveyed parish by parish the history, people, topography and customs of the county, literally defining Dorset. The engravings for the first edition were sponsored by landowners, from the Earl of Ilchester to James Frampton; Rackett himself drew many of the illustrations for the second edition, which Dr. Richard Pulteney supervised into the presses. It is therefore with some justification that this exhibition, and its accompanying catalogue, is entitled *Georgian Faces: Portrait of a County*. The exhibition approximately covers the period from the death of George I in 1727 until the end of the century; roughly from the beginning of Hutchins's research to the publication of the second edition. It is with Hutchins in mind that the exhibition and catalogue are ordered: not chronologically, or by artist, but by sitter. This means the portraits are grouped along social lines, from the King and powerful landowners to the 'merchant princes' of prosperous Poole, the scientists and antiquarians of Blandford and finally painters and architects.

Several parameters determined the choice of pictures; only sitters who lived in or regularly visited Dorset are included. This means important collections of eighteenth-century portraits that have arrived in the county subsequently, most notably those from Holland House, have been omitted. The modest nature of the exhibition has also meant pictures have been borrowed for the importance of the sitter, and not always their artistic merit. Another priority has been to show less well-known pictures from the County's museums as well as from private collections. Although it is an attempt at showing the breadth of rural achievement, it is in no sense encyclopaedic, several notable faces are absent including people who were born in the county but made their careers elsewhere, for example Thomas Coram and Thomas Masterman Hardy.

Three of the artists represented in the exhibition – Sir James Thornhill, Giles Hussey and Thomas Beach – were all born in Dorset, and I have attempted to show that the county was an important influence on their careers. Thornhill returned to Dorset later in life when building a house near Stalbridge, as his London practice began to wane. The Roman Catholic Giles Hussey, employed by other recusant families, revealed a very specific patronage circle within the county. Despite his metropolitan training, Beach remained reliant on Dorset patrons throughout his career. This has been neatly illustrated by the recent discovery of his diary for the year 1798, which shows his peripatetic existence, and the houses and families he visited in the county. The tradition of local patronage endured into the nineteenth century, when Alfred Stevens was sent to study in Italy through the assistance of the Reverend Thomas Rackett.

I would like to extend my thanks to the Paul Mellon Centre for British Art for supporting my research and the London Library in allowing me to be a Carlyle member whilst working on the catalogue. I am particularly grateful to Jonathan Yarker for helping me with the structure and direction of the project, to Francesca Radcliffe for her work on the index, to Eliza Oxley and Rosemary Goad for their careful editing and to Roger Peers both for editing and advising on all things Dorset.

I am indebted to Jon Murden for his enthusiasm and unwavering support. In addition I would like to express my thanks to Mark Pomeroy, Archivist of the Royal Academy of Arts; Emma Floyd, Librarian at the Paul Mellon Centre for British Art; Lynda Brooks, Librarian, and Ben Sherwood,

Linnean Society Library; Alastair Laing and James Grasby, National Trust; Ann Smith, Archivist at Sherborne Castle; the librarians at the Heinz Library and archivists at the Dorset History Centre. The Public Catalogue Foundation was also instrumental in the discovery of some of the portraits and their subsequent illustration in the catalogue.

I am also indebted to the following for their help, support, advice and encouragement: Brian Allen; Liz Arkell; John Astle; Alexandra Ault; Hugh Beach; Sue Beckett, Charles Beddington; Hugh Belsey; Mark Bond; Venetia Chattey; David Clammer; George Clarke; Jane Cunningham; Eddie and Dione Digby; Peter Down, Rosemary Dunhill; Anthony du Boulay; Elizabeth Einberg; Katharine Eustace; Mary Frampton; Michael Honeybone; Lucy Howarth; Anthony Jaggard; Maureen Keats; Laurence Keen; Lawrence Klein; Helen Kennett; John Kenworthy-Brown; Alex Kidson; Polly Legg; Victoria McDonagh, Brigid Martin; David Orr; Anthony Pitt-Rivers; Roger Quarm; Geoff Quilley; Francesca Radcliffe; Jane Roberts; Ingrid Roscoe; Ann Ross-Skinner; Guy Schwinge; Robin Simon; Julia Smith; George, John and David Solly; Greg Sullivan; Sue Taylor; Charlotte Townshend; Marjorie Trusted; Dick Vane-Wright; Duncan Walker; Elizabeth Waller; George Wickham; Amina Wright and Alison Yarrington.

Above all, I am deeply indebted to the private owners who have loaned their portraits for the exhibition.

Gwen Yarker, Curator

Explanation and Abbreviations

A Note on Hutchins

John Hutchins's *History and Antiquities of the County of Dorset* was first published in 1774 in two volumes, by John Nichols of London, the year after Hutchins died. Hutchins was helped in the project by various antiquarians including Richard Gough. A second edition, edited by Richard Gough and John Bowyer Nichols, with significant contributions by Dr. Richard Pulteney and the Reverend Thomas Rackett, was produced in four volumes between 1796 and 1815. A third edition in four volumes appeared between 1861 and 1874, edited by William Shipp and James Whitworth Hodson, and was re-issued in 1973. Although I have consulted all three editions, including an extra-illustrated second edition in the Dorset County Museum with inserted manuscript material, the references throughout are generally to the third, and most comprehensive edition.

Abbreviations:

DNH&AS: Dorset Natural History and Archaeological Society.
DHC, DCRO: Dorset History Centre, (formerly Dorset County Record Office).
NPG: National Portrait Gallery.
ODNB: Oxford Dictionary of National Biography.

Frequently cited sources:

Beach, 1934: E. Beach, *Thomas Beach A Dorset Portrait Painter,* London, 1934.

Frampton, 1885: *The Journal of Mary Frampton from the Year 1779 until the Year 1849,* ed. Harriot Georgiana Mundy, London, 1885.

Graves and Cronin, 1899: A. Graves & W.V. Cronin, *A History of the Works of Sir Joshua Reynolds,* London 1899–1901.

Hutchins: J. Hutchins, *History and Antiquities of the County of Dorset,* London, 1774; 1796–1815; 1861–1874.

Mannings, 2000: David Mannings, Joshua Reynolds, Martin Postle, *Sir Joshua Reynolds: A Complete Catalogue of His Paintings,* New Haven and London, 2000.

Nichols, 1812–1816: J. Nichols, *Biographical and Literary Anecdotes of W. Bowyer, and of many of his learned friends, containing an incidental view of the progress and advancement of literature in this Kingdom, from the beginning of the present Century to the end of the year 1777, etc*, London, 1812–1816.

Oswald: A. Oswald, *Country Houses of Dorset,* London, 1935.

Sloman, 2002: S. Sloman, *Pickpocketing the Rich: Portrait Painting in Bath* 1720–1800, exh. cat., Bath, (Holburne Museum of Art), 2002.

Vertue, 1929–47: G. Vertue, eds. L. Cust and A. Hind, 'The Notebooks of George Vertue', *The Walpole Society,* London, 1929–47.

Waterhouse: E. Waterhouse, *British 18th Century Painters in oils and crayons,* Suffolk, 1981.

Whitley: T. Whitley, *Artists and their friends in England 1700–1799*, London, 1928.

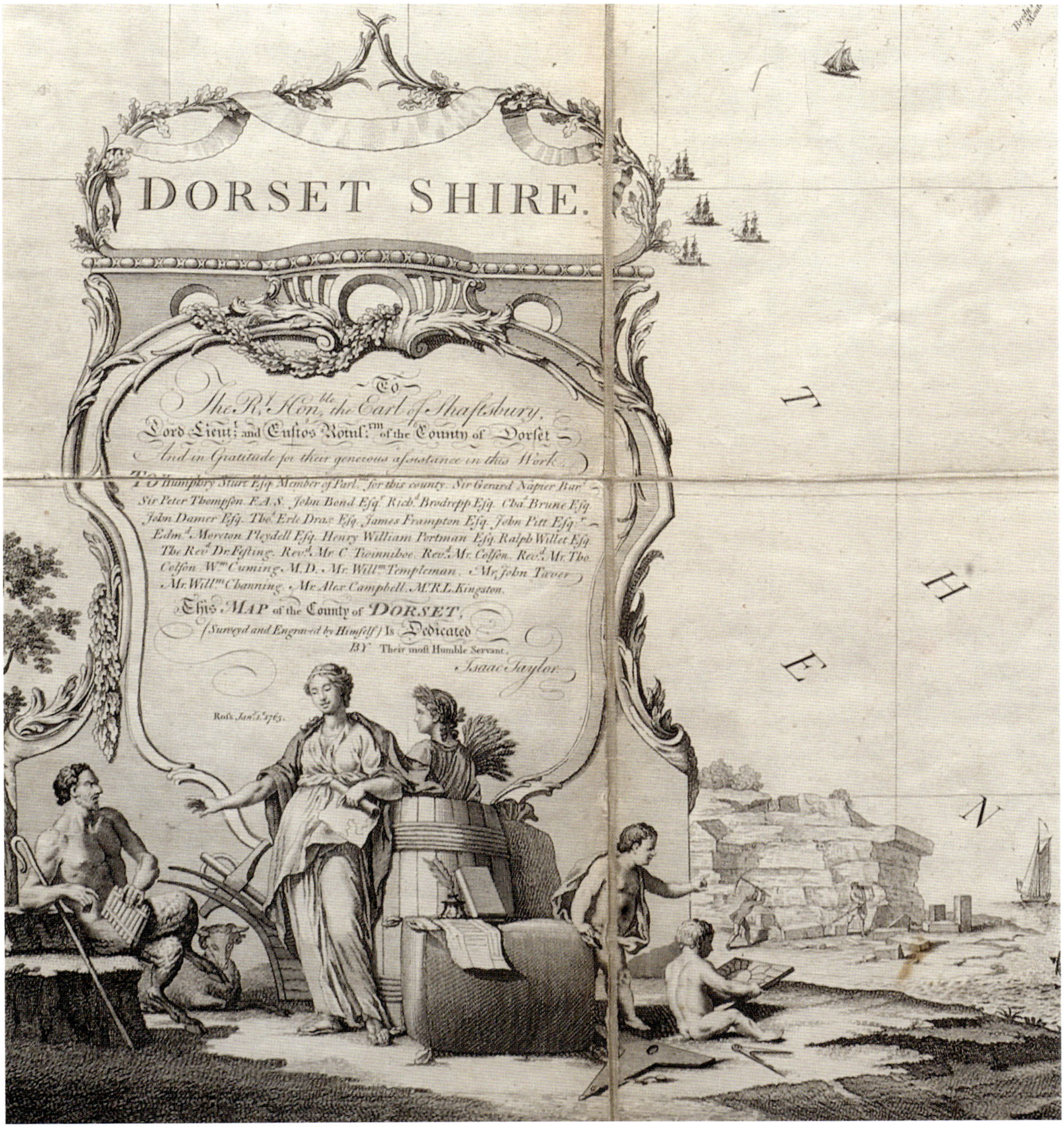

Detail from map *Dorsetshire* by Isaac Taylor, 1765.

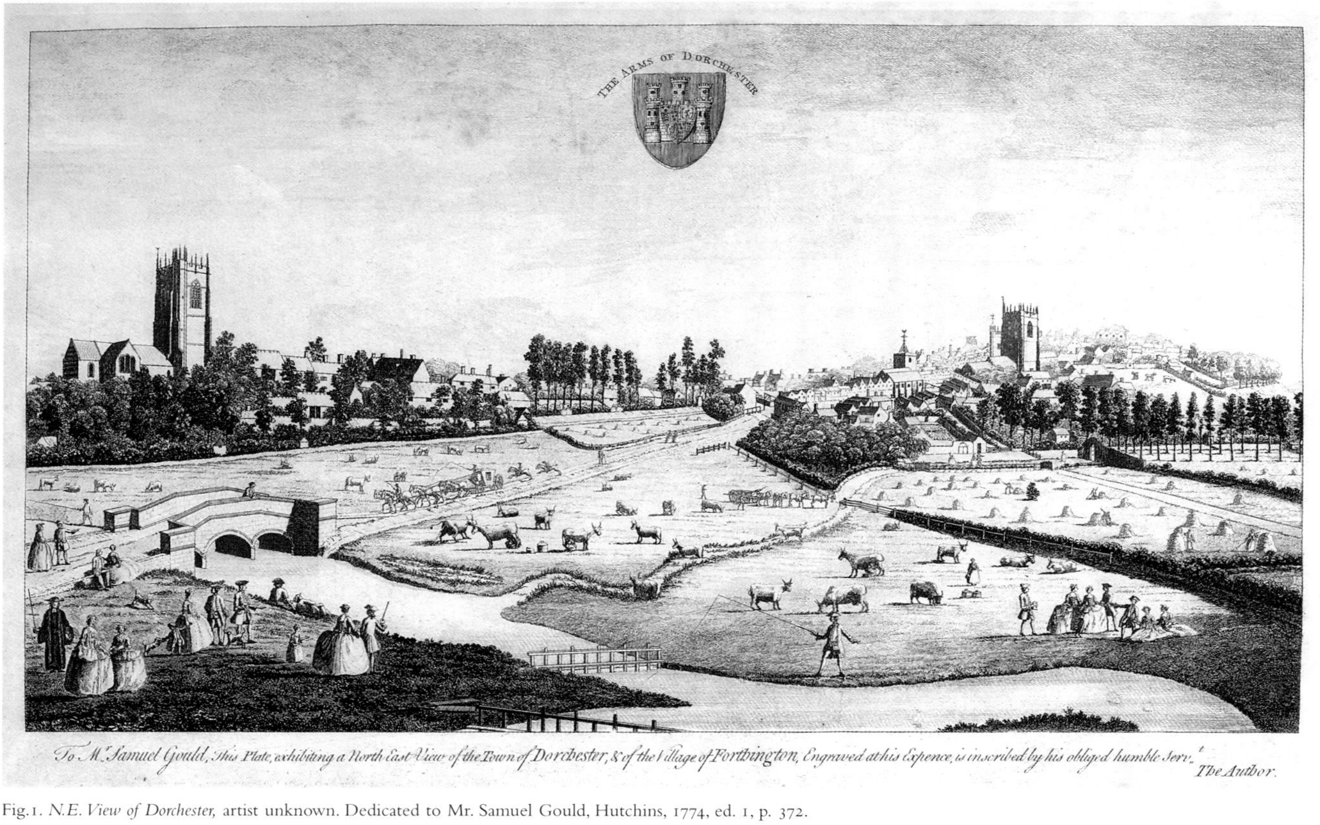

Fig.1. *N.E. View of Dorchester,* artist unknown. Dedicated to Mr. Samuel Gould, Hutchins, 1774, ed. 1, p. 372.

A Portrait of Dorset in the Eighteenth Century

Introduction

The view of Dorchester dedicated to Samuel Gould in 1774 (fig. 1) offers an instructive portrait of the county in the eighteenth century as an ordered, productive landscape, populated by affluent, fashionably dressed figures. In fact Dorset went through a period of almost continual change from the accession of George II in 1727 until his grandson George III's last visit to Weymouth in 1805. Increased mechanization of agriculture and major urban building projects – in Blandford Forum, Gillingham, Wareham and Dorchester itself – changed the face of the county; not to mention the rapid expansion of Poole as a mercantile centre and Weymouth as a fashionable resort.[1] Increased affluence and the enclosure of land saw the rise of the great estate, and the building and remodelling of important houses from Vanbrugh's Eastbury near Blandford Forum in the 1720s to William Chambers's Milton Abbey (fig. 15) in the 1770s, completed by James Wyatt. These social changes inevitably resulted in certain frictions, precipitating the foundation of the Dorset Militia in 1757, and the Dorset Volunteer Rangers in 1794. *Georgian Faces: Portrait of a County* includes portraits of many of the people who witnessed this period of change, and were active participants in shaping Dorset during the eighteenth century.

The anonymous engraving of Dorchester suggests a finite, contained world, but the presence of a stage-coach on the London road reminds us that increased mobility was to revolutionise the speed at which news, people and ideas travelled. Many of Dorset's wealthiest residents owned houses in London – which by the mid-century could be reached in a day – and those fashions, ideas and intellectual currents which shaped eighteenth-century London quickly percolated into the county. By the 1780s Blandford Forum became the centre of a group of scientists and antiquarians, including Dr Richard Pulteney (cat. 54), the Reverend Thomas Rackett (cat. 43) and Tiberius Cavallo (cat. 55), of national and international significance, positioning Dorset as an unlikely centre of enlightenment thought and scientific discovery.[2] Travel also brought tourists to Dorset, including Voltaire, Alexander Pope, Joseph Banks and Horace Walpole, and at the end of the century the whole court. This essay will illustrate the shifting political, social and economic landscape they experienced, positioning the sitters of *Georgian Faces* in their immediate local and broader national contexts.

Landowners and the Land

Gould's engraving comes from John Hutchins's ambitious *History and Antiquities of the County of Dorset*, published in 1774.[3] The *History* offers a fascinating lens through which to read the county during the century.

Impressive in scope, Hutchins chronicled the county parish-by-parish, listing buildings, monuments, family pedigrees and histories in two richly illustrated volumes. Such an arrangement reveals the preoccupation with land and its ownership; eligibility to vote relied on a property qualification, and was the principal source of wealth. Hutchins's dedication in the first edition (fig. 2) neatly articulates the social

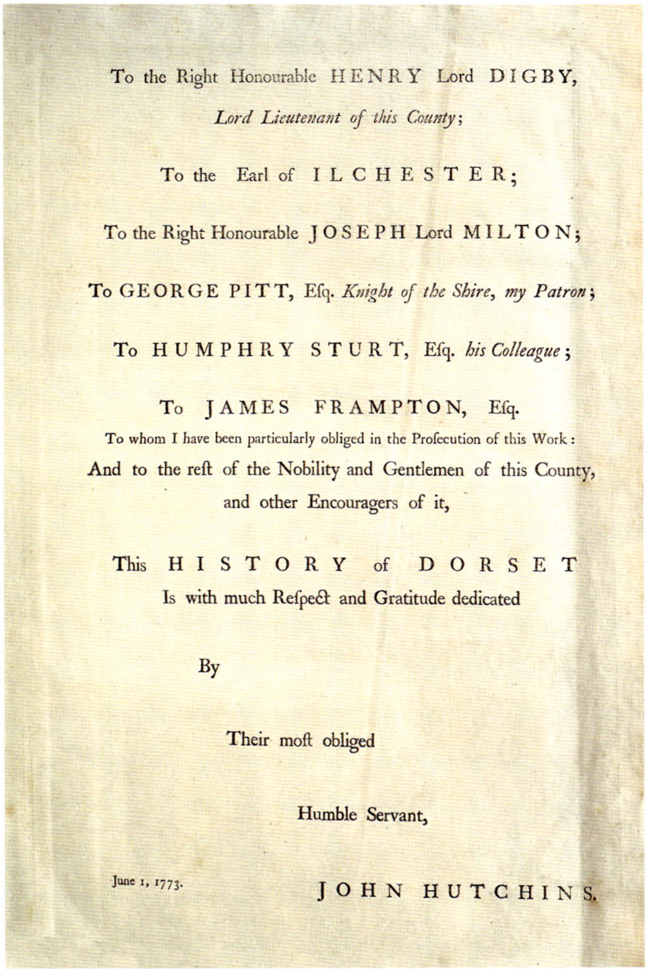

To the Right Honourable HENRY Lord DIGBY,
Lord Lieutenant of this County;

To the Earl of ILCHESTER;

To the Right Honourable JOSEPH Lord MILTON;

To GEORGE PITT, Efq. *Knight of the Shire, my Patron*;

To HUMPHRY STURT, Efq. *his Colleague*;

To JAMES FRAMPTON, Efq.
To whom I have been particularly obliged in the Profecution of this Work:
And to the reft of the Nobility and Gentlemen of this County,
and other Encouragers of it,

This HISTORY of DORSET
Is with much Refpect and Gratitude dedicated

By

Their moft obliged

Humble Servant,

June 1, 1773. JOHN HUTCHINS.

Fig. 2. *Dedication*, John Hutchins, 1774, ed. 1,1.

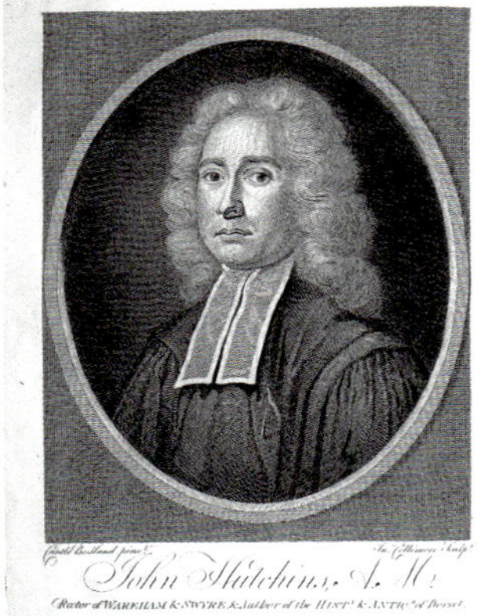

Fig. 3. *The Reverend John Hutchins (1698–1773)*, after Cantlo Bestland, by John Collimore, Hutchins, ed.2,4,xxvii.

stratification of the county: at the head the Lord Lieutenant (cat. 9) and major landowners, the Earl of Ilchester (cat. 15), Lord Milton (fig. 14), Hutchins's patron George Pitt (cats. 26,27), Humphrey Sturt (fig. 6); then James Frampton senior and other members of the gentry like John Bragge (cat. 38), the Bonds (cats. 33–35) and Trenchards (cat. 40); followed by professional men like Dr William Cuming (fig. 24) and some tradesmen, who all enabled the first edition to be completed. Hutchins (fig. 3) wrote his history by studying the papers of those same Dorset families, who, at their own expense, supplied him with engravings of their houses, and then subscribed to the volumes.[4]

Landowners formed the largest unit of political and economic power in the county, with its population of 113,583, reaffirming the grip of the aristocracy on government, especially the executive machinery of local government. Even gentry with a modest estate needed a capital outlay of about £30,000. Apart from agriculture, the other industries consisted chiefly of Portland and Purbeck quarrying, hemp and net production and some shipbuilding. Ball clay-mining near Wareham by men like Thomas Hyde (cat. 50) resulted in 1,400 tons of white potter's clay supplied to Josiah Wedgwood's pottery business from Dorset by 1771.[5]

Dorset's economy was primarily agricultural; during the period many estates were radically overhauled. In the 1760s, several landowners like Humphrey Sturt and James Frampton senior employed Isaac Taylor to survey and draw up highly detailed estate maps as part of the drive to make land holdings more efficient and improve profitability.

In 1764 Taylor was employed to document Frampton's Moreton estate in considerable detail (fig. 4), listing the revenue from every field. The plan of the estate included Taylor's drawing of Frampton's new manor house, possibly designed by Blandford Forum builder and architect, Francis Cartwright (fig. 5). In 1782 Frampton wrote to his thirteen-year old son, James: 'my general plan, besides rebuilding the old Family mansion, etc., has been by some few purchases, and ornamenting the Estate, round it, to contribute towards making the whole as compleat as the nature of the Country would well admit of.'[6]

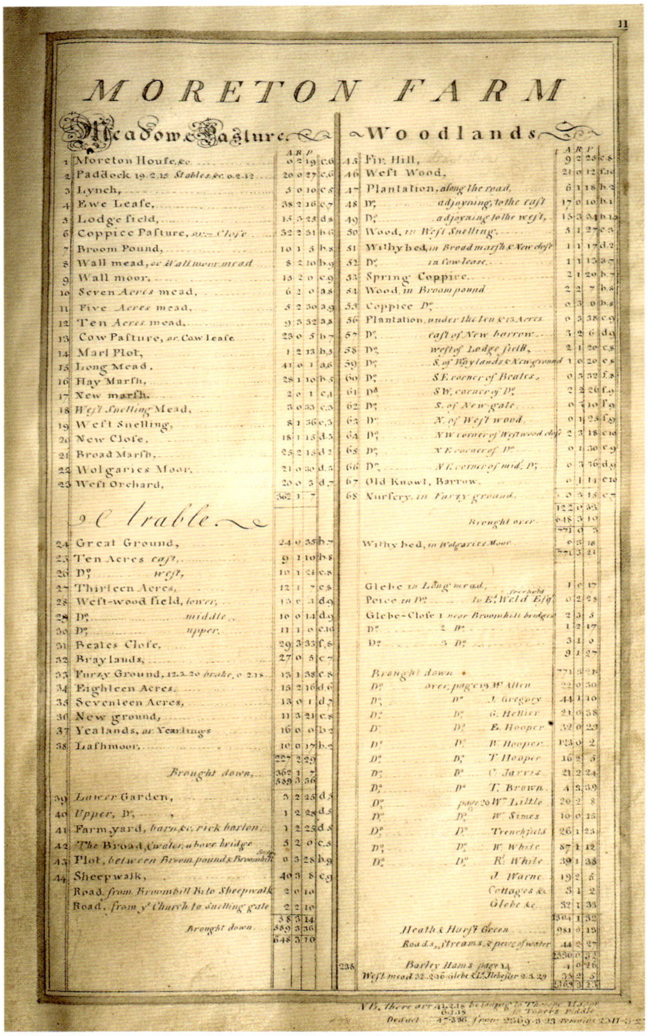

11

MORETON FARM

Meadow & Pasture.

		A	R	P	
1	Moreton House, &c.	0	2	19	c.6
2	Paddock 19.2.15 *Stables &c.* 0.2.12	20	0	27	c.6
3	Lynch,	3	0	10	c.5
4	Ewe Lease,	38	2	16	c.7
5	Lodge field,	15	3	25	d.8
6	Coppice Pasture, *or Close*	32	2	31	b.6
7	Broom Pound,	10	1	5	b.8
8	Wall mead, *or Wall moor mead*	8	2	10	b.9
9	Wall moor,	15	2	0	c.9
10	Seven *Acres* mead,	6	2	0	a.8
11	Five *Acres* mead,	5	2	30	a.9
12	Ten *Acres* mead,	9	3	32	a.8
13	Cow Pasture, *or* Cow lease	23	0	5	b.7
14	Marl Plot,	1	2	13	b.5
15	Long Mead,	41	0	1	a.6
16	Hay Marsh,	28	1	10	b.5
17	New marsh,	2	0	1	c.4
18	*West Snelling* Mead,	3	0	33	c.3
19	West Snelling,	8	1	36	c.3
20	New Close,	18	1	15	d.3
21	Broad Marsh,	25	2	15	d.2
22	Wolgaries Moor,	21	0	30	d.3
23	West Orchard,	20	0	3	d.7
		362	1	7	

Arable.

		A	R	P	
24	Great Ground,	24	0	35	b.7
25	Ten Acres *east*,	9	1	10	b.8
26	D° *west*,	10	1	23	c.8
27	Thirteen Acres,	12	1	7	c.8
28	West-wood field, *lower*,	13	0	3	d.9
29	D° *middle*	10	0	14	d.9
30	D° *upper*,	11	1	0	c.10
31	Beales Close,	29	3	33	f.8
32	Braylands,	27	0	5	c.7
33	Furzy Ground, 12.3.20 *brake*, 0.2.18	13	1	38	c.8
34	Eighteen Acres,	15	2	16	d.6
35	Seventeen Acres,	13	0	1	d.7
36	New ground,	11	3	21	c.8
37	Yealands, *or* Yearlings	16	0	0	b.2
38	Lashmoor,	10	0	17	b.2
		227	2	29	
	Brought down,	362	1	7	
		589	3	36	
39	*Lower* Garden,	3	2	25	d.5
40	*Upper*, D°,	1	2	28	d.5
41	Farm yard, *barn &c. rick barton*	1	2	23	d.5
42	*The* Broad, *water above bridge*	5	2	0	c.5
43	Plot, *between Broom pound & Broomhill*	0	3	28	b.9
44	Sheepwalk,	40	3	8	c.9
	Road *from Broomhill Br. to Sheepwalk*	2	0	10	
	Road, *from yᵉ Church to Snelling gate*	2	2	10	
		58	3	14	
	Brought down	589	3	36	
		648	3	10	

Woodlands.

		A	R	P	
45	Fir Hill,	9	2	25	c.8
46	West Wood,	21	0	12	f.10
47	Plantation, *along the road*,	6	1	18	b.2
48	D° *adjoyning, to the east*	17	0	10	b.1
49	D° *adjoyning to the west*,	15	3	34	b.12
50	Wood, *in West Snelling*,	5	1	27	c.3
51	Withy bed, *in Broadmarsh & New close*	1	1	17	d.2
52	D° *in Cow lease*	1	1	13	a.7
53	Spring Coppice,	2	1	20	b.7
54	Wood, *in Broom pound*	2	2	7	b.8
55	Coppice *D°*	0	3	0	b.8
56	Plantation, *under the Ten & 13 Acres*	0	3	38	c.9
57	D° *east of New barrow*	3	2	6	d.9
58	D° *west of Lodge field*,	2	1	20	c.8
59	D° *S. of Braylands & New ground*	1	0	20	c.8
60	D° *S.E. corner of Beales*,	0	3	32	f.8
61	D° *S.W. corner of D°*	2	2	26	f.9
62	D° *S. of New gate*	0	3	10	f.9
63	D° *N. of West wood*	0	1	25	f.9
64	D° *N.W. corner of Westwood close*	2	3	18	c.10
65	D° *N.E. corner of D°*	0	1	30	c.9
66	D° *N.E. corner of mid. D°*	0	3	36	d.9
67	Old Knowl, Barrow,	0	1	14	c.10
68	Nursery, *in Furzy ground*,	0	3	15	c.7
		122	0	33	
	Brought over	648	3	10	
		771	0	3	
	Withy bed, *in Wolgaries Moor*	0	3	18	
		771	3	21	
	Glebe *in Long mead*,	1	0	17	
	Peice *in D°* *freehold to Ed. Weld Esq.*	0	2	28	
	Glebe-Close 1 *near Broomhill bridge*	2	3	5	
	D° 2 *D°*	1	2	17	
	D° 3 *D°*	3	1	0	
		9	1	27	
	Brought down	771	3	21	
	D° over, page 19 Wᵐ Allen	22	0	30	
	D° D° J. Gregory	44	1	10	
	D° D° G. Hellier	21	0	38	
	D° D° E. Hooper	32	0	23	
	D° D° W. Hooper	123	0	2	
	D° D° T. Hooper	16	2	5	
	D° D° C. Jarvis	21	2	24	
	D° D° T. Brown	4	3	39	
	D° page 20 Wᵐ Little	20	2	8	
	D° D° W. Simes	10	0	15	
	D° D° Trenchfield	26	1	23	
	D° D° W. White	87	1	12	
	D° D° R. White	39	1	38	
	J. Warne	19	2	5	
	Cottages &c.	3	1	2	
	Glebe &c.	32	1	33	
		1304	1	32	
	Heath & Hurst Green	981	0	13	
	Roads, Streams, & peice of water	44	2	27	
		2330	0	32	
235	*Barley Hams page 14*	4	0	26	
	West mead 32.2.36 Glebe Cl. Ilchester 2.3.29	35	2	5	
		2369	3	23	

Fig. 4. *Moreton Farm*, list and value from the Survey of Moreton Estate, Isaac Taylor, 1764–1770.

The acceleration of the agricultural revolution through developments in mechanization required the consolidation of traditional strips of land into larger fields. Between 1733 and 1778 Frampton senior reclaimed and enclosed heathland and using chalk marl planted conifers at Moreton Heath.[7] Arthur Young wrote in 1771 that all the land 'from Moreton to Dorchester is inclosed,' at least part of this formed Frampton's 10,000 acre estate.[8] Frampton made improvements in the development of water meadows along the rivers Frome and Piddle.[9] At Crichel, Humphrey Sturt (fig. 6) improved agriculture for his tenants, introducing the cultivation of new crops and experimenting with land reclamation and drainage on heathland.[10] Landowners also looked to diversify; Sturt by keeping carp in his new lake, which he sold in London and Bristol and

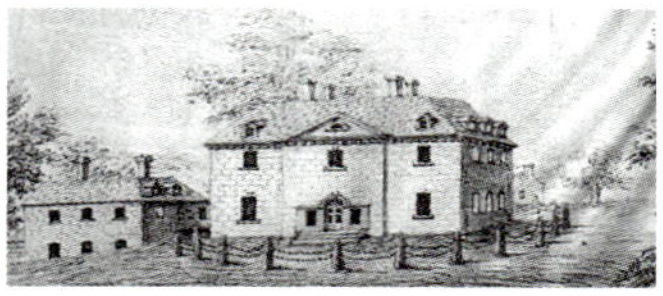

Fig. 5. *Moreton House*; detail from the Survey of Moreton Estate, Isaac Taylor, 1764–1770.

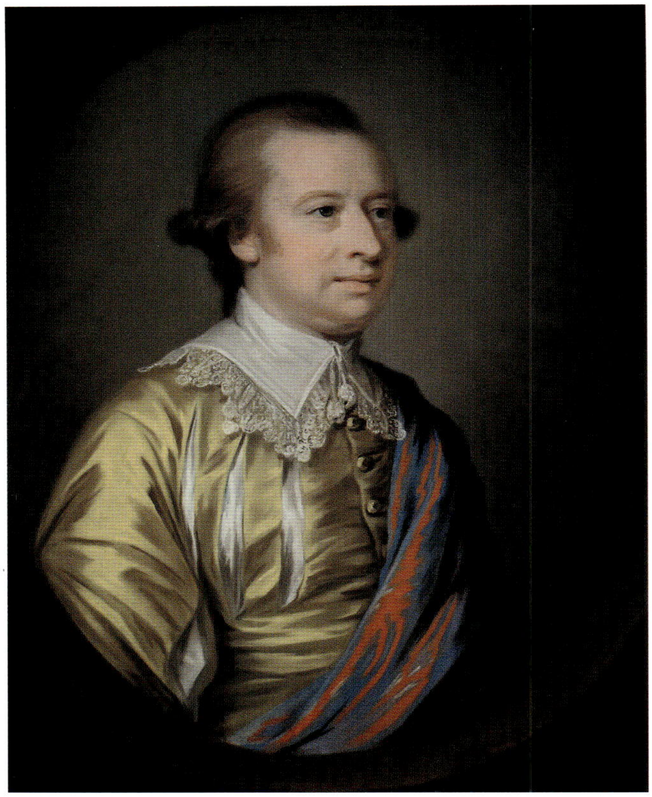

Fig. 6. *Humphry Sturt (1725–1786)*, pastel on paper, Katharine Read, c. 1760.

believed to be more profitable than revenue from his land.[11]

Thomas Erle Drax sought to promote mineral water from his estate at Charborough. Maps defining geology and rock structure were eagerly scrutinized for potential business opportunities. The close link between manor house, land and agricultural labourers is clearly demonstrated in George Egan's 1760 painting showing John Fry Hussey's Edmondsham House, Cranborne (fig. 7). Commissioned by Hussey as a gift to his wife, it shows the essential relationship between house and estate.

Political Dorset

As already noted, landowning came with political opportunities and responsibilities. Whilst peers were members of the House of Lords and eligible to become lord-lieutenant, the gentry could become members of the Commons, magistrates and holders of other local offices. For much of the century Dorset returned predominantly Whig MPs, and up to 1832 Dorset sent 20 members to Parliament, eighteen for the boroughs and two for the county. In the absence of ideological divisions the two parties were primarily concerned with the preservation of power based on patronage and kinship, directed by common economic concerns. Parliament existed to represent the people who mattered, with family relationships and personal loyalties paramount. Those politicians with a powerful following were the real powers in the land.[12] Dorset seats were the subject of considerable bribery and corruption at elections. At the beginning

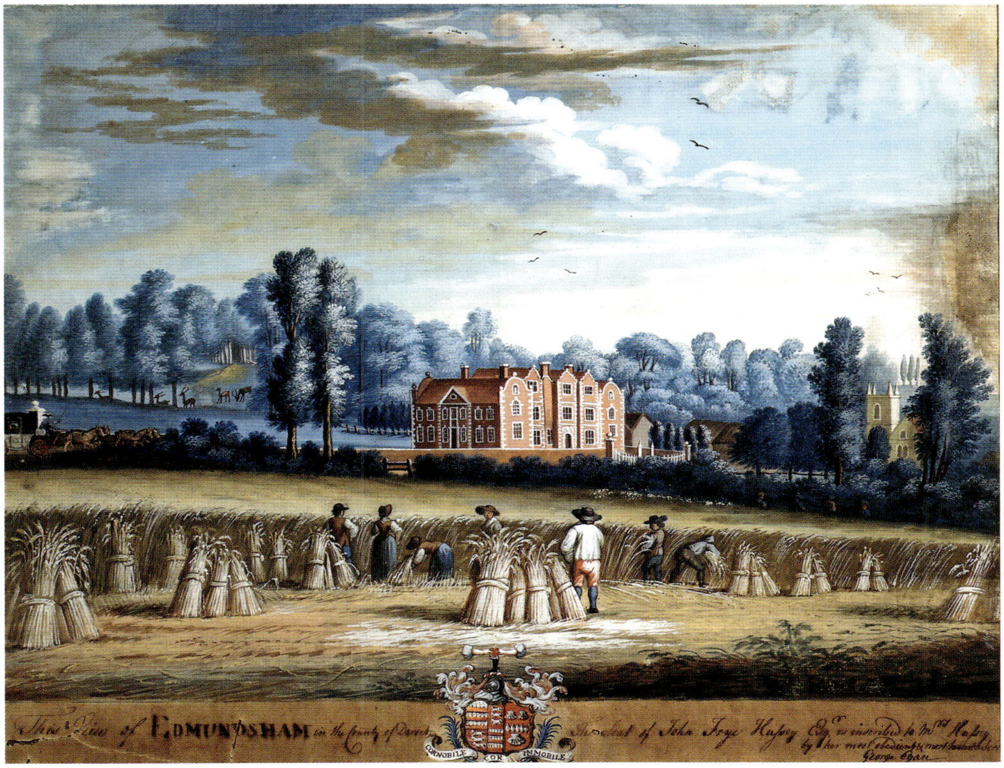

Fig. 7. *Edmunsham (sic) House,* bodycolour, George Egan, c. 1760.

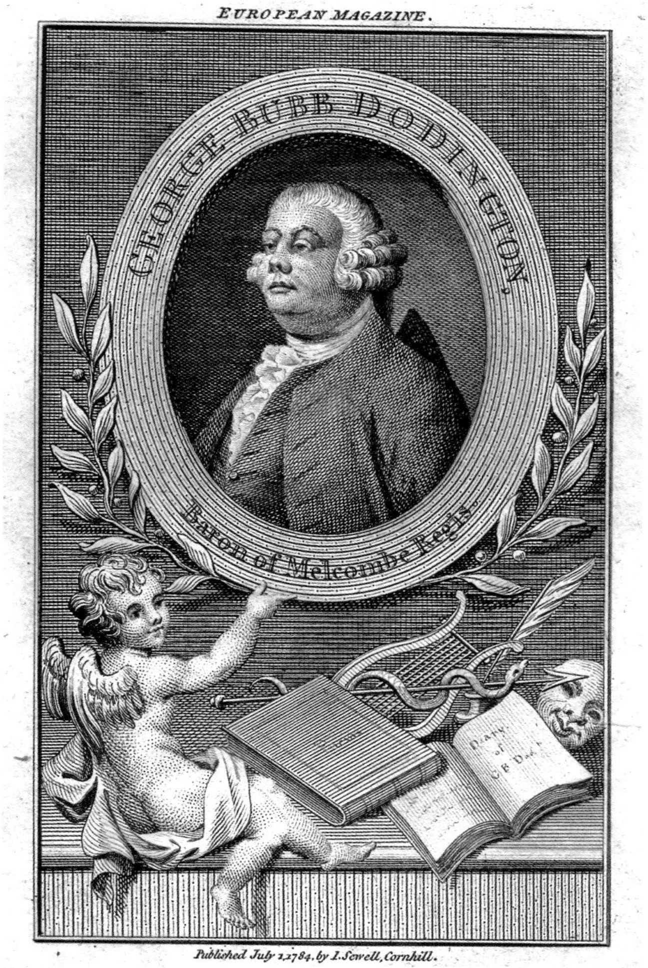

Fig. 8. *George Bubb Dodington, Baron Melcombe (1690/91–1762),* after an unknown artist, from the *European Magazine,* 1784.

of the century parliamentary seats in Dorset were simply purchased; the architect Christopher Wren bought his Dorset seat in 1701–1702.[13] The combined towns of Weymouth and Melcombe Regis returned four members to parliament, the only borough in the country apart from London, to do so, and was for a time represented and controlled by George Bubb Dodington (fig. 8), who spent his life in ill-judged political intrigue. Dodington was lampooned in William Hogarth's satire *Chairing the Member,* the last painting in his *Election* series (Sir John Soane Museum). Hogarth shows a corrupt Whig election campaign of 1754 with the fat candidate (resembling Dodington) precariously borne aloft on a tipping chair and ironically positioned under a goose in flight. The four paintings contain numerous allusions to the scheming and trickery that often took place to secure a seat.[14]

As Dodington's diary makes clear, intricate arrangements were made to ensure votes for the right candidate. In 1753 he arranged 'Lord Milton, Messrs. Drax, Trenchard, and most of the Whig party', for the election of Knights of the Shire (representatives of counties sent to advise the government) at the Antelope tavern in Dorchester. Dodington wrote: 'There could be no doubt of the Whigs carrying the election if they resolved upon it, because, to my knowledge, two-thirds of the property of the county were in their hands'.[15]

On the opposing Tory side, Henry Bankes (cat. 25) was an active friend and supporter of William Pitt the Younger. He was member for the rotten borough of Corfe Castle, from 1780 till 1826, after which he was elected for the county.[16] An accomplished scholar and trustee of the British Museum, for which he was the powerful parliamentary advocate, he fiercely opposed the1832 Reform Bill.[17] George Pitt, later Lord Rivers, who lived at Stratfield Saye in Hampshire, but owned the largest acreage of land in Dorset, represented Shaftesbury as a Tory MP in 1742 and Dorset from 1747–1774.[18] By the mid-eighteenth century party politics were largely dynastic; Pitt's son, George Pitt, 2nd Lord Rivers (cat. 23) took over his father's seat in 1774, serving as Tory MP for the county until 1790.

Dorset Families

Political loyalties were often cemented through familial connections. It is a feature of the genealogy of Dorset's most prominent families in the eighteenth century that although leading cosmopolitan social lives in London, they were frequently closely related. The Fox-Strangways of Melbury and Digbys of Sherborne Castle intermarried a number of times during the century, forging a powerful union of two Whig families. Originally from a relatively modest background, the Fox family rose to great prominence through the financial acumen of Sir Stephen Fox.[19] In 1736 Fox's eldest son, Stephen, (cat. 4) married Elizabeth Strangways Horner and acquired the large Strangways estates of Melbury and Abbotsbury. The Prime Minister, Robert Walpole, made him Lord Ilchester in 1741, and it is instructive that Fox displayed his patron's portrait prominently in the saloon of his principal residence, Redlynch House.[20] Sir Stephen Fox's daughter, Charlotte (cat. 5) married Edward Digby, (cat. 7) the eldest son of William, 5th Lord Digby (cat. 6). The voluminous correspondence of their sons Edward, 6th Lord Digby (cat. 8) and Henry, 7th Lord Digby (cat. 9) with their uncle Stephen, details not only the political unity, but the warmth of their involvement in each other's lives; they frequently visited each others' estates and discussed projects.

Whilst landowners were required to pursue political careers, younger siblings often had to find an alternative outlet for their energies. The respective occupations of the close-knit Digby (cats. 8–13) brothers, revealed through their portraits, demonstrate society's expectations dependent on their position within the family, as landowner or sailor, soldier or churchman. Whilst Edward Digby had political ambitions, his brother Henry pursued a career as a diplomat in Dresden and Vienna. Following Edward's death, Henry succeeded to the title and inherited Sherborne Castle. The third brother Robert joined the navy, a popular and potentially profitable career. William Digby (cat. 11) became Dean of Durham, his brother Stephen (cat. 12) became a Colonel and a courtier and married his cousin Lucy Fox-Strangways, and the youngest, Charles, (cat. 13) also a clergyman, was rector of Kilmington, Somerset.[21]

For landowners the year was dictated by a combination of the political calendar, the agricultural seasons and sport. Lovers of field sports like the Ilchesters and Digbys were mainly in the country between September and January; the Digbys returned to Dorset in June or July and departed for their London home in Lower Brook Street in January.[22] Between February and June Lord Ilchester, together with all but three of his youngest children and their governess, removed to their London house in Burlington Street. When in Dorset, the Reverend Thomas Rackett, (cat. 43) who enjoyed shooting, frequently dispatched pheasants and hares to London friends. Races outside Blandford Forum were a popular summer diversion; and it was from his Dorset experiences that Peter Beckford (cat. 22) wrote the pioneering book *Thoughts on Hunting*, 1781. Focusing on all aspects of the sport, he demonstrated his expertise in managing hounds and offered detailed advice on all aspects of animal welfare. Hunting and shooting were important sports generating considerable fellowship between landowners. John Trenchard writes of enjoying 'much with my Dogs and guns' and of 'some noble hunting with George Pickard's Hounds'.[23] The sport fostered close friendship between neighbours; Peter Beckford often stayed at Charborough when he hunted on Drax land. Beckford and Drax were both Dorset landowners whose wealth came through ownership of sugar plantations in the West Indies.

When in the country life consisted of attending balls, visiting and entertaining friends. In December 1791 Frances Bankes, wife of Henry Bankes (cat. 25) set out to impress her country neighbours by giving a ball celebrating completion of the remodelling of the Pratt interior of Kingston Hall by Robert William Brettingham. She wrote to her mother-in-law that 70 guests were seated at trestle tables in the new eating room, with the same number again in the north parlour.[24] Tea was served using kettles of water kept permanently boiling on Mr Bankes's dressing room fire.

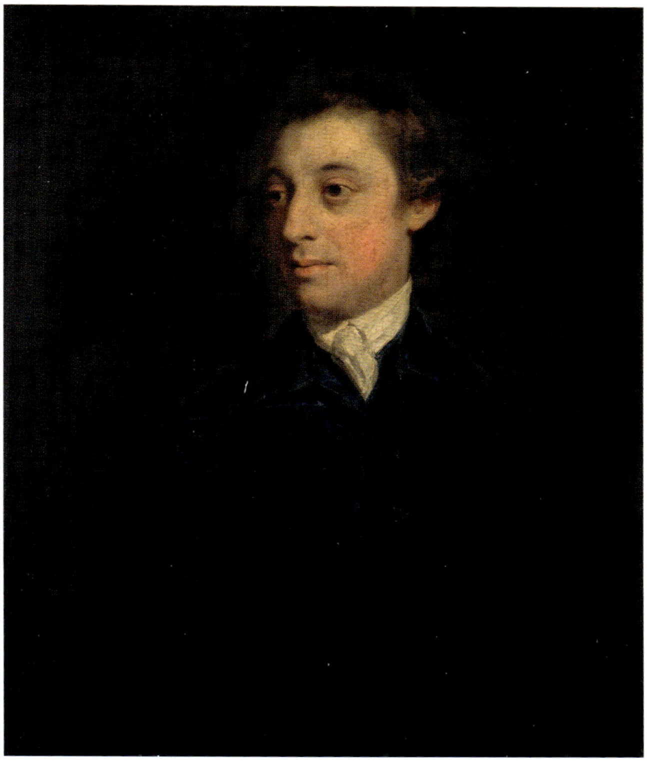

Fig. 9. *William Chafin*, oil on canvas, Thomas Beach, c. 1761.

Guests included Lady Digby, the Trenchards and the Sturts, and those the *Times* described as *Members of the County*, such as the Bonds.[25] It was evidently an eagerly anticipated occasion, John Trenchard wrote to Ozias Humphry that, 'Mrs Banks (sic) gives a huge great Ball and Supper where my Appearance must be recorded. Everybody will be very fine'.[26] To the cosmopolitan Mrs Bankes this 'unremarkable affair' had the desired effect of impressing the neighbourhood.

Women, disenfranchised and excluded from local politics, were responsible for running the household and managing children's education.[27] Recreation time was spent visiting, sewing and sketching together, writing journals or perhaps creating silhouette cut-outs such as those made by Princess Elizabeth (cat. 67) and Mary Frampton (cat. 66). Others created gardens, such as the first Countess of Ilchester at Abbotsbury in 1765. Women's portraits often alluded to their domestic activities such as Lady Caroline Damer (cat. 19) shown engaged in tambourwork or Mrs Weld (cat. 32) holding a skein of wool. In aristocratic households, like the Ilchesters, the eldest son was either tutored at home or attended public school followed by university; many went to Eton, and others like Henry Bankes went to Westminster. In Dorset schools for the offspring of local gentry included excellent grammar schools at Wimborne and Milton Abbas, where John Hutchins taught, and where Thomas Rackett the Elder (cat. 41), William Chafin (fig. 9) and Thomas Masterman Hardy (fig. 10) were pupils.

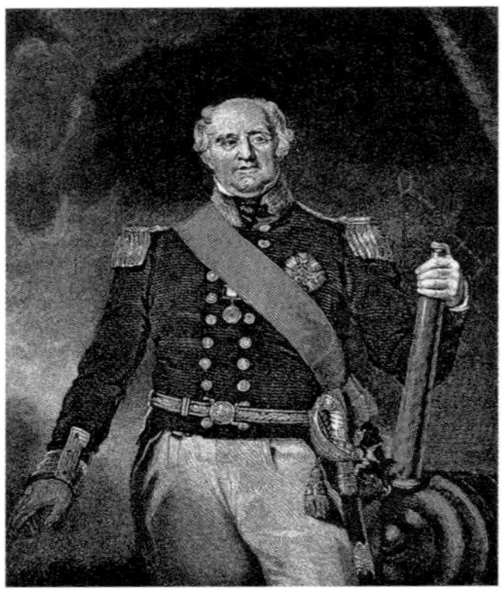

Fig. 10. *Sir Thomas Masterman Hardy Bt. (1769–1839)*, after Richard Evans by H. Robinson, 1846.

Educating daughters changed as the century progressed. In the 1760s two of Stephen Fox's daughters attended a fashionable school in Bath and were contemporaries of Fanny Burney. Most of the towns in Dorset had girls' boarding schools, though later in the century they became less fashionable and there was a change to private governesses. A governess mainly educated the daughters of the second Earl of Ilchester at home.[28]

Dorset was home to several prominent recusant families. Excluded from the British education system on account of their Roman Catholicism, they frequently sent their children to schools abroad. The Weld family and the artist Giles Hussey (cat. 58) from Marnhull were educated in France and Italy. Edward Weld was at St Omer and the Jesuit University of Rheims before setting off on a Grand Tour in 1761, during which time he sat to Pompeo Batoni, whilst his sister Mary (cats. 59, 60) became a nun at Artois. Aside from the strong European links between Roman Catholic families, the male offspring of many aristocrats and the wealthiest gentry often visited the Continent to finish their education. The aristocracy often undertook a costly Grand Tour, a custom since the seventeenth century – the 3rd Earl of Shaftesbury (cat. 20) lived in Naples, where he wrote on art and sculpture. Tours lasted anything between one and four years. George Pitt, later Lord Rivers, toured Italy as a young man with Edward Holdsworth as his tutor between 1740 and1742, and his son-in-law, Peter Beckford, was in Italy between 1765–6, returning with his family in 1783 and remaining in Florence until 1799.

Houses and Gardens

At the centre of Dorset's large estates was the country house, a locus for family, politics and artistic patronage. The agricultural boom from the 1730s onwards resulted in the construction of several important dwellings, such as the palatial baroque Eastbury, begun in 1725 by John Vanbrugh for George Bubb Dodington, of which only part of the stables court remains. The Palladian architect Henry Flitcroft built St Giles, the home of the Earl of Shaftesbury, (fig. 11) and also worked for Sir Stephen Fox at Redlynch in Somerset.

Later in the century other fashionable architects were employed: Robert Adam with unexecuted designs for a bridge and façade at Sherborne Castle and Highcliffe for the Earl of Bute; William Chambers and James Wyatt for Lord Milton at Milton Abbey; Humphrey Sturt at Crichel between 1772–1780; and Henry Portman at Bryanston in 1778.[29] But it was Dorset's own architects, the Bastard family (cats. 51,52) who worked most consistently on the county's houses, often completing projects begun by

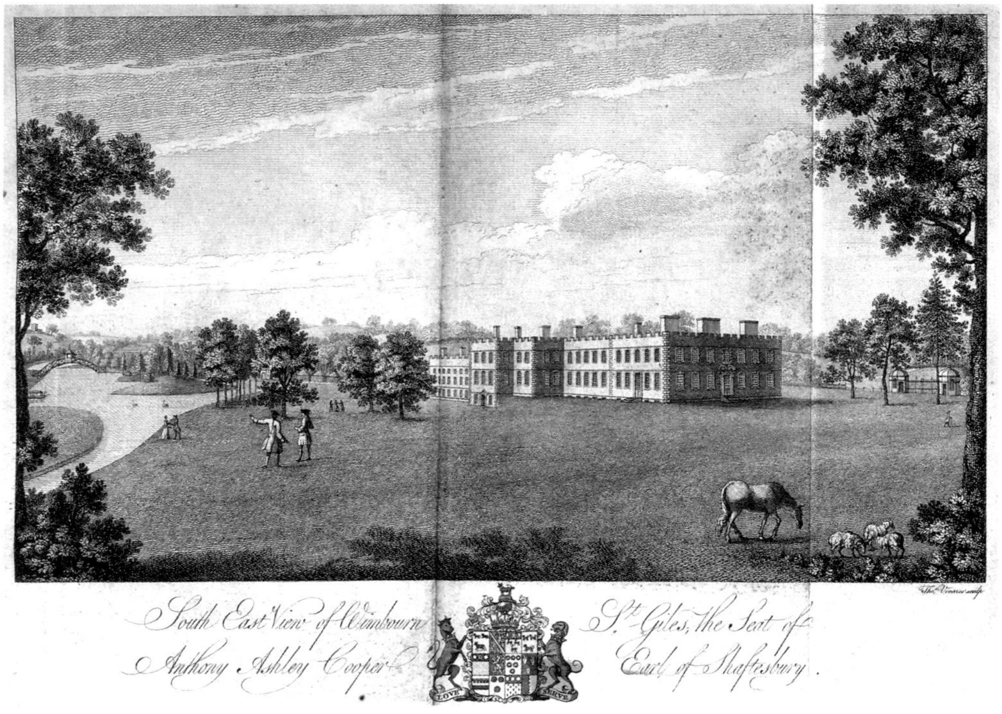

Fig. 11. *S.E. View of Wimbourn (sic) St Giles*, folded, Thos. Vivares, Hutchins, ed.1,2, p. 216, 1774.

fashionable London practitioners. This tradition of local intervention should not be misread as parochialism. The little known Dorset builder and architect Francis Cartwright, who built both Came House in 1756 for John Damer and probably Moreton for James Frampton senior (fig. 5), was a highly competent master of domestic Palladianism and another, James Hamilton, was working in Weymouth.

The eighteenth century witnessed a rise in theories relating to the construction and laying out of landscapes and parks; as a result the picturesque creations of such gardeners as 'Capability' Brown are a feature of several Dorset estates, with one of his earliest projects being at Sherborne Castle (fig. 12). During a visit to Dorset in 1762 the writer and collector Horace Walpole commented that Melbury and its adjacent church, 'tho exceedingly old, looks as if designed for ornament by modern taste'.[30]

Pryce's engraving of Melbury was used as an illustration in the first edition of Hutchins (fig. 13), setting the house and church against a parkland landscape with trees, and in the foreground, an expanse of water complete with decorated chinoiserie barge. Walpole's observation reminds us that more often than not 'design' was necessary and often projects required the wholesale destruction of existing houses, or even villages. The most striking example was the town of Middleton or Milton, near Blandford Forum.

Joseph Damer (fig. 14) purchased the old Abbey house from the heirs of Sir Jacob Bancks in 1752.

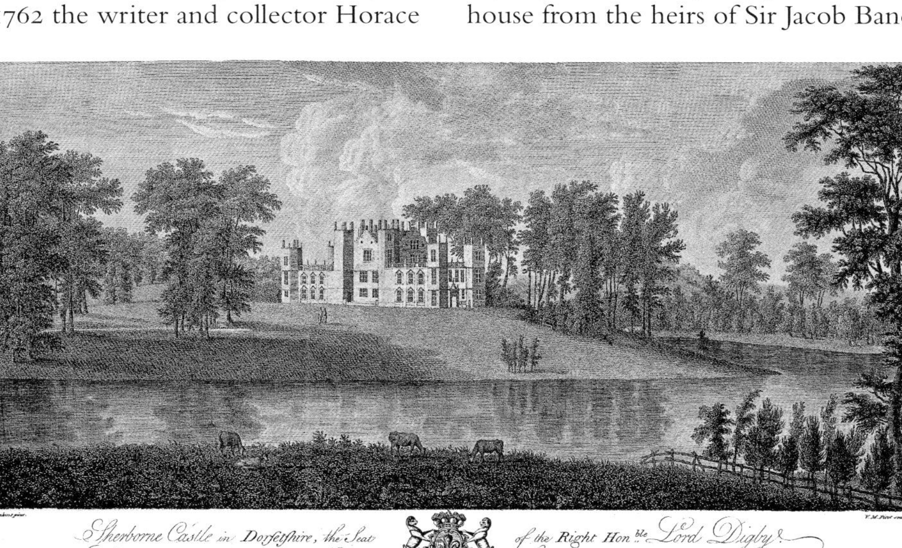

Fig. 12. *Sherborne Castle*, after W. Tomkins by V.M. Picot, Hutchins ed.1, 2, p. 390, 1774.

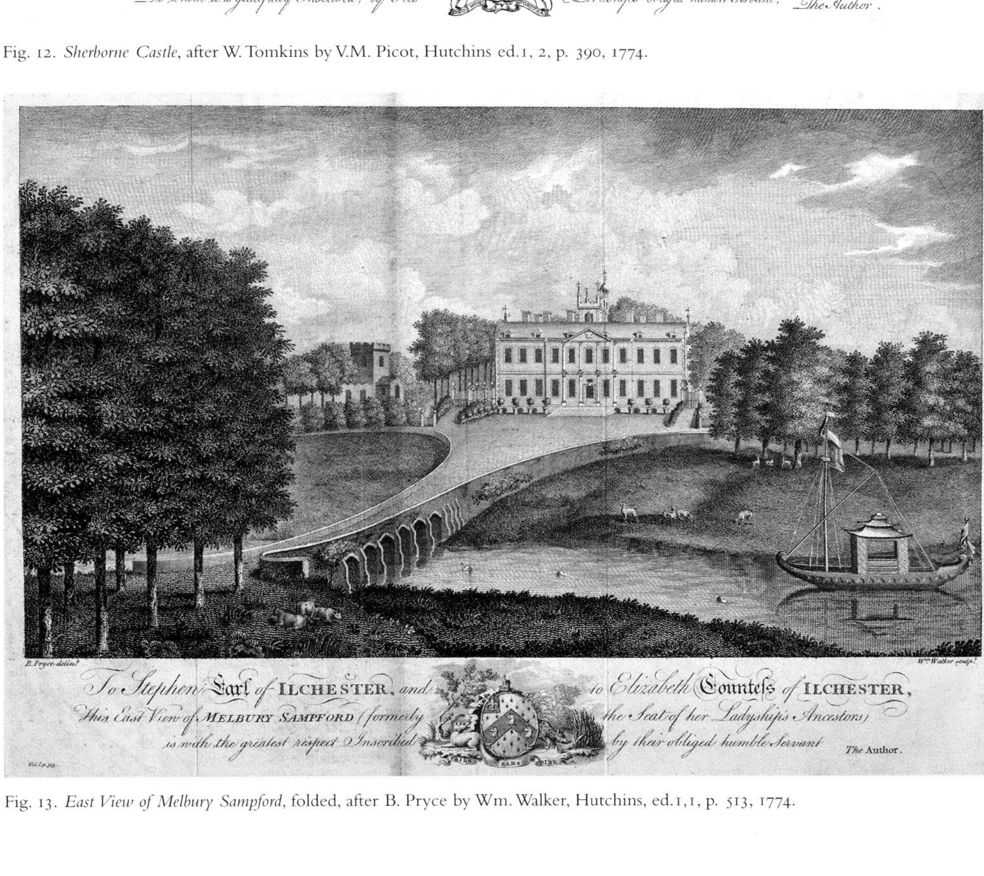

Fig. 13. *East View of Melbury Sampford*, folded, after B. Pryce by Wm. Walker, Hutchins, ed.1, 1, p. 513, 1774.

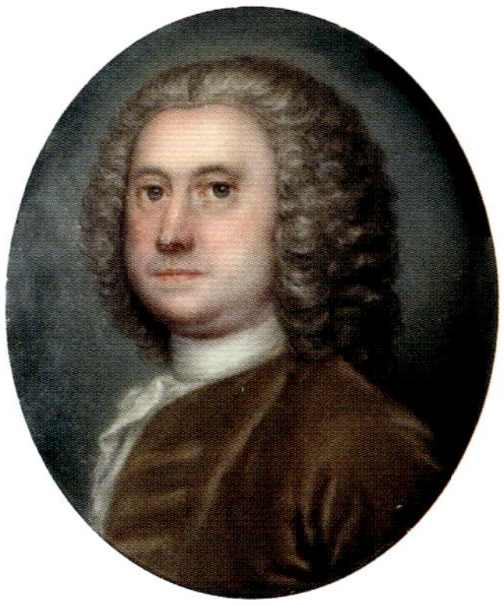

Fig. 14. *Joseph Damer, 1st Earl of Dorchester, 1717–18–1798,* enamel, artist unknown, c. 1750.

Damer immediately implemented a grand scheme to remove the old town south of the abbey, replacing the decaying house with a magnificent new structure and grounds (fig. 15).[31] Created Baron Milton in 1764, Damer enlisted 'Capability' Brown to reshape the entire valley.[32]

Lord Milton systematically set about removing the town, house by house as leases fell in or occupants moved. He then flooded the valley to make an ornamental lake. Milton commissioned William Chambers to create a new model village half a mile to the south-east of the house, and to design a new house in the Gothic style.[33] The resulting Gothic mansion, finished by Wyatt, with its neighbouring Abbey church, set in its carefully sculpted valley, is one of the most striking picturesque landscapes of the eighteenth century. Until the eighteenth century the old manor house of Crichel stood in the village street of More Crichel. Sturt rebuilt the house (fig. 16), removed and relocated the entire village, except the church, and

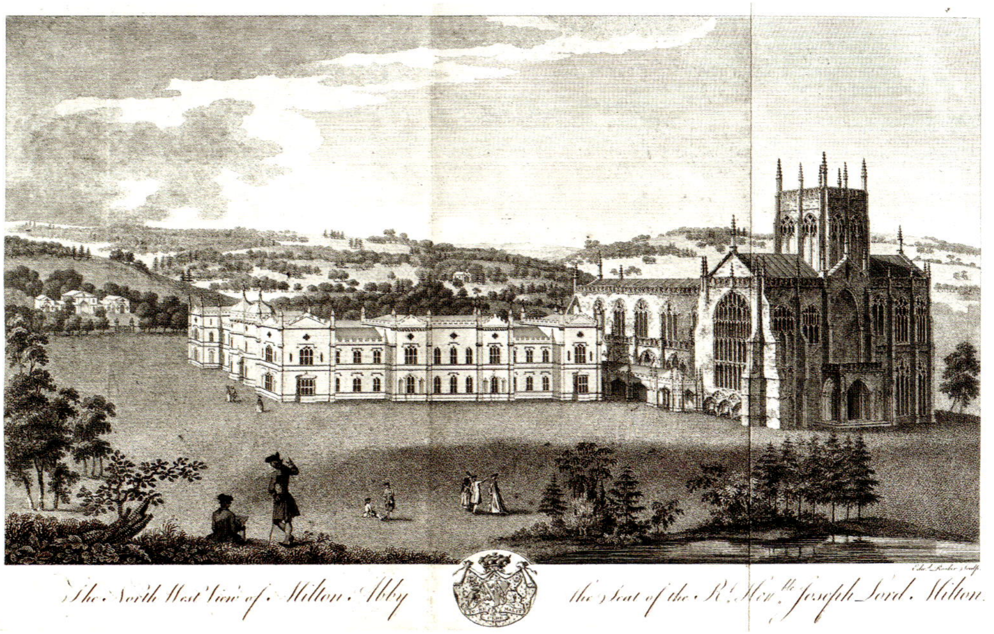

Fig. 15. *The N.W. View of Milton Abbey,* folded, Edwd.Rooker, Hutchins, ed.1,2, p. 438, 1774.

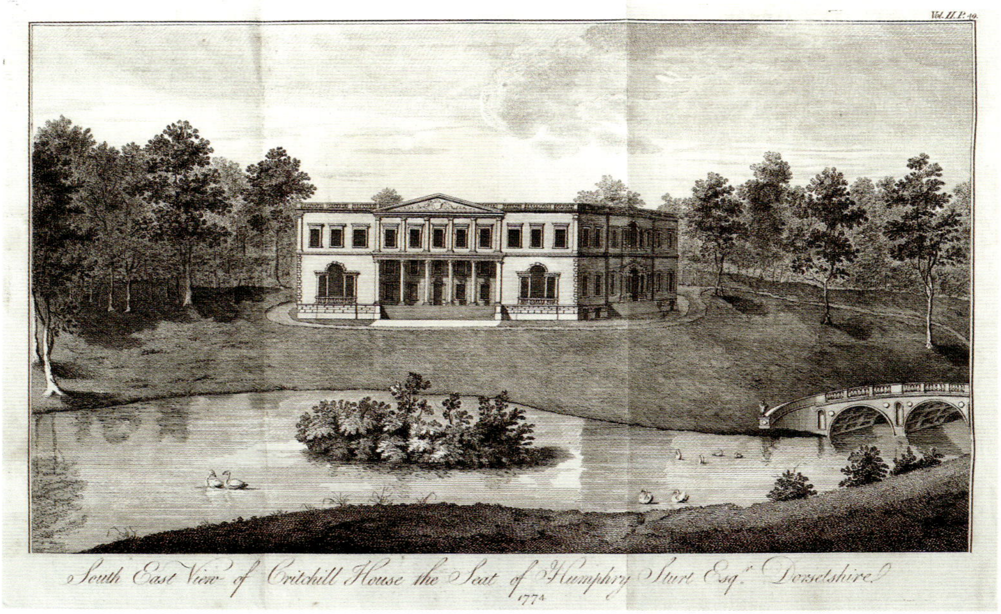

Fig. 16. *S.E. View of Critchill (sic) House the Seat of Humphrey Sturt Esq,* folded, artist unknown, Hutchins, ed. 1, 2 p. 49, 1774.

he too partly flooded a valley to create a picturesque setting of lake and park.[34]

The Dorset Militia

Land ownership came with responsibilities. By 1750, many labourers in Dorset were unable to find regular work, leading to food riots, a situation worsened by the poor harvest of 1756; this unrest continued throughout the eighteenth century. The Dorset Militia was formed in 1757 under Lord Rivers, ostensibly as a response to the threat of invasion posed by France at the beginning of the Seven Years War, but also as a control over potential domestic unrest. Rivers, Colonel for 40 years, recognized that since men in the militia were less likely to riot, it offered the benefit of controlling the populace. This however did not extend to his own officers, and in 1797 Rivers published 'The Present State of the Dorset Militia', in which he accused his son and a kinsman W.M. Pitt (cat. 18) of encouraging the militia officers to seek his removal as Colonel in favour of Lord Milton.[35] By 1800 and no longer the Colonel, Lord Rivers still maintained that enrolling men into the volunteer force and properly managing them had been highly effective in turning 'insurrection into defence'.[36] Lord Rivers sat for several portraits wearing the uniform of Colonel of the Dorset Militia. His mounted portrait by Thomas Gooch (cat. 26) shows him surrounded by the tents of the militia camp with their followers and children. Through an Order in Council dated 14 May, 1798 the Sea Fencibles were formed, mostly of fishermen, to protect the coast on shore and afloat as the threat of invasion from across the Channel became a reality. Their duties included guarding the Martello towers, patrolling the beaches and preparing to attack French ships before they reached shore.

Dorset urbanism: unlikely centres of enlightenment

The eighteenth century witnessed the rise of several prosperous towns in Dorset with an independent middle class, who pursued careers as doctors, scientists and antiquarians, contributing to an intellectual life at a local and national level. Poole was Dorset's largest and most prosperous port, from which Wareham clay was exported to potteries in the north of England. During the century Poole's merchants grew rich on the fat profits of the Newfoundland fishing trade. Born in Poole, Sir Peter Thompson (cat. 47) became a rich Bermondsey merchant, diligent public servant and MP who served on 90 committees, prepared seven bills and took a prominent part in the building of Westminster Bridge. It is likely that his portrait by Thomas Frye, a previously unpublished painting from Poole Museum, was painted to commemorate either his appointment as High Sheriff in 1745, or his knighthood the following year. Thompson had powerful ties with Poole and somewhat unusually retired to the town, living in a princely house on Market Street built by John Bastard. There he pursued his antiquarian interests, corresponding with Hutchins and loaning him various important manuscripts relating to the history of Poole and Dorset.

New fortunes allowed merchants to pursue interests previously the preserve of aristocrats. Joseph Gulston (cat. 49), a City of London merchant with estates in Hertfordshire and Northamptonshire and a director of the South Sea Company, was MP for Poole from 1741 to 1765. His son Joseph (fig. 42) indulged the expensive habit of antiquarian book and print collecting. He was MP for Poole in 1780, but lost his seat in 1784, apparently through neglecting to get out of bed until too late in the day to solicit the five votes needed from Quaker constituents. That same year his dire financial difficulties resulted in the sale of most of his books and two years later of his print collection of over 40,000 items.[37]

Blandford Forum

By the second half of the century there was significant local interest in botany, antiquities, fossils, geology and insects. The Dorset circle of polymath amateurs, who researched and collected in various fields and corresponded with a wide network of scholars, presented papers at learned societies in London.[38] Blandford Forum emerged, having been rebuilt by the Bastard brothers following the disastrous fire of 1731, as a cultural hub and home to this group of empiricists, including Dr Richard Pulteney (cat. 54), Thomas Rackett, Henry Seymer (cat. 53) and Tiberius Cavallo. The most important resident was Pulteney, a physician, cardiologist and botanist who regularly contributed to the *Gentleman's Magazine* from 1750, and was Thomas Rackett's early mentor. In 1781 he wrote '*A General View of the Writings of Linnaeus*', containing Linnaeus's first English biography. A Fellow of the Linnean and Royal Societies, Pulteney was a highly influential figure in London. Pulteney's circle regularly carried out errands for each other, conveying shell and fossil collections, packets of minerals, books and microscopes to and from London.[39] Pulteney also encouraged the work of his neighbour Henry Seymer of Hanford, a dedicated naturalist and owner of an extensive garden of exotic plants. Like Rackett and Pulteney, Seymer was a taxonomist applying Linnaeus's binomial system to shells and butterflies as well as to plants. Interested too in entomology, conchology and mineralogy – especially fossils – Seymer 'had always agents in town on the look-out to secure any collections that might be brought to this country by voyagers; and he procured many rare species in consequence of the celebrated voyage of the immortal Cook'.[40] From 1772 the Duchess of Portland with her avid interest in natural science visited Seymer and exchanged specimens.[41] Seymer's exotic garden plants were supplied by Blandford Forum-born nurseryman John Galpine, son of John Kingston Galpine, an associate of the Linnean Society in 1798, for whom Rackett and his circle were sponsors.

The Reverend Thomas Rackett was prominent in local antiquarian discoveries, recording Dorset's history, topography, distinguishing features, architecture and archaeology. He was a Fellow of the Society of Antiquaries, one of the few institutions engaged in collecting British archaeology, to which Dorset discoveries were reported by Rackett and associates.[42] Rackett collaborated with fellow antiquaries, Sir Richard Colt Hoare of Stourhead and William Cunnington, to excavate prehistoric barrows in Dorset.[43] Rackett and Pulteney worked closely with another antiquarian, Richard Gough, on the second edition of Hutchins, improving it by publishing their recent research on shells and plants of Dorset, and adding over twenty of Rackett's sketches in an attempt to integrate images with the written word.[44] At Spetisbury Cavallo and Rackett studied the sky through a telescope, laying down a meridian line in the rectory garden. Both knew astronomer William Herschel; Rackett produced the earliest known sketch of Herschel operating his telescope from his observing chair at Datchet.[45]

This group had an impact on the court when resident at Weymouth. Queen Charlotte and the princesses pursued their interest in the natural world, scouring the beach for seashells and seaweed and consulting local experts over their discoveries. In 1797 Queen Charlotte sought advice over her fern collection from Wiltshire-based botanist Aylmer Bourke Lambert, who spent summers in Dorset with Seymer.[46] In 1805 Queen Charlotte canvassed Dr William Maton's help in identifying a species of bladderwrack in Weymouth. There for the 'season', Maton, a rising physician, natural philosopher and antiquarian, was hoping to secure royal patronage. He wrote to Thomas Rackett at Spetisbury requesting him to send his copy of the third edition of the *Linnean Transactions* for the Queen to read an article on *fuci*.[47]

The Court at Weymouth

The national spotlight was thrown on Dorset when George III (cat. 1) and members of the court came to stay at Weymouth (fig. 17) in 1789. Seaside resorts were in vogue by the late eighteenth century and Weymouth's benefits were promoted by the local

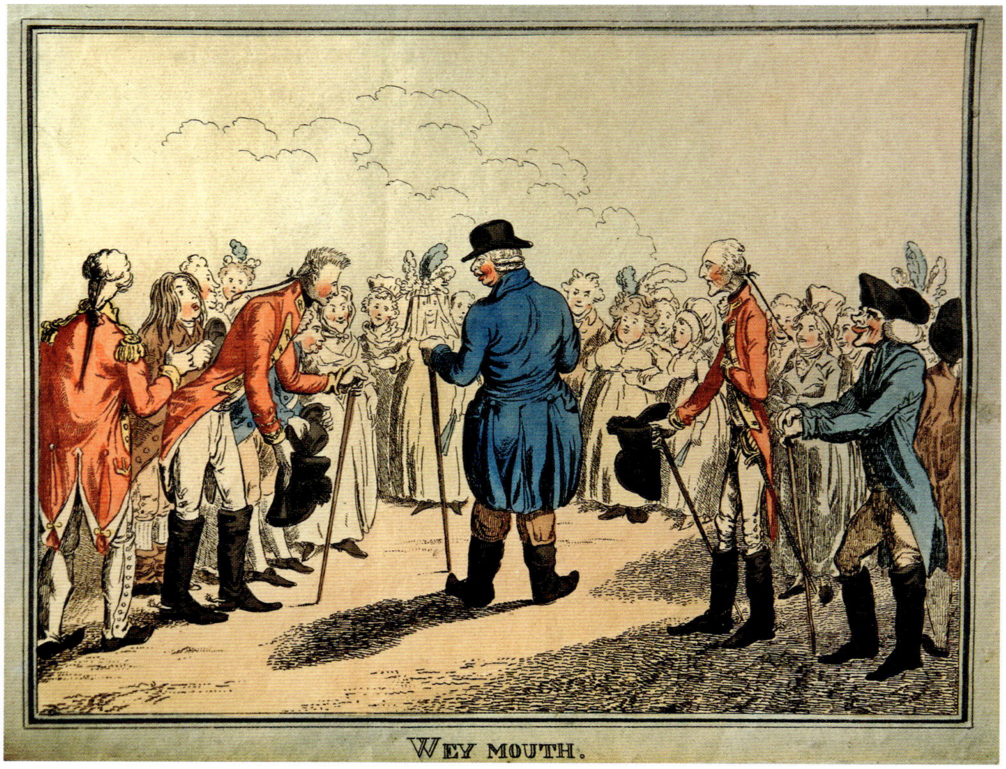

Fig. 17. *Wey Mouth,* James Gillray, hand-coloured etching, published by Hannah Humphrey, 1797. George III is shown addressing Lord Cathcart (1755–1843), then major-general, who stands hat in hand on the left. General David Dundas, who was based near Dorchester, is on the right.

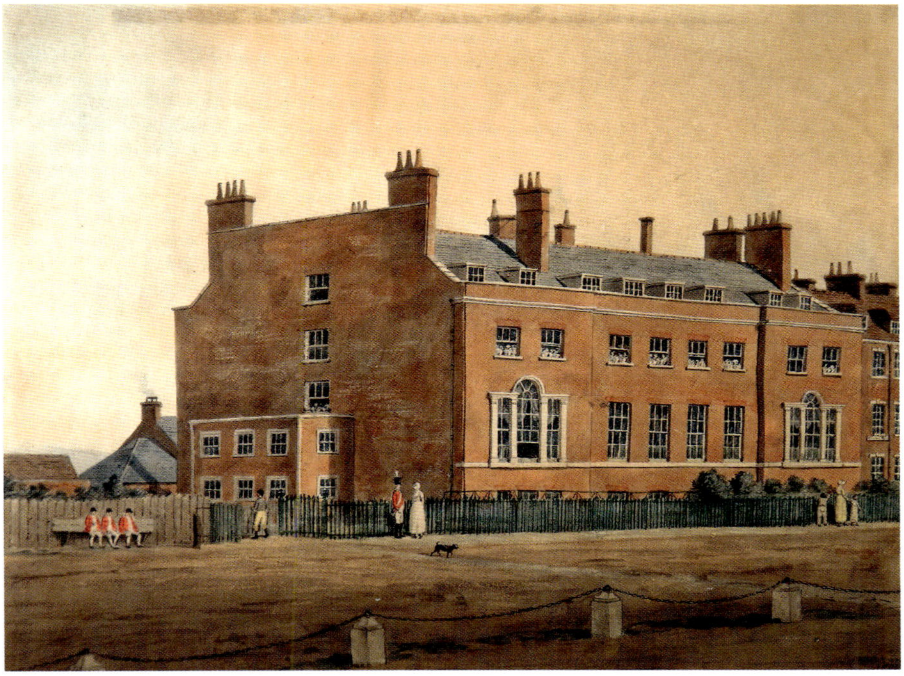

Fig. 18. *Gloucester Lodge,* watercolour on paper, John Upham, 1809.

physician Dr John Crane, who advocated sea air, sea-bathing and drinking seawater as medically beneficial.[48]

By 1780 the King's brother, William Henry, Duke of Gloucester (cat. 2) had built a house in Weymouth and offered it to the King following his serious illness of 1788. The following year the King, Queen and their three elder daughters – Charlotte, Augusta and Elizabeth – visited Weymouth, staying from June to the end of August.[49] Altogether the royal family visited twelve times between 1789 and 1805, always staying at Gloucester Lodge (fig. 18). The Royal Mail delivered government dispatches to the King at seven o'clock every morning via a messenger. The King transacted his business in time for the papers to be returned to London by four o'clock in the afternoon. In this way the business of government was maintained. The *Times* recorded that the Royal Mail delivered all food, water and provisions for the royal party each day from the royal palaces.[50] The King rose early to walk and rode out for several hours each day; he also swam from a bathing machine (fig. 19). In the evenings the royal family frequently attended performances by Sarah Siddons, Philip Kemble, John Quick or the card magician Highman Palatine.[51]

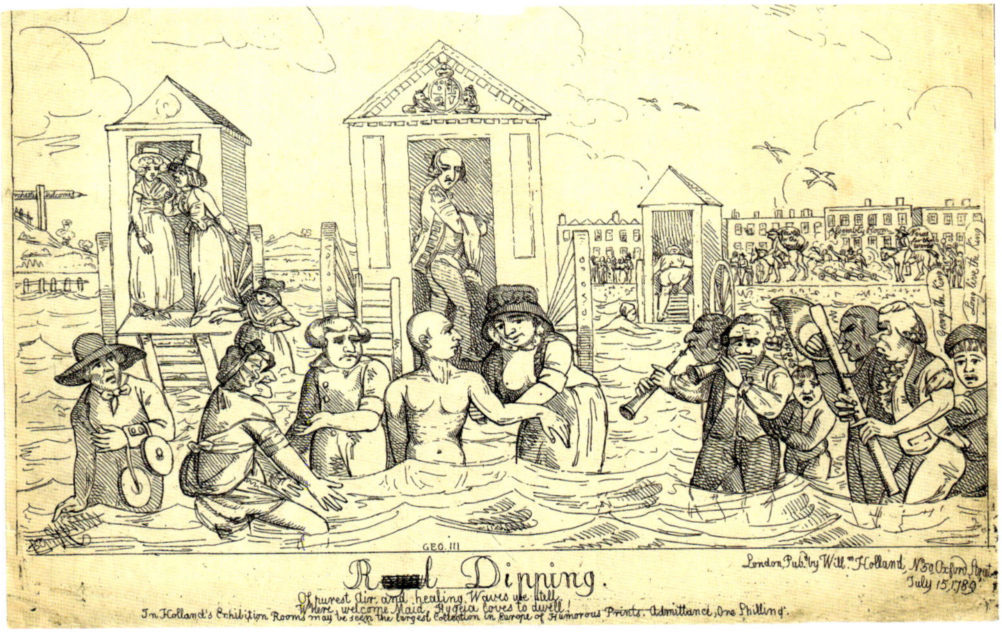

Fig. 19. *Royal Dipping,* John Nixon, etching, published by William Holland, 1789. The King, naked, is being dipped in the sea whilst the band plays 'God Save Great\George the King\Long live the King'.

George III and his family became a fixture in the county, being entertained by Dorset's aristocrats and landowners. During his first summer at Weymouth the King visited the Ilchesters at Redlynch, Somerset, Lionel Damer at Came House near Dorchester, Lord Milton at Milton Abbey, sailed on board the *Southampton* to the Welds at Lulworth Castle, and stayed at Sherborne Castle. On visiting the various houses, the King often asked to see portraits, particularly of people he knew, frequently commenting on likenesses. At Herringston he instantly recognized the portrait of his physician Sir Edward Wilmot (cat. 24) hanging in the dining-parlour.[52] He visited the Roman Catholic Weld family (cats. 31, 32) at Lulworth Castle twice (fig. 34). Thomas Weld went out of his way to welcome and impress the King, ensuring, according to Hutchins, that 'the choicest productions of every kind were laid before them with a generous profusion, and in the most splendid style, the whole being served up on entirely new services of gold and silver, on every piece of which was engraved "*Long Live the King*"'.[53]

Because George III was ostensibly convalescing at Weymouth there is no evidence of artists commissioned to record officially the royal visits. But a number of artists and print sellers cashed in on the royal presence; during the 1790s James Fittler and John Love produced a series of twelve large views of Weymouth and its coastal neighbourhood. One of the views was claimed to be engraved from a drawing by Princess Sophia. John Love went further, exhibiting a 'Transparent Painting covering the whole of the bow window of my Billiard and Exhibition Room ... being the First Transparent Painting ever exhibited in this Town. Lit from behind by the Patent Lamps, there shone out from its three panels the symbolic figures of Fame, Britannia, the British Lion and Neptune: the whole being embellished and surrounded by Bays, Laurels, Ears of Wheat and Cornucopiae'.[54] It was perhaps for a print for Love and Fittler that William Delamotte, the son of the local book-seller and librarian, produced his large watercolour *Weymouth Bay* (fig. 20) in 1794, showing the sun's rays over Weymouth, flattering the sovereign, alluding to his benevolence to the town and to Delamotte, whom George III sponsored through the Royal Academy Schools.[55]

By the end of the eighteenth century the renewed threat from France meant land and coastal defences had to be put in place, and volunteer forces raised in addition to the militia and regular army. By the late 1790s there was a build-up of troops around Weymouth as far as Dorchester, where a barracks was built in 1795. George III often rode out to inspect the troops (fig. 21). On Wednesday 17 September 1794 the King and Queen, accompanied by the Duke of Gloucester and Prince Ernest, inspected the Corps of the Dorset Volunteer Rangers under Maiden Castle and expressed their thanks 'at seeing them so alert and forward in their manouevres'.[56] The Dorset Volunteer Rangers (DVR), a corps of light cavalry, was founded by George Damer, Lord Milton (cat. 28), in 1794 and made up of prominent local landowners.[57] The volunteers were armed civilians officially sanctioned to defend the county from potential invasion.

The Volunteer Rangers were also responsible for preventing civil insurrection in the county. One of the officers, James Frampton (cat. 29) wrote an account of the Rangers: 'I thought it highly proper for everybody to shew themselves in such times as these and ready to do their utmost to defend their property and the County at large from all innovations the followers of

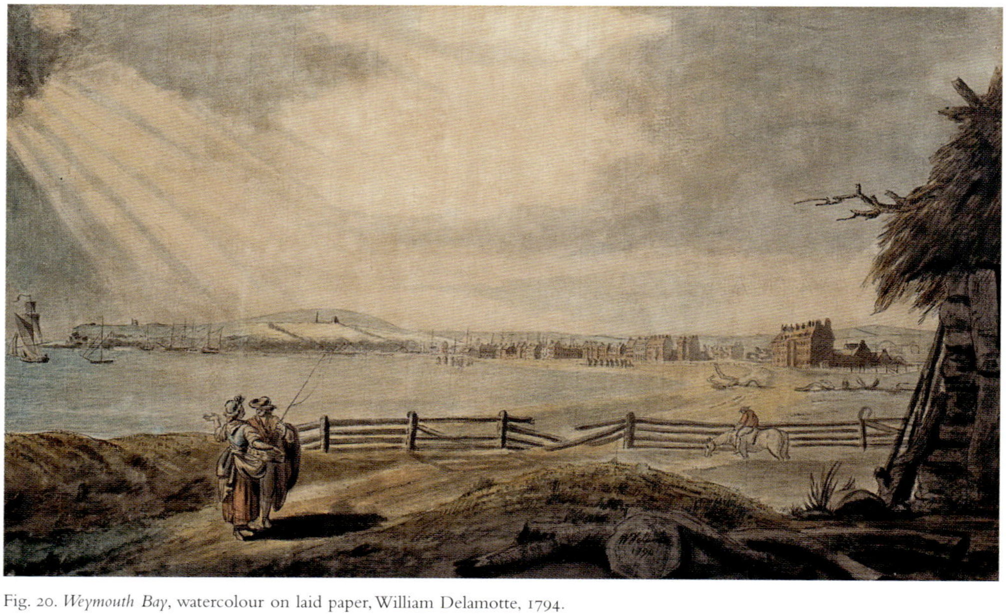

Fig. 20. *Weymouth Bay*, watercolour on laid paper, William Delamotte, 1794.

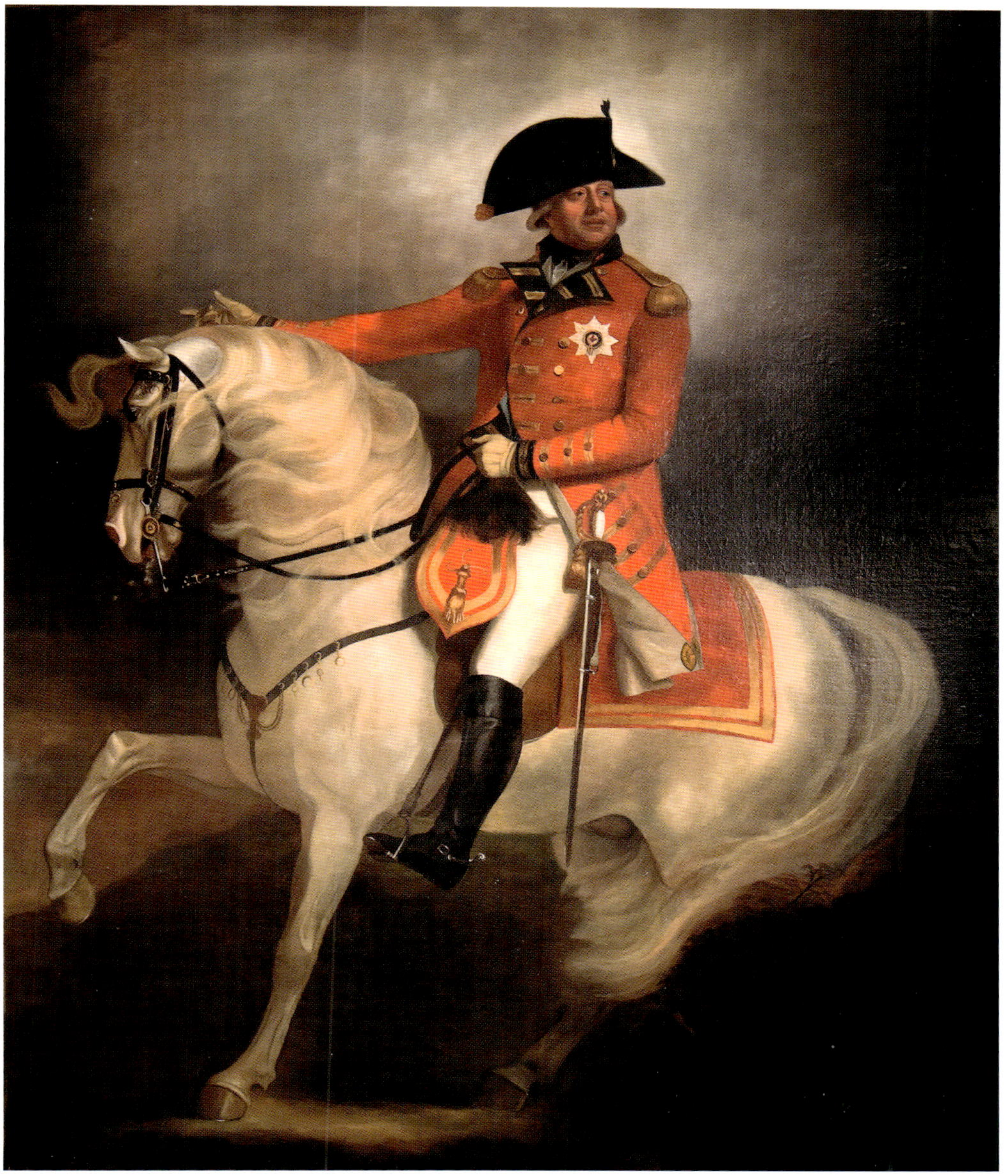

Fig. 21. *King George III Reviewing the 10th Dragoons,* oil on canvas, after William Beechey, early 19th century.

the French system might try to introduce'.[58] Frampton had experienced at first hand the 'innovations' of the 'French system'. Travelling in France in 1790 he visited Saint-Cloud to see the King and Queen, and on 18 July 1791 witnessed the brutal suppression of the crowd by the national troops in Paris.[59]

The fear was not completely without foundation. Dorset had undergone massive change during the century; mechanization of agriculture and reformation of land had resulted in the enclosure of much of the county, whilst the growth of towns like Poole and Blandford Forum had precipitated the rise of a new middle-class. This flux inevitably resulted in conflict. By the beginning of the nineteenth century disquiet led to rick-burning and the Swing Riots, culminating in the conviction and subsequent transportation of six Tolpuddle labourers by the Dorchester Justices. But it was also as a result of this changing landscape that amateurs such as Hutchins resolved to record the county. Indeed it was the network of natural philosophers and antiquarians, like Thomas Rackett and Richard Pulteney, as well as conscientious landowners like James Frampton, who paved the way for the founding of the Dorset County Museum in 1845 and later the Dorset Natural History and Archaeological Society.

1 See J. Bettey, *Dorset,* Plymouth, 1974, p. 146; by 1800 Poole's population was about 5,000 and Weymouth's 4,000.

2 There was common ground with the Lunar Society in the Midlands, engaged in parallel activities, albeit more structured.

3 Samuel Gould was the Dorchester bookseller responsible for distributing Hutchins in 1774.

4 Dorchester-based William Cuming was physician to the nobility and gentry, which enabled him to persuade the landowners to contribute engravings to Hutchins. The volumes attracted considerable national interest amongst antiquarians though Horace Walpole thought the content dull. On 5 June 1775 he wrote to William Cole, 'I have just run through the two vast volumes of Hutchins's Dorsetshire. He has taken infinate (sic) pains; indeed all but those that would make it entertaining.'

5 The clay pits here were described as between 12 and 14 feet deep. See W. Maton, *Observations relative Chiefly to the Natural History, Picturesque Scenery and Antiquities of the Western Counties of England, made in the years 1794 and 1796*, 1797, Salisbury, p. 11.

6 Letter from James Frampton Senior to James Frampton Junior, Moreton, 25 July 1782, intended for his son to read when an adult, private collection.

7 See H. C. Prince, J. N. Jennings, C. H. B. Sperling, A. S. Goudie, D. R. Stoddart and G. G. Poole, 'Discussion. Marlpits or Dolines of the Dorset Chalklands?', *Transactions of the Institute of British Geographers,* n.s., 4, No.1, 1979, pp. 116–124.

8 In 1771 Young reviewed Dorset's agriculture, comparing it unfavourably with his native East Anglia, regarding certain aspects of Dorset farming practice as 'barbarous' and 'vile'. A. Young, *The Farmer's Tour through East England*, London, 1771, 3, pp. 320,368, 343.

9 J. Bettey, *Dorset,* Plymouth, 1974, p. 53. In 1779 George Boswell of Puddletown wrote his influential *Treatise on Watering Meadows* giving specific details on creating and managing water meadows.

10 Sturt shipped ash from soap factories in London to enrich his fir plantations on Brownsea Island.

11 Ed J.C. Mansel-Pleydell, 'Journal of an Excursion to Eastbury and Bristol etc in May and June 1767, Sir Joseph Banks Bart, With Notes by S.G. Perceval, Esq., of Henbury and Bristol', *Proceedings of the Dorset Natural History and Antiquarian Field Club,* 21, 1900, pp. 143–149.

12 It was common for the principal landowners of opposing parties to agree each to take one of the county seats.

13 Advantageous for Wren, who was responsible for the Portland stone quarries providing stone for St Paul's Cathedral.

14 Dodington's Whig ambitions, scheming and vast size saw him lampooned in Hogarth's cartoon '*The Five Orders of Periwigs*' 1761.

15 7 August 1753, ed. H. P. Wyndham, *The Diary of the Late George Bubb Dodington, Baron of Melcombe, From March 8, 1749 to February 7 1761*, London, 1785, pp. 245–246.

16 Letter from James Byres to Charles Townley, Rome, 13 December 1782, 'I had the honour of sending you by Mr Banks (sic) who meant to be in England before the meeting of Parliament'. This was Henry Bankes, a neighbour of Charles Townley in Westminster. See I. Bignamini and C. Hornsby, *Digging and Dealing in Eighteenth Century Rome,* New Haven and London, 2010, 2, p. 141.

17 Bankes was the author of *The Civil and Constitutional History of Rome from the Foundation to the Age of Augustus,* London, 1818.

18 24,942 acres in 1883, see J. Bateman, *The Great Landowners of Great Britain,* London, 1883, p. 381.

19 Stephen Fox's youngest son, Henry Fox, became the first Lord Holland and was the father of Charles James Fox, the leading Whig, for much of the second half of the century.

20 Ed. Paget Toynbee 'Horace Walpole's Journals of Visits to Country Seats, Etc,', *The Walpole Society,* 16, 1928–29, pp. 44–48.

21 Their one sister Charlotte died aged nineteen in 1753.

22 Sherborne Castle Estates Archive, Game Books, 1753–1793.

23 Royal Academy Library, HU/4/50, John Trenchard to Ozias Humphry, London, 1 Sep 1790; HU/4/104, John Trenchard, Lytchet, to Ozias Humphry, London, 18 Oct 1794.

24 DHC, Box D/BKL 8C/67, Folder 6; Frances Bankes, Kingston Hall, to her mother-in-law Mrs Bankes, Westminster, 25 December 1791,

25 A. Sebba, *The Exiled Collector, William Bankes and the Making of an English Country House,* London, 2004, p. 20.

26 Royal Academy archive, Humphry Correspondence, HU/4/60, John Trenchard, Warmwell, to Ozias Humphry, 2 Dec 1791.

27 See J. Martin *Wives and Daughters. Women and Children in the Georgian Country House*, London, 2004; ed. Joanna Martin, *A Governess in the Age of Jane Austen. The Journals and Letters of Agnes Porter,* London, 1998.

28 See ed. Joanna Martin, *A Governess in the Age of Jane Austen. The Journals and Letters of Agnes Porter,* London, 1998, pp. 52,79; Agnes Porter was governess to the Ilchester family between 1788–1797.

29 Portman cultivated exotic plants with his Bryanston gardener Alexander Brown. See R. H. Jeffers, 'Richard Pulteney M.D., F.R.S. (1730–1801), and His Correspondents', *Proceedings of the Linnean Society of London,* 171, 1, 1959–1960, pp. 15–26.

30 Ed. Paget Toynbee 'Horace Walpole, 'Journals of Visits to Country Seats etc', Contained in 2 MS notebooks inscribed 'Book of Materials Sept 1759 and Book of Materials 1771', *The Walpole Society* vol. 14, p. 47.

31 Damer commissioned John Vardy to build Milton (later Dorchester) House at Park Lane.

32 See P. Willis, 'Capability Brown's Account with Drummond's Bank, 1753–1783', *Architectural History,* 27, 1984, pp. 382–391.

33 When Young visited in 1771 he wrote that, 'His Lordship designs soon to build a very magnificent house in the Gothic stile, (sic) for the better uniting with the church', A. Young, *The Farmer's Tour through East England*, London, 1771, 3, p. 376.

34 Humphrey Sturt lived at nearby Horton House and inherited Crichel from a Napier uncle. According to Pevsner the church was rebuilt in 1850, N. Pevsner, J. Newman, *Dorset*, London, 1972, p. 299.

35 G. Pitt, *The present State of the Dorsetshire Militia, set forth in a series of letters between the Colonel [Lord Rivers,] and some of the principal officers of that regiment, from September 1793 to this time,* London, 1797.

36 See A. Gee, *The British Volunteer Movement, 1794–1814,* Oxford, 2003, p. 118, fn. 30, Home Office, 50/47, Rivers to Henry Dundas, Stratfield Saye, 16 May 1800.

37 *Gouty Gulston the Antiquarian at Antwerp* by Thomas Rowlandson, c. 1797, posthumous pencil, pen, ink and watercolour drawing, private collection.

38 Hutchins paved the way with his *History*; during its production he wrote about Dorset in the *Gentleman's Magazine* in 1767 and 1778.

39 Linnean Society manuscript archive, Pulteney folder of correspondence. In 1793 Tiberius Cavallo sent a microscope from London to Pulteney in Blandford via Thomas Rackett.

40 Nichols, 1812–1816, 8, p. 201, information given to Nichols by A. B. Lambert, Vice-President of the Linnean Society.

41 The first images of Homer's Swallowtail (Lepidoptera: Papilionidae) Dr. D. Vane-Wright, *The Linnean,* 2004, 20, 4, pp. 31–41.

42 Rackett's protégé Dr William Maton gave related papers at the Society of Antiquaries of London.

43 A popular activity also recorded by Joseph Banks on Cranborne Chase in 1767, see J.C. Mansel-Pleydell, 1900.

44 Richard Gough initially helped Hutchins with the first edition. See Bodleian Library Ref, MSS. Top, Dorset, d. 3–4, Correspondence of Richard Gough, John Nichols, and J.B. Nichols, concerning the second edition of Hutchins.

45 *William Herschel,* Thomas Rackett c. 1782, watercolour, private collection. There is another version by Rackett in the Lewis Walpole Library attributed to John Inigo Richards.

46 Linnean Society manuscript archive, from Aylmer Bourke Lambert to Richard Pulteney, 8 August 1797.

47 DHC, D/RAC/34, Correspondence between William Maton and the Reverend Thomas Rackett. Letter from Maton in Weymouth to Rackett at Spetisbury Rectory, dated 10 August 1805, referring to the King's health, *'The monarch has talk'd to me a good deal about his eyes, which are certainly better. I much doubt (but this is entre nous) whether there had ever been any cataract. The occulists are sometimes overknowing'*. Maton's efforts were rewarded; he became physician-extraordinary to Queen Charlotte in1816, attended the Duke of Kent in his last illness in 1820 and was physician-in-ordinary to the infant Princess Victoria.

48 J. Crane, *An Account of the Nature, properties, and Medicinal Uses, of the Mineral Water at Nottington, near Weymouth, Dorset . . . With a view of the well in its present state,* Dorchester, 1780; J. Crane, *Cursory Observations on Sea-Bathing,* Weymouth, 1795. Crane was the residing physician at Weymouth and his pamphlets were sold at Peter Delamotte's and John Love's circulating libraries in Weymouth.

49 F. Fraser, *Princesses. The Six Daughters of George III,* London, 2004, pp. 124–125.

50 The *Times*, 6 July 1789.

51 The *Times,* 13 July 1789.

52 Hutchins, ed.3, 2, p. 528.

53 Hutchins, 3rd ed., l, p. 375. The French royal family sought shelter at Lulworth following the revolution of 1830.

54 V.J. Adams, 'John Love (of Weymouth)', *Dorset Worthies*, 10, DNH&AS, Dorchester, 1965.

55 Dorset silversmith John Bridge was introduced to King George III through his cousin, a farmer called upon to entertain the King at Weymouth. The farmer mentioned to the king his cousin was a partner in a London firm of goldsmiths; once back in London George III summoned John Bridge. The king was sufficiently impressed with Bridge's work that the firm of Rundell and Bridge became 'by appointment'.

56 DHC, D/FRA/X3, manuscript by J. Frampton, *Account of the Origin and proceedings of the Dorset Yeomanry Cavalry from 1793–1814,* p. 19.

57 A card dated 4 June 1801, lists the officers' duties of the DVR as '*Engaged to serve in case of riots and tumults, in any part of the adjoining counties; and in case of invasion, in any part of Great Britain'*, private collection (fig. 31).

58 DHC, D/FRA/X3, manuscript by J. Frampton, *Account of the Origin and proceedings of the Dorset Yeomanry Cavalry from 1793–1814,* p. 2.

59 Frampton, 1885, p. 62. Frampton's step-brother Charlton Byam Wollaston, Paris, to his mother Phillis Frampton, Moreton, 18 July 1791.

(Cat. 28) *Opposite*

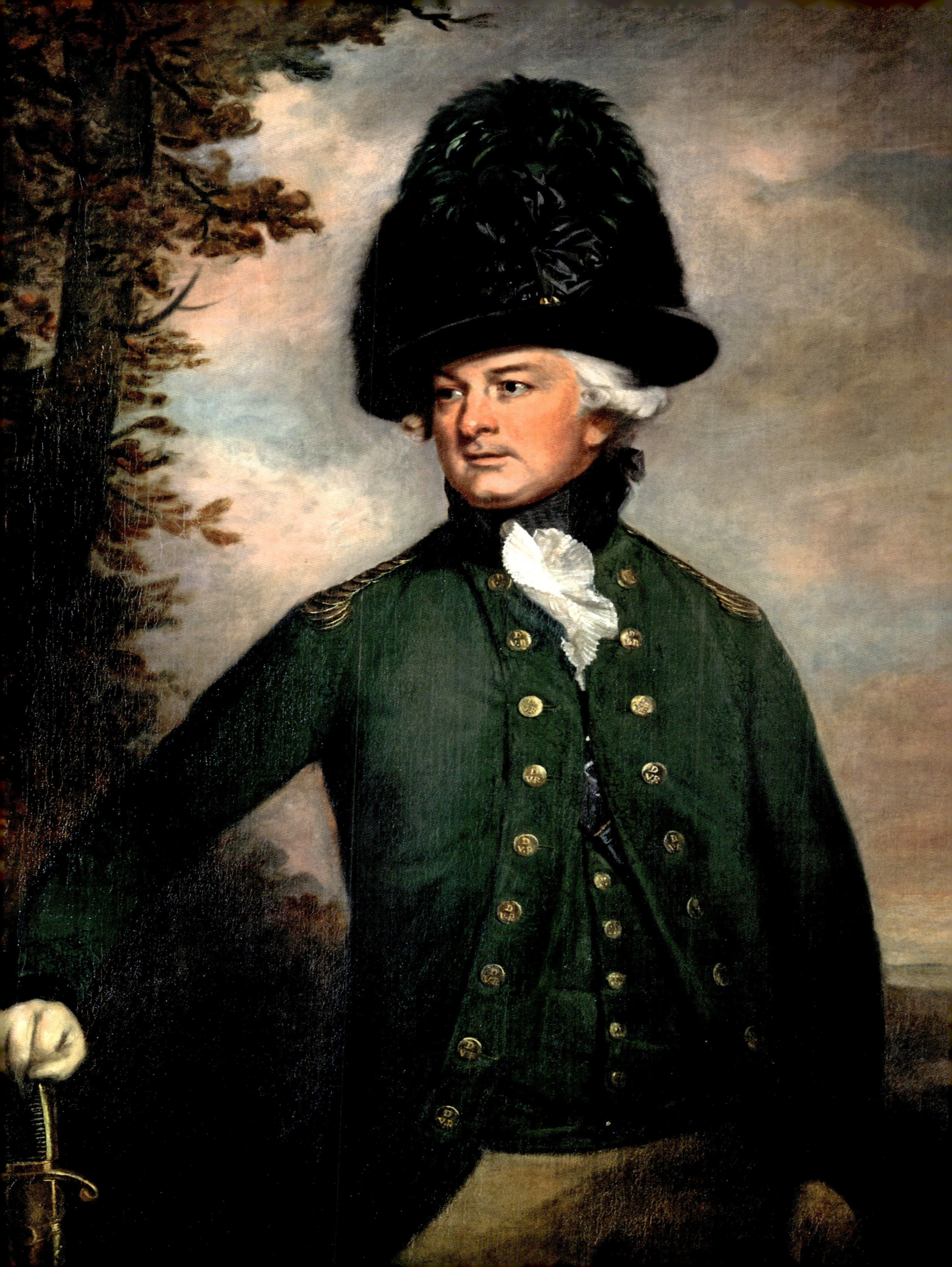

Portraiture and Dorset

Introduction

Writing in 1755 the French miniaturist Jean André Rouquet commented in his *L'Etat des Arts, en Angleterre* on 'how fond the English are of having their pictures drawn.'[1] The predominance of portraiture was reflected in the composition of the art market, and seen as one of the reasons a national school of history painting failed to emerge, a situation that prompted William Hogarth to complain 'Portrait painting is the chief branch of art by which . . . a money lover can get a fortune.' Portraiture was therefore both the principal form of art produced in Britain during the eighteenth century and the principal means by which an artist could make a living. Private patrons overwhelmingly desired portraits; of themselves, members of their family and in the newly commercial age, their houses, estates and animals. Portraiture conferred status upon the sitter, whilst the display of pictures celebrated loyalties, both political and familial. This essay examines portraiture and patronage in Dorset during the century, setting the paintings included in *Georgian Faces* in both their local and national contexts. It will also examine the careers of three Dorset-born painters, Sir James Thornhill, Giles Hussey and Thomas Beach, demonstrating how important their Dorset background was for each during their careers. Both Thornhill and Hussey attempted to forge careers not as portraitists, but as history painters; whilst Thornhill was successful and able to forge a political career in Dorset, Hussey a generation later was forced, finally, to turn to portraiture. The role of the local market is particularly marked in the work of Thomas Beach, a situation greatly illuminated by the recent discovery of his manuscript diary for 1798, presented here for the first time. Beach's journeys to Dorset reveal the sophisticated strategies he used to serve both metropolitan clientele, such as the Earl of Ilchester and Lord Rivers, and more local Dorset patrons. Whilst neither Dorset sitters nor Dorset artists could claim responsibility for any of the major developments of the English school during the century, the very conservatism of a rural audience and its choice of painters are instructive.

James Thornhill and the dominance of portraiture

At the beginning of the century there were continual attempts to promote art in Britain and place painting on a more professional footing. Painters and patrons felt that British art would benefit from the regulation and structure of a continental-style academy, not least to encourage a European hierarchy of genres, which privileged history painting over portraiture. In 1711 Godfrey Kneller become governor of an academy attached to his own house in Queen Street, London. Kneller was the most prominent portraitist of the period, famous for his three-quarter length portraits of members of the Kit-Kat club, which included the Dorset-born Matthew Prior, and which set the standard for the elegant representation of contemporary sitters in the manner of Van Dyck. The bust-length portrait of John Bond (cat. 33), signed and dated 1723, is a late instance of Kneller's work. As a portraitist Kneller felt it unnecessary to promote history painting.[2]

In 1719 Kneller's academy moved to the Covent Garden house of the painter James Thornhill. Thornhill was born at Melcombe Regis, the son of grocer Walter Thornhull and Mary Sydenham.[3] After his father abandoned the family, Thornhill joined the London household of his great-uncle the physician Dr Thomas Sydenham, who left him on his death in 1689 sufficient money to take up a trade. Thornhill became apprenticed for seven years to another relation, Thomas Highmore, Serjeant-Painter to the King. Thornhill was not a portraitist, but a decorative history painter (fig. 22).

The taste at the end of the seventeenth century for large-scale allegorical frescos had seen the arrival of several decorative artists from Europe, but Thornhill, an adept courtier, won several key commissions over his foreign rivals. The size and prodigious quantity of Thornhill's work required the employment of large numbers of studio assistants. One such was Dietrich Ernst Andreae, described by the engraver George Vertue as having 'workt for Sr J. Thornhill.'[4] Thornhill relied on painters like Andreae to complete many of the more complicated poses in his elaborate, decorative allegories.

In the 1720s the taste for Thornhill's brand of decoration began to decline, the rise of Palladianism rendering full-bodied Baroque decoration obsolete. Thornhill turned to Dorset for commissions and to foster his nascent political career. In 1718 he decorated the stairway and ceiling at Charborough Park with the *Judgement of Paris* and from 1720 worked at Sherborne House for Henry Seymour Portman.[5] It was probably

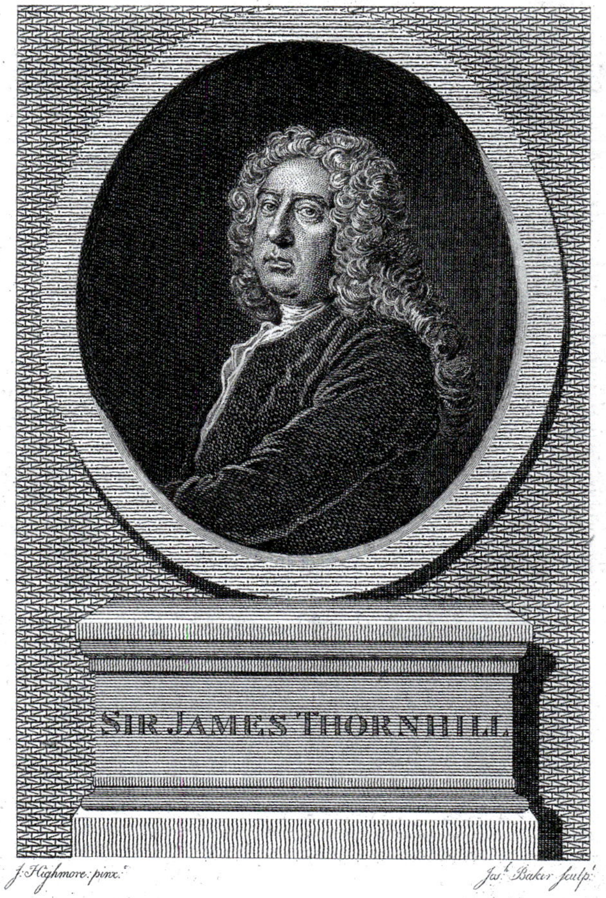

Fig. 22. *Sir James Thornhill,* after Joseph Highmore, engraved by Joshua Baker, 1732.

whilst working with Thornhill in Dorset that Andreae completed his portraits of John and William Bastard (cat. 51,52). Thornhill also worked at Eastbury for Bubb Dodington, who was undoubtedly instrumental in encouraging him to enter the corrupt world of Weymouth politics. In 1721 Thornhill was granted the Freedom of the town and in gratitude he painted the Royal coat of arms (fig. 23) and *The Last Supper* for St Mary's Church, Melcombe Regis. Thornhill also built an almshouse, at his own expense, for distressed mariners, a strategy ensuring his election as Whig MP for Melcombe Regis. As his political aspirations increased, his artistic ones seemingly waned. In 1732 he was appointed a Commissioner assessing claims for the rebuilding of Blandford after the disastrous fire; and working with the Bastard brothers, he also produced an early design for the new Town Hall (Sir John Soane Museum).

Thornhill consolidated his life in Dorset by building a house at his family's former estate, Thornhill near Stalbridge, between 1720 and 1725, and it was here that Thornhill spent his last years as a country gentleman, visited by fellow artists such as the portrait painter Jonathan Richardson, between July and August 1733. By the time of Richardson's visit to Dorset in 1733 to paint Thornhill's portrait (cat. 56), he was visibly ailing. Of his death in 1734 Walpole wrote *'affected with the gout and his leg swelling, he set out for his seat at Thornhill near Weymouth, where four days after his arrival he expired in his chair . . . aged fifty-seven'.*[6] Thornhill was buried in nearby Stalbridge church; his widow inherited the Dorset house, though she finally moved to London to live with her daughter Jane and son-in-law, William Hogarth.[7]

The decline in Thornhill's artistic fortune was emblematic of the lack of interest in history painting. Less than fifty years after his death, when Hutchins was trying to write an account of the artist's life in Dorset, he found direct information scarce. In 1767 Hutchins approached Horace Walpole for biographical detail but was informed that despite 'turning over Vertue's MSS' Walpole observed that 'there is nothing, but some few notices relating to his works,' suggesting Hutchins contact Thornhill's daughter.[8] Walpole who subscribed to Hutchins's *History* made his lukewarm view of Thornhill clear, 'He had some merit, and we have few good painters; but surely Sir James was not one of the first class!'[9]

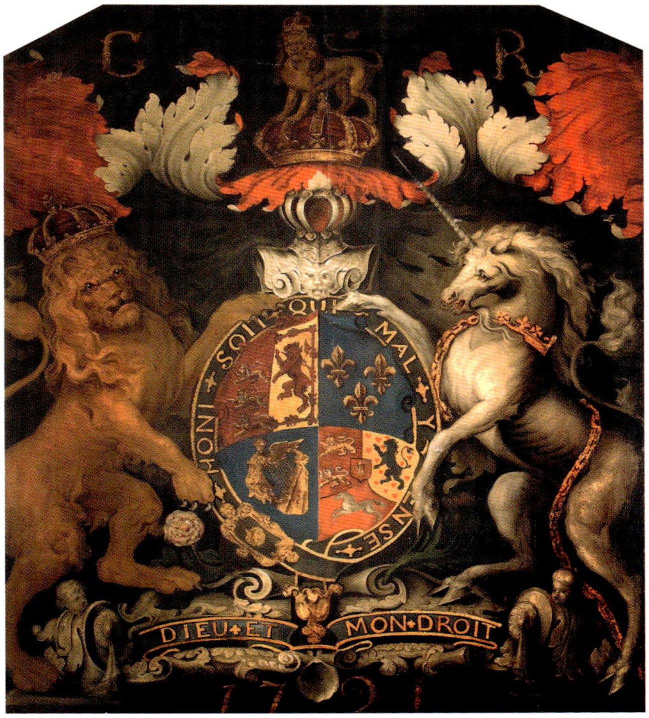

Fig. 23. *Coat of Arms of George I,* oil on panel, Sir James Thornhill, 1721.

Giles Hussey and the failure of history painting

Thornhill encouraged history painting through the academy he ran at his Covent Garden house and through the writings of his friend, Jonathan Richardson. Richardson briefly taught another Dorset artist, Giles Hussey (cat. 58). Hussey, the sixth son of John Hussey of Marnhull, came from an ancient Dorset family of landowners and farmers and was born at Nash Court, about six miles from Thornhill. As a Roman Catholic, Hussey was educated abroad at the English Benedictine college at Douai and St Omer c. 1717–22.[10] Back in England in 1727 he was an indentured apprentice to Jonathan Richardson, but left him after one month for the continental appeal of Venetian history painter Vincenzo Damini. He assisted Damini on his fresco commission for Lincoln Cathedral, travelling with him to Italy in 1730. In Bologna Hussey studied drawing, composition and design, acquiring a considerable reputation. In 1734 Sir John Evelyn read a letter to the Society of Antiquaries in London which stated '*one Hussey, a Dorsetshire Gentleman was the Most Celebrated Master in Drawing*'.[11]

Hussey returned from Italy in 1737 following his father's death, with the help of Sir Hugh Smithson, later 1st Duke of Northumberland. He arrived back with a dazzling reputation and high expectations, completing a number of history paintings for Smithson, including a painting of *Bacchus* (Syon House). In 1745 Hussey was elected to the Spalding Gentlemen's Society, where he was described as 'History Painter of the Schools of Rome and Bologna'.[12] But despite his reputation, Hussey found there was little market for his paintings of antique deities. He was forced to turn to portraiture, frequently clothing his sitters in ancient Greek or Roman costume.[13]

By 1768 a disappointed Hussey finally abandoned London for Dorset. He inherited the family estate at Marnhull in 1773 where he largely remained, working on an elaborate theory of beauty based on harmonic proportion and drawing portraits for a circle of Catholic patrons, in particular the Arundells of Wardour Castle and the Weld family at Lulworth.[14] Between the early 1770s and 1785 Hussey produced a number of profile drawings for Thomas Weld showing his family, relations and contacts of which at least twenty-four are still known.[15] Amongst the profiles in ovals was a self-portrait of Hussey aged 63, dated 1773, the year he inherited the family estate, later reproduced as a print (cat. 58).

With the income from his Marnhull estates, Hussey was able to indulge his theoretical ideas and his profile portrait drawings were drawn as if on the musical scale, since Hussey believed the human face was in harmony with itself (fig. 50). In 1779 Hussey wrote to a Dorset neighbour, 'the order of nature in harmonical progression of numbers becomes the rule of art, from which we cannot deviate without error, and consequent reproof'.[16] This led to the highly distinctive qualities of his instantly recognisable faces as he forced these head and shoulder portraits into his tightly conceived formula, described in detail in Hutchins's Second Edition.[17] Thomas Weld commissioned Hussey to produce a drawing of Lulworth Castle, engraved by Basire, for inclusion in Hutchins's *History* of 1774, *S.W. View of Lulworth Castle taken from the Grove*, undoubtedly at the request of Dr William Cuming (fig. 24), local physician and another of Hussey's sitters from the Weld group, who used his role as physician to encourage donors to give plates of their houses for the *History*.[18]

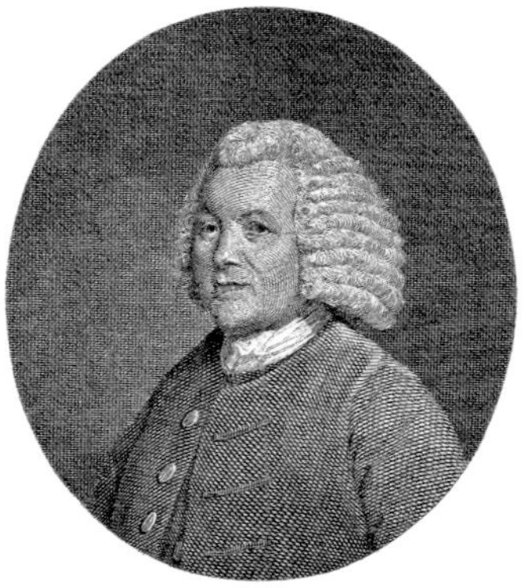

Fig. 24. *Dr William Cuming*, engraving after Thomas Beach by William Sharp, 1785.

London painters, Dorset sitters

Portraiture therefore remained the most commercially viable option for a young painter. In the 1740s, Jonathan Richardson's principal pupil, Thomas Hudson, emerged as the most fashionable practitioner. George Vertue observed that 'he has great business and much merritt, his drawings of portraits true fair and Easy, his draperys well disposd and his actions natural, his flesh colours well imitated & his manner agreeable', adding that his paintings 'supplyes the want of Sr. G. Kneller – in most cases.'

A successful painter like Hudson would have required a considerable studio to assist in the production of portraits. Typically the portraitist would only be responsible for the head, hands and pose of the figure, leaving details of costume to an assistant or contracting it out to a drapery painter. The most successful drapery painter of the period was the Dutch artist Joseph Van Aken. George Vertue described that many of the successful portraitists of the 1740s, including Hudson and Allan Ramsay, painted with his assistance, 'whose draperys silks satins Velvets, gold & embroideryes which he dos paint for several of them painters extreamly well – and is a great addition to their works and indeed puts them so much on a Level that its very difficult to know one hand from another'.[19] Allan Ramsay's early portrait of Mary Bond (cat. 35) provides an instance of this kind of collaboration; a drawing for her costume by Joseph Van Aken survives in the National Gallery of Scotland. The confusion mentioned by Vertue persists. Van Aken was almost certainly partly responsible for the portrait of Joseph Gulston, here attributed to Thomas Hudson (cat. 49).

A portrait of Gulston signed by Allan Ramsay and dated 1746, shows Gulston in a pose derived from Van Dyck's portrait of the *Earl of Carnarvon* (Wilton House).

It was during the 1740s that the two most prominent portraitists of the century emerged, Joshua Reynolds and Thomas Gainsborough. The Devon-born Reynolds was a member of Hudson's studio, establishing himself in London as an independent master, following the support of several local patrons. At the same time Gainsborough, who had trained in the circle of the second St. Martin's Lane Academy, finding insufficient work in London, moved back to his native Suffolk. Their two careers represented the options open to a British portraitist, either to forge a career in the highly competitive metropolitan market, or move to one of the thriving rural centres; it is instructive that both painters relied on patronage from their home counties at the beginning of their careers, much as Thomas Beach would two decades later.

Reynolds developed a highly sophisticated portrait style during the 1750s, exemplified in his group portrait of *Charles James Fox, Lady Sarah Bunbury and Lady Susan Fox-Strangways* of 1764 (private collection). Susan Fox-Strangways was the daughter of the 1st Earl of Ilchester (cat. 4) and sister of the 2nd (cat. 15), she is shown walking in the garden of Holland House with her cousins.[20] Reynolds frequently staged his grander sitters in semi-historical guises, borrowing poses from Old Master paintings. At the same date Reynolds had a lucrative practice producing head and shoulder portraits of more modest patrons with the assistance of his studio, which by 1760 included the Dorset-born Thomas Beach.

In 1759 Gainsborough moved from Suffolk to the fashionable resort of Bath, by then established as a lucrative centre for portraitists, attended as it was by a constant stream of potential clients. Like Reynolds, Gainsborough produced ambitious portraits of prominent sitters such as the 1st Lord Rivers in 1769 (Cleveland Museum of Art, Ohio), which he showed at the Royal Academy, whilst perfecting a highly commercial head and shoulders format for less wealthy clients. In 1767 Gainsborough painted the modest portraits of John Bragge (cat. 38) and his wife Elizabeth. Famed for his speed of execution, a simple portrait like of those of the Bragges would have been completed in a matter of days.

Thomas Beach

Thomas Beach modelled his own practice very much in the commercial shadow of Reynolds and Gainsborough. Whilst adopting the style and highly regulated life of Reynolds, he followed Gainsborough to Bath in 1771, using it as a base for his summer tours, visiting patrons in Somerset and Dorset. Despite being one of Reynolds's most capable imitators and establishing a prolific portrait practice telling us much about the strategies of itinerant artists in the eighteenth century, Beach has received little scholarly attention.[21]

Born at Milton Abbas, in 1738, the third of four children of Thomas and Ursula Beach, little is known about his early life. Beach's artistic ability, first revealed at school, resulted in Lord Milton sending him to train with Joshua Reynolds in 1760, studying also at the second St. Martin's Lane Academy.[22] As Reynolds's assistant, Beach transferred the outline of Reynolds's designs to canvas and applied the under painting, known in the eighteenth century as 'dead colouring', to portraits.[23] In the two years he was with Reynolds, Beach learnt not only technique, but the process of managing a portrait practice and cultivating patrons. Beach undoubtedly met Dorset clients sitting for Reynolds, for example several of the Digby brothers (cats. 9–13) and Charles Blair of Winterborne Whitechurch. In consequence perhaps, in 1765 Beach painted Blair's portrait in Dorset and members of Blair's family between 1777 and 1782.[24]

Recognizing Bath's potential, Beach moved to the city in 1771 with the guarantee of visiting Dorset gentry. By 1778 he was living in rooms in 2 Westgate Buildings, strategically placed to attract custom on the direct carriage route between the Circus and Pump room. Beach rented his rooms from Charles Davis and his family of artists' colourmen and Beach's diary reveals his close relationship with them.[25] It was during this period that he established his pattern of painting society portraits in Bath during the winter season and in summer visiting Dorset and Somerset country houses. This astutely doubled his local client base. For example he painted Seymer family portraits in Bath and then visited the family in Dorset at Hanford. Throughout his time in Bath Beach kept in contact with London, becoming a fellow of the Society of Artists, the year after his move to Bath, and Vice-President in 1780.[26] He consistently submitted portraits to their annual exhibition, until the decline of the Society during the 1780s when he began to send portraits to the Royal Academy. Adept at self-promotion, in 1778 Beach organized Bath's first public art exhibition at his rooms, promoting his work and the arts in general.[27] He organised concerts in his rooms with key musicians such as the violinist Johann Peter Salomon and the great castrato Giusto Ferdinando Tenducci, regularly visited the Pump Rooms and the theatre where many of the actors and musicians sat to him, including Sarah Siddons and John Philip Kemble.[28]

Without extant letters and associated biographical material, Beach's working life has been pieced together through his pocket diary for 1798. It provides a clear account of Beach's commercial strategy and working life. In the manner of Reynolds, Beach's short daily entries name the sitters, duration of sitting, supplementing this with the names of visitors, and the progress made on each portrait. He seems generally to have had about three pictures in production at any one time. We also know that Beach was employed to clean Old Master paintings either *in situ* or at his rooms; on 29 May 1798 he mentions cleaning paintings by Van Ostade and Guercino. Highly productive, the diary records Beach painting thirty-two portraits in Bath and Dorset during the course of 1798.

Beach in Dorset

Beach's Dorchester relations provided a guaranteed base when he was working in the county every summer from 1762. Henry Seymer's (cat. 53) diary for 1765 noted Beach painted family portraits at Hanford. In 1772 Peter Beckford, (cat. 22) William Churchill, Richard Howard and Henry Portman sat wearing the colours of the Beckford Hunt. This was an early example of Beach using a Dorset-based organisation to sustain a number of commissions from potentially lucrative clients, a pattern he would repeat in the 1790s in his portraits of the Dorset Volunteer Rangers. This kind of corporate portraiture became popular from the 1760s onwards, a particular feature of the provincial master. In 1762 Joseph Wright of Derby had painted six members of the Markeaton Hunt. The Fox-Strangways portraits of 1777 and 1778 indicate Beach was probably staying at Redlynch in Somerset. Beach was in Dorset in 1777 painting members of the Michel and Blair families. Henry Portman of Bryanston, the great property developer who built much of Marylebone, was painted along with four members of his family in 1780.[29] In 1788 Beach was at Blandford to paint one of two versions of *Dr Richard Pulteney* (cat. 54) and in 1782 Mrs Siddons reported dining with Beach in Dorchester; the following year he painted members of the Steward family (cat. 39) in Weymouth.

The Diary of 1798

On Saturday 23 June, Beach packed up his painting box and left Bath for Somerset and Dorset, returning to Bath by Thursday 13 December.[30] In Somerset he visited friends and patrons of thirty years standing, the Phelips at Montacute House, where he 'Cleand a Picture of the Dog', and the Helyars of Coker Court near Yeovil, but painted only one portrait, that of his Somerton cousin James Bryer. The first Dorset visit was to the Seymers at Hanford where he remained for the month. At Hanford he was treated as one of the family, included in all their activities, dining, walking out, meeting mutual friends, attending church and playing cards; families even placed their transport at his disposal. Beach immediately began working on Mrs Seymer's portrait, having painted Henry Seymer in Bath earlier that year. The diary gives revealing detail about his working method; as at Bath, mornings were devoted to sittings. The first day was spent dead colouring the whole painting. The next three sittings were for face and drapery, one afternoon devoted to painting background, then one more drapery session and another to finishing the background; in Mrs Seymer's case this included a porch. There was then a final session for face and drapery and one last sitting with the sitter before the portrait was finished. When staying with Lord Rivers at Stratfield Saye in 1771, Gainsborough also referred to this process and to painting the drapes with no assistant.[31] At Hanford Beach '*cleaned and varnished Archbishop Wake*' and other family portraits and a painting by Francesco Albani. Hanford was fourteen miles from Beach's family home at Milton Abbas and in addition to looking up old neighbours, he called on Lord Milton, now the Earl of Dorchester, presumably to discuss the commission of portraits of the officers of the Dorset Volunteer Rangers for Milton's library. Two days after Mrs Seymer's portrait was completed a copy was commissioned from Beach by a relative, Mr Ker.[32] It is instructive that Mrs Seymer was required to sit for her copy, despite Beach having the first version at hand. At Blandford Beach ordered clothes, stocked up on artist's supplies such as turpentine, caught up with old friends like Dr Pulteney and John Galpine and courted potential commissions.

The diary shows Beach to have been both highly sociable and industrious. He worked the entire week except Sunday with no assistance, managing all aspects of arranging sitters, payments, ordering materials from London and assiduously maintaining contacts to guarantee a steady stream of commissions. Whilst staying with the Seymers at Hanford on 26 July Beach recorded a letter from 'Mrs Pleydell asks the price of a child's picture', exactly a month later Beach had travelled to Whatcombe and records the completion of his portrait of 'Master Pleydell' (private collection).[33] The diary records Beach's arrival at Whatcombe on 19 August, the following day 'after breakfast began Master Pleydell's Picture – Dead coloured the whole' he then paints in order his face, hands and drapery, completing it five days later. Beach generally wrote ahead to the next patron on his itinerary, ensuring transport and other arrangements, travelling from Whatcombe to Melcombe where he started a portrait of Edmond Morton Pleydell's sister, Cornelia Stuart (private collection).[34] His major expense was travel, paying drivers, coachmen and for the transportation of his paintings. His outgoings seemed to be larger than his income, payment for paintings seemed particularly slow for 1798.

While constantly on the move, Beach made regular purchases of turpentine, linseed oil, tacks and transparent paper, and carried colours and canvasses with him. Earlier in the year he had purchased fitches (brushes) from Cohen at Charing Cross and also received parcels of colours and pencils from London by mail. At Dorchester he ordered an easel; straining frames were made by local carpenters often at estates where he was staying, and frames were ordered from carver William Griffier. Briefly married, Beach mainly lived a bachelor existence. He is thought to have retired to Dorchester, perhaps where he produced his two final self-portraits in 1801 (cat. 57) and 1802 (NPG). He died in Dorchester on 17 December 1806, aged 68, and was buried in the churchyard of All Saints beside the widow of his brother William. In 1905 a memorial brass was placed in the church to celebrate his life, this is now in St Peter's Church in Dorchester.

Unlike Reynolds or Gainsborough, Beach did not attempt either history painting or landscape, content to practice solely as a portraitist. He was capable of highly dramatic theatrical compositions like his double portrait of *Elizabeth Siddons and John Philip Kemble* in the dagger scene from Macbeth (Garrick Club, London) painted in 1786. But Beach was most successful in communicating a good likeness of his sitters, usually in half-length, shown close to the picture plane framed by a feigned oval and often animated through a slightly open mouth, or tilted head. This simplicity appealed to his rural clients and allowed Beach to replicate his formula whilst travelling around. The conservatism of his compositions belies considerable skill in execution and freedom in handling.

Hanging portraits in Dorset

With no forum for the public display of art in the county – although altarpieces by Thornhill could be seen in Weymouth and Folke – civic patronage was rare and country houses became the principal place where art was viewed. As political influence resided in the ownership of land, country houses assumed a new importance during the eighteenth century as a place for entertaining, canvassing and consolidating local support. Increased mobility during the century meant that country houses were more accessible to neighbours and tourists, giving the furnishing of interiors and the display of portraiture a new importance. In John O'Keeffe's 1793 comedy, *The London Hermit, or Rambles in Dorsetshire*, the fictional Squire Whimmy wished 'to oblige the world of taste and fashion, by showing them my house, pictures, gardens and improvements'[35] One of the ways in which a landowner could celebrate his tenure was in the form of a portrait and this often specifically highlighted his 'improvements'; Beach's portrait of Thomas Weld shows the Catholic landowner holding plans of the chapel he has built by John Tasker.[36]

Joseph Banks, the great scientist, made a tour of the county in 1767 and specifically records being disappointed in his attempts to see the pictures at Lord Portman's house Bryanston, though more fortunate when visiting John Bankes at Kingston Hall, near Wimborne; allowed to view the house, he observed that though the pictures were fine, Mr Banks had no catalogue and knew nothing about them![37] Joshua Reynolds visited with Samuel Johnson in 1762; he left notes in the house (still preserved in the library) observing 'that he never had fully appreciated Sir Peter Lely till he has seen these portraits'.[38] In 1797 William Maton reported that 'Mr Weld has the goodness to permit strangers to see the internal part of his noble house every Wednesday.'[39] He admired the 'elegance and commodiousness of the apartments' and particularly noted that amongst the treasures on show was 'a collection of portraits in pencil by that very ingenious artist and eccentric character Giles Hussey.' The increased interest in painting as a polite art during the eighteenth century resulted in the inclusion of several 'catalogues' in the second edition of Hutchins.[40] The hang at Milton Abbey is described in detail; giving an impression of the portraiture and its use. The principal rooms for entertainment, the drawing-room and saloon, are described as 'full of pictures', set off with simple pea-green or French grey furniture and the dining parlour was hung with 'state' portraits of *Joseph Damer* after Pompeo Batoni, and his wife, *Lady Caroline Sackville,* which were copies by Angelica Kauffmann. Caroline Sackville was the daughter of the Duke and Duchess of Dorset and brought her Sackville fortune to the union, so full-length portraits of her parents were also hung in the dining room.[41] Marriage was frequently the stimulus for portraiture, John Downman's image of the *Reverend John Richards* and Gainsborough's portrait of *John Bragge* and his wife were both painted to celebrate nuptials. At the end of the century Joseph Damer commissioned Thomas Beach to paint the portraits of the first officers of the Dorset Volunteer Rangers; Beach's portrait of the

Prince of Wales was given pride of place over the fireplace, whilst the officers were installed above the bookcases at Milton Abbey.

The connoisseur Horace Walpole recorded his travels through Dorset in 1762, noting key portraits in each house he visited. Walpole's descriptions give a vivid idea of how a nexus of family and political connections was played out through portraits in the semi-public interiors of Dorset's country houses. At Redlynch, Somerset, home of Lord Ilchester, Walpole listed a portrait of Lord Ilchester's Whig patron, Walpole's father *Sir Robert Walpole in hunting dress* (private collection). Melbury is described as being 'most richly and abundantly furnished with pictures, tapestry, fine tables . . . & many family pictures.' The staircase was dominated by a vast painting of Thomas Strangways with his wife Susanna Rideout and six of their children; begun in the late seventeenth century it was altered and largely repainted by Thomas Hill between 1720 to 1722, incorporating contemporary portraits of the earlier sitters, positioned in front of the new east front of the house itself.[42] This probably explains Elizabeth Fox-Strangway's (cat. 17) description of Melbury in 1794 as 'this gloomy mansion of our forefathers.'[43] This celebration of ancestors reflected a new historicism in the display of portraits around 1750; Walpole recorded the installation of a copy of Van Dyck's portrait of the seventeenth century courtier *Sir Kenelm Digby* in the library of Sherborne Castle.[44] It was Walpole himself, at his country villa Strawberry Hill, who had started a new fashion for genealogy and the antiquarian preservation of portraits. Edward, 6th Lord Digby, followed Walpole's lead, employing the Dorset architect Francis Cartwright to design a delicate Gothic interior in which to house the portrait of his illustrious forbear.

Copyists were frequently employed to replicate family portraits both ancient and modern. At Redlynch Walpole noted Ranelagh Barrett's copy of *Queen Elizabeth's Procession to Blackfriars*, a celebrated painting in the collection of the first Earl of Ilchester's nephew, Henry, 7th Lord Digby, at Sherborne Castle. Portrait copies were accorded the same status as the primary version and crucially served to cement familial connections. After Edward Digby's untimely death in 1757 at the age of 27, Barrett made two copies of his portrait by Pompeo Batoni. The primary version remained at Sherborne Castle with Henry Digby, one copy was possibly owned by his younger brother Robert, and a second was installed over the fireplace in the Saloon at Redlynch.[45] It is likely that Barrett, who was described by George Vertue as having 'much busines and employment . . . for persons of quality,' travelled to Dorset to copy the Digby portraits. Equally, multiple versions were a feature of studio practice.

Conclusion

It was an eighteenth century convention for patrons to sponsor talented local artists and send them to train with an established practitioner in London. Dorset has examples of this, such as Lord Milton sending a local village boy Thomas Beach to Joshua Reynolds. George III sent William Delamotte, Weymouth son of the local bookshop keeper, to the Royal Academy Schools, and later the Reverend Thomas Rackett sponsored Alfred Stevens's study in Italy.[46] Whilst Dorset was not at the forefront of artistic taste during the century, the range of portraiture in this exhibition, which includes family group portraits and marriage pictures, celebrates military standing and commercial prowess. That Dorset produced three painters and also architects able to satisfy demand to an exacting standard reveals the power of patronage operating in the county during the eighteenth-century.

1 J.A. Rouquet, *The Present State of the Arts in England*, London, 1755, p. 45.
2 For a discussion see I. Bignamini, 'George Vertue, Art Historian, and Art Institutions in London, 1689–1768', *The Walpole Society*, 1988, 54, p. 34.
3 Mary Sydenham, daughter of the governor of Weymouth was from a renowned Parliamentary Dorset family.
4 Vertue, 1929–47, 3, p. 62 and 4, p. 145.
5 Christopher Pitt of Blandford dedicated a poem to Thornhill's Charborough commission, *To Sir James Thornhill, on his excellent Painting the Rape of Helen, at the Seat of General Erle in Dorsetshire'*, 1718. Thornhill's other Dorset commissions included the decorative scheme at Minterne for the Churchills, of which a small fragment still remains.
6 H. Walpole, *Anecdotes of Painting in England*, London, 1782, 4, p. 46.
7 It is likely that Hogarth visited Dorset to stay with his brother-in-law John Thornhill, where he painted the portrait of *Thomas Coombs* (cat. 62).
8 ed. W. S. Lewis, *The Correspondence of Horace Walpole,* vol. I, p. 334. Horace Walpole to John Hutchins, from Arlington Street, 17 February 1767. See too Hutchins ed.3, 2, pp. 461–463.
9 Horace Walpole to John Hutchins, Paris, 22 September, 1765, ed.3, vol.2, pp. 461–2.
10 There is a comprehensive account of Hussey and his theories in Hutchins, ed.2, 4, pp. 154–160 and ed.3, 4, pp. 307–314.
11 Society of Antiquaries library, Minutes, 1732–7, 15 June 1734, 2:42. 4.
12 Giles Hussey aroused the concern of Vertue, a significant member of the Spalding Gentlemen's Society and a fellow Catholic. Hussey's membership of the Society was proposed and accepted in November 1745, though he ceased being a member by 1747.
13 He allegedly burned many of his portraits and felt he had been the victim of a whispering campaign, see J. Shackleton, '*A Portrait of Giles Hussey, 1709–1788, A biography of the Dorset artist'*, 1999, privately published, p. 69.
14 Lady Arundell owned a number of Hussey's pencil sketches and drawings, including a self portrait, coloured with a thin water-colour wash. See J. Shackleton, *A Portrait of Giles Hussey, 1709–1788,* 1999, private publication, p. 66.
15 Sotheby's, 12 March 1987, lots 1–24.
16 Hutchins, ed.3, 4, p. 310.
17 Hutchins, ed.2, 4, p. 154–160 and ed.3,4, pp. 307–314.
18 A copy was in George III's 'Topographical Collection' now in the British Library.
19 Vertue, 1929–47, 3, p. 117.
20 Lady Susanna Sarah Louise Fox caused a scandal when she eloped with actor William O'Brien in 1764 under the pretext of sitting for her portrait to pastellist Katharine Read. The couple eventually retired to Stinsford House, near Dorchester. J. Martin, *Wives and Daughters in the Georgian Country House*, London, 2004, p. 40.
21 At the beginning of the twentieth century Beach's descendant, Elise Beach, began compiling a catalogue of Beach's known work. She had access to family papers and his only extant diary for 1798, for her account of Beach's life. Helped in her research by Hilda Finberg, she published her book before their research was complete. Brinsley Ford archive, Paul Mellon Centre for British Art.
22 Beach's younger sister Frances, known as Fanny, later kept house for him at Strand-on-the-Green, London, where their near neighbours were the Zoffanys.
23 See Mannings, 1, p. 9. Paintings were sent out to artists like John Giles Eccardt for completion. Reynolds also employed journeymen. Horace Walpole records

that 'Peter Toms, reckoned the best painter of draperies in London, paints for Reynolds.'

24 I am indebted to Charles Beddington for making this connection.

25 See Sloman, 2002, p. 66, 231n. S. Sloman, 'Artists' Picture Rooms in 18th-Century Bath', *Bath History*, 6, 1996, p. 149. The partnership, Charles Davis & Son, at 2 Westgate Buildings, was dissolved on 5 January 1794, the business was continued by Charles Davis jun., who advertised 'funerary achievements, pictures cleaned, lined & repaired, colours and oils for house painting, gold leaf etc'.

26 Whitley, 1, p. 394 notes that Beach tried to revive the Incorporated Society's failing fortunes by exhibiting his portraits of Mrs Siddons at their annual exhibition amongst a number of other Bath portraits. In 1783 Beach sent 16 portraits to the Society's exhibition and was made President. He continued to support it until the Society came to an end in 1791.

27 Sloman, 2002, p. 17.

28 Sloman, 2002, p. 16.

29 One of Beach's portraits of Henry Portman belongs to The Trustees of the Portman Settled Estates. Sloman, 2002, p. 27, refers to Beach's portrait of Henry William Portman, which was sold at Christie's, 24 November, 1978, lot 80.

30 Beach, 1934, pp. 35–47.

31 ed. J. Hayes, *The Letters of Thomas Gainsborough*, New Haven and London, 2001, p. 78. Gainsborough was there to paint the grand portraits of Rivers's daughter and son-in-law, Lord and Lady Ligonier (Huntingdon Library, California).

32 Henry Seymer junior married Grace Ker a kinsman of Lord Rivers, thence the family name became Ker-Seymer.

33 Beach painted a portrait of Edmond Morton Pleydell, his sisters Anne and Mary, and his son Edmond Morton who died young. Hutchins, ed.3., 1, p. 199.

34 Cornelia Pleydell married Hon. Archibald Stuart, son of the Earl of Moray, at the same date Beach painted a portrait of their son, Francis Archibald Stuart playing a drum (private collection). See E. Beach, 1934, cat. nos. 271–273.

35 J. O'Keeffe, *The London Hermit*, or *Rambles in Dorsetshire,* London, 1793, p. 3.

36 See T. Holt 'Thomas Weld's New Chapel at Lulworth – Some Contemporary Correspondence', *DNH&AS Proceedings*, 1C, 1977, pp. 33–41; J. Manco and F. Kelly, 'Lulworth Castle from 1700', *Architectural History*, 34, 1991, pp. 145–170.

37 Ed. J.C. Mansel-Pleydell ,'Journal of an Excursion to Eastbury and Bristol etc in May and June 1767, Sir Joseph Banks Bart. With Notes by S.G. Perceval, Esq., of Henbury and Bristol', *Proceedings of the Dorset Natural History and Antiquarian Field Club,* 21, 1900, pp. 143–149.

38 Hutchins, ed.3, 3, p. 237.

39 Devon Record Office, 219/2/10a-b, the original MS. of W. Maton's *Tour in the Western Counties*, 1797, p. 24. (Complete with Thomas Rackett's sketches).

40 There is evidence that Hutchins was read by those with a particular interest in art. The antiquarian William Musgrave lists portraits mentioned in Hutchins in his 'Lists'. See A. Meyer, 'Sir William Musgrave's 'Lists of Portraits'; with an account of head-hunting in the eighteenth century', *The Walpole Society*, 1998, 54, pp. 454–503.

41 See Hutchins, ed. 2, 4, pp. 220–222. See too J. Harris, *Sir William Chambers*, 1970, p. 226; G. Beard, *Craftsmen and Interior Decoration in* England 1660–1820, Edinburgh, 1981; G. Beard and C. Gilbert (eds.), *Dictionary of English Furniture Makers 1660–1840*, 1986. In 1771 the London framer and gilder Robert Ansell was asked to provide an estimate for gilding for Lord Milton at Milton Abbas on behalf of William Chambers.

42 See O. Millar 'Artists and Craftsmen in the Service of Sir Stephen Fox and His Family', *The Burlington Magazine*, 137, No. 1109, 1995, pp. 518–528.

43 DRO D/FS1, box 241; correspondence from Elizabeth Fox-Strangways to the 2nd Earl, 1794.

44 See S. Barnes, N. De Poorter, O. Millar and H. Vey, *Van Dyck; A Complete Catalogue of the Paintings,* New Haven and London, 2004, cat. no.4, pp. 94–98. Although none of the Van Dycks were in the collection of Sherborne Castle an early eighteenth century copy of the family portrait and Sir Kenelm were installed there.

45 Ed. P. Toynbee, 'Horace Walpole's Journals of visits to country seats, etc.' *Walpole Society*, 16, 1927–8, p. 44, Walpole, on his visit to Redlynch described the double cube Saloon, 'hung with green damask and pictures'.

46 DHC, DAC/RAC/70, R. Poley, Blandford to the Reverend Thomas Rackett, Spetisbury, 10 July 1834. Poley sought Rackett's financial support for Alfred Stevens's study in Italy.

Catalogue

1. **Studio of Sir William Beechey** (1753–1839)

George III (1738–1820)
oil on canvas, 1799–1800
76.8×64.8 cm

Provenance: Artist's studio; Royal Female Orphanage, Beddington Park; Collection of the Shaftesbury Society; Leggatt Bros. 1970; Bequest of Lord Kenyon, 1993.
Literature: J. Ingamells, *Mid-Georgian Portraits, 1760–1790,* London, pp. 191–203
Exhibited: Smithsonian, 2007.

National Portrait Gallery

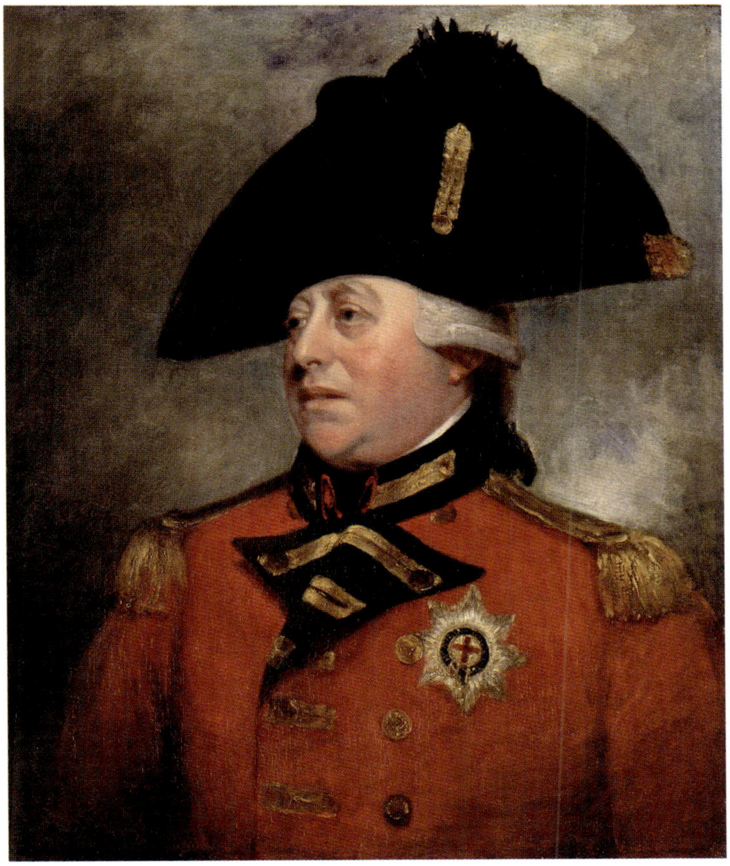

George III was the first Hanoverian monarch born and raised in England. He ascended the throne in 1760 and, during his long eventful reign lasting until 1820, gained India, won and lost America and defeated revolutionary France and Napoleon. He took a personal interest in government, though his firm views sometimes amounted to obstinacy, resulting in disaster when he refused to recognize American colonists' grievances of no taxation without representation. Following illness in 1788, his recovery was publicly celebrated on 10 March 1789 and in June that year the King came to Weymouth for the first time to take the water cures.[1]

In 1761 the King married Charlotte of Mecklenburg-Strelitz, (1744–1818); both took a keen interest in the upbringing and education of their fifteen children. They presented the nation with the powerful image of a highly domesticated royal family. Industrious George had a range of interests including farming, mechanics and books, and owned an important library.

This head and shoulders portrait of the King is one of several versions and was painted by Sir William Beechey's studio in about 1799–1800. There were difficulties in painting the King's portrait at this time due to the nature of his illness; the competently painted portrait head is supported on a somewhat pedestrian body. The King is shown with grey eyes and white powdered hair, wearing a general's uniform of red coat and white breeches together with the star of the Garter.[2] The portrait is a studio version of the full-length portrait of the King in the uniform of a general at Buckingham Palace, painted by Beechey for George III at the same time and exhibited at the Royal Academy in 1800 (fig 25).[3] A handwritten label on the frame of this portrait states it was given by Beechey to the Royal Female Orphanage at Beddington Park in 1809.

Admired for his direct but decorative portraits, Beechey was appointed portrait painter to the Queen in 1793. He was elected to the Royal Academy in 1798, and knighted the same year that he exhibited *His Majesty Reviewing the Third Dragoon Guards and the Tenth Light Dragoons,* his major work commissioned by the King, (destroyed in the Windsor Castle fire in 1992).[4]

1 Between November 1788 and February 1789 the King had his first attack of the genetic disorder porphyria.
2 Other half-length versions of this portrait are at Deakin University Art Gallery, Burwood, Victoria, NSW; the Royal College of Physicians; Weymouth Museum and a miniature version by William Grimaldi in the Royal Collection.
3 The Royal Collection, Sir William Beechey, *George III*, 1799–80.
4 A version of this painting is also in Weymouth Museum (fig. 21).

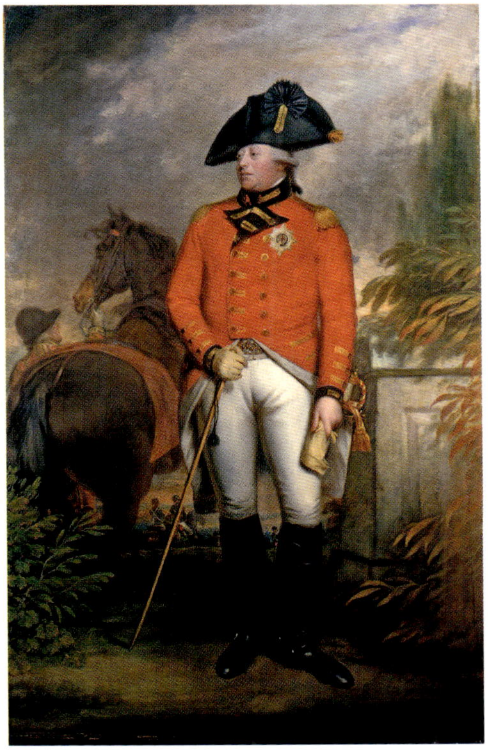

Fig. 25. *George III,* William Beechey, oil on canvas, 1799–1780.

2. **Hugh Douglas Hamilton** (1736–1808)
Prince William Henry, 1st Duke of Gloucester (1743–1805)
pastel on paper, 1773
26×20 cm
Inscribed: *'Hamilton Delin[t] 1773'*
Provenance: Sitter, probably given to Dr Edward Wilmot, then by descent.

3. **Hugh Douglas Hamilton** (1736–1808)
Maria Walpole, Duchess of Gloucester (1736–1807)
pastel on paper, 1772
26×18 cm
Inscribed: *'HDHamilton Delin[t] 1772'*
Provenance: Sitter, probably given to Dr Edward Wilmot, then by descent.

Private Collection

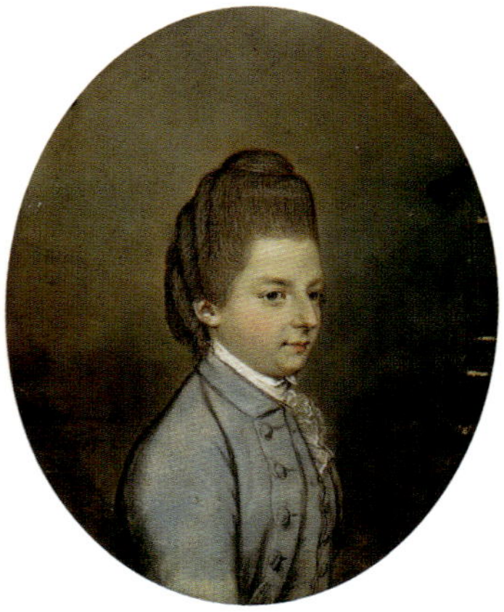
3.

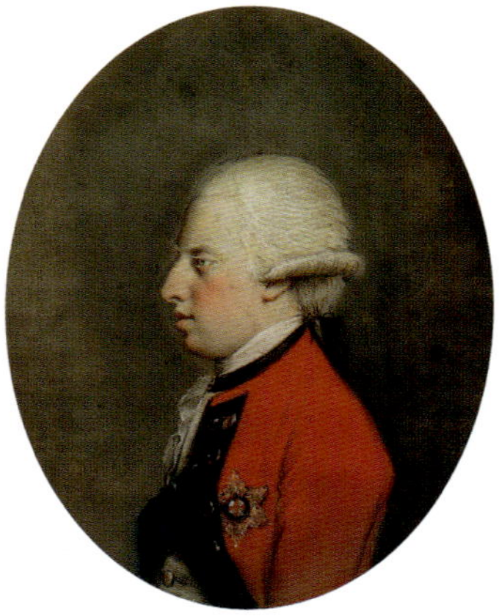
2.

Prince William Henry was third son of Frederick, Prince of Wales and his wife, Augusta, and younger brother of George III. In 1766, he secretly married Maria Waldegrave (*née* Walpole) whom Horace Walpole regarded as a great beauty.[1] The couple kept their marriage secret until the late summer of 1772 when Gloucester, travelling in Italy, learned that his wife was pregnant, forcing him to inform the King. George III cut off Gloucester's allowance, banned them from court and immediately investigated the legitimacy of the marriage.[2]

These previously unrecorded pastel portraits dated 1772 and 1773 were consequently completed in the midst of the marriage crisis. It is possible that the portrait of Maria, shown wearing a simple riding habit, was done before the announcement of their wedding in September 1772, whilst William's portrait of the following year shows him dressed as a general wearing the Garter, and possibly commemorates their marriage becoming public knowledge.

Hamilton was an Irish artist who moved to London in about 1764 and set up a highly lucrative practice as a pastellist, where he charged nine guineas a portrait.[3] His finish varied between slight sketches of unblended strokes with graphite visible, and others which were highly finished. Hamilton exhibited another portrait of the Duke with eleven other sitters at the Society of Artists in 1770, described by Horace Walpole as 'very pretty. These drawings are upon a flesh-coloured chalk, and here and there a touch of crayons'.[4] A portrait of Maria, similarly posed, is dated by Hamilton, 1770 (Gorry Gallery, Dublin).

In 1771, before embarking on his continental tour, the Duke of Gloucester stayed in Weymouth, with the wealthy philanthropist and developer Ralph Allen.[5] The Duke was so impressed by the town that by 1780 he had built his own house, Gloucester Lodge (fig. 18).[6] In June 1780 the King received the Duke for the first time in eight years, and from 1789 Gloucester lent his Weymouth house for use as the summer residence of his brother.[7]

The Duke of Gloucester took part in local activities while staying at Weymouth. Mary Frampton recorded 'He shoots at Moreton and although he was treated apart from the other guests he asked to dine at Moreton instead of merely taking luncheon which threw the household into confusion and panic over protocol etc.'[8] The Duke was in Weymouth in 1786 and again in August 1788 when *The Salisbury & Winchester Journal* reported his arrival 'the guns were fired to announce the happy tidings, and the people in general were eager to testify their joy; flags were displayed, and illuminations shone in every part of the town'.[9] The welcome extended to Mr. Love's Musical and Circulating Library exhibiting a transparent painting, with the following lines:

'Hail, Weymouth! hail this doubly glorious morn,
The Prince's birth, and Glo'ster's wish'd return!
May the salubrious breezes of this place
Establish health in his illustrious race'.

In 1791 John Love and James Fittler published *Views of Weymouth* dedicated to the Duke of Gloucester.

The Duke may have presented the portraits to Dr Edward Wilmot (cat. 24), formerly physician-in-ordinary to George III, who had retired to live with his daughter near Dorchester in about 1761. It is likely that he remained on good terms with the Duke, who experienced similar ill health to the King, and who may have continued to consult him.

1 Maria was the second daughter of Sir Edward Walpole, a younger son of Sir Robert Walpole, the prime minister. She married James Waldegrave, 2nd Earl Waldegrave who died in 1763.
2 The Royal Marriage Act, 1772 was passed the year before their secret marriage was known.
3 See N. Jeffares, *Dictionary of Pastellists before 1800*, Norwich, 2006, p. 226.

4 A. Graves, *The Society of Artists of Great Britain 1761–1791; The Free Society of Artists, 1761–1783*, London, 1907, 1770, no. 214.
5 Ralph Allen discovered Weymouth in about 1750 and by 1758 had built a house on the waterfront where he entertained the young Duke of York.
6 Gloucester Lodge was built on the waste ground between Stacie's Hotel, Assembly Rooms and the precincts of old Melcombe.
7 It is thought the Duke of Gloucester suffered from a medical condition similar to the King's, hence they were united in their desire to seek a cure.
8 Frampton, 1885, p. 27.
9 *The Salisbury & Winchester Journal*, 18 August 1788.

4. **William Hoare** (1707–1792)

Stephen Fox-Strangways, Ist Earl of Ilchester (1704–1776)
oil on canvas, 1740s
75×62 cm
Provenance: Sitter, then by descent.

Sherborne Castle

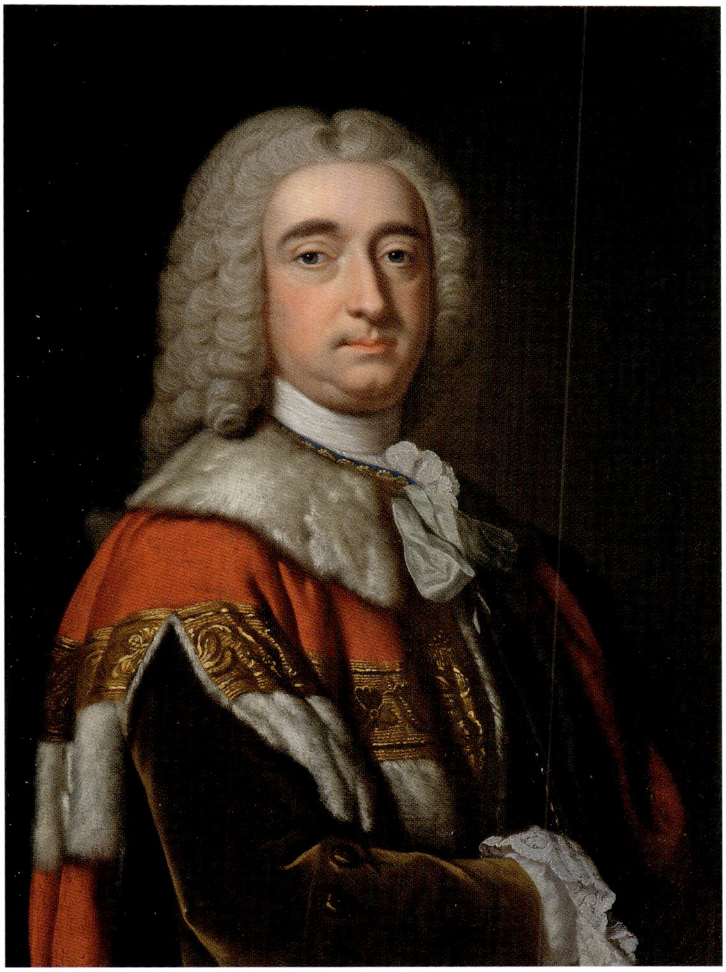

Stephen Fox, Ist Earl of Ilchester, was the son of Stephen Fox, the Paymaster of the Forces to Charles II, and who amassed a vast fortune. Fox travelled abroad on the Continent as a young man in 1723, visiting the Low Countries, France and Italy under the supervision of John Wigan. In Venice in 1724 he sat to Rosalba Carriera, visiting again in 1728 accompanied by Lord Hervey. By 1736 Stephen Fox was married to the heiress Elizabeth Strangways Horner (1722–1792) the only daughter of Thomas Strangways Horner, of Mells Park, Somerset, and his wife Susannah, the daughter and co-heiress of Thomas Strangways of Melbury House, Melbury Sampford, Dorset. At his marriage Stephen Fox retired to lead the life of a country gentleman, mainly at the house he built at Redlynch, Somerset. An important politician at the centre of a powerful Whig coterie, Fox was MP for Shaftesbury between 1726 and 1734 and briefly member for Hindon. From 1735 to 1741 he again represented Shaftesbury and by 1739 held the office of Joint Secretary of the Treasury.

Elizabeth and Stephen had five daughters, and one son Henry Thomas Fox-Strangways (cat. 15).[1] An important union between two great Dorset families took place when Stephen's sister Charlotte married Edward, son of the 5th Lord Digby in 1729 (cats. 5, 7). Stephen Fox was raised to the peerage in 1741 and created first Earl of Ilchester by George II in 1756; two years later he became the owner of Melbury and added his wife's name Strangways to his own, which his children and their descendants continued to use. Aged 72, Stephen Fox died in 1776; his wife survived him as Dowager Countess of Ilchester until 1792, and was an important influence on the Fox-Strangways family.

Shown in his peer's robes, William Hoare's head and shoulder portrait commemorates Fox's elevation to the peerage.[2] Seated, he wears a full-bottomed grey wig, with peer's robes over a brown velvet coat. Probably painted in Somerset, Hoare was the natural choice for Fox as the first fashionable portrait painter to settle in Bath, and a regular visitor to relations nearby at Stourhead. Hoare made at least two further versions of the portrait for the family, this version probably accompanied Charlotte when she married Edward Digby. Stephen Fox appears in Hogarth's informal *Conversation Piece* at Ickworth, c. 1740 together with his brother Lord Holland (father of the famous Charles James Fox), the Duke of Marlborough and the Earl of Bristol.

1 The daughters were Susannah, who married the actor William O'Brien, Charlotte, Juliana, Lucy who married Colonel Stephen Digby (cat. 12) and Christiana Caroline Henrietta (Harriot) (cat. 17) Two of his daughters, at school in Queen Square, Bath, were contemporaries of Fanny Burney, see ed. J. Martin, *A Governess in the Age of Jane Austen. The Journals and Letter of Agnes Porter*, London, 1998, p. 51.
2 By 1763 Fox was admitted to the Privy Council.

5. **Attributed to Enoch Seeman** (1690–1744)
Charlotte Digby, neé Fox (1707–1778)
oil on canvas, c. 1729
76×61 cm
Provenance: Sitter, then by descent.

Sherborne Castle

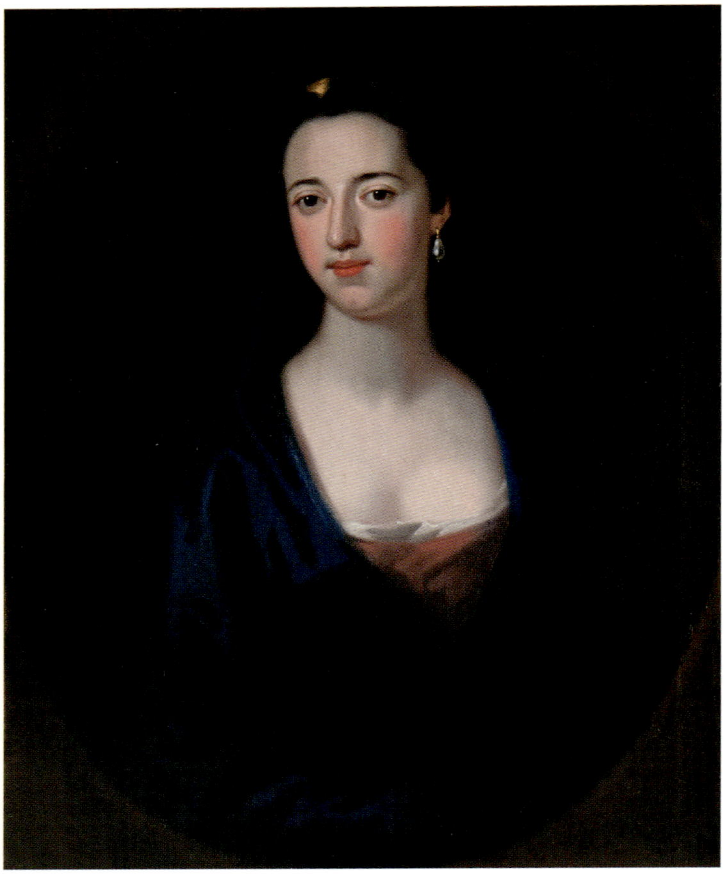

The daughter of Sir Stephen Fox and sister of the 1st Earl of Ilchester (cat. no. 4) and Henry, 1st Baron Holland, Charlotte came from a powerful Whig family. In 1729 she married Edward Digby (cat. 7) fourth surviving son of the 5th Lord Digby (cat. 6), forging a union between the two dynasties. Charlotte and Edward had six sons (cats. 8–13) and one daughter, who appeared as a small child in a portrait with her mother and oldest brother Edward, attributed to Robert Taylor. Charlotte suffered losses throughout her life: in 1746 her husband Edward died, in 1753 her daughter Charlotte, and in 1757 her eldest son Edward (cat. 8) died in Ireland. Charlotte remained an important influence on her sons and their families and close to her brother's family, the Fox-Strangways living nearby at Melbury. After Edward inherited Sherborne Castle in 1752, she acted as chatelaine for him. Wealthy in her own right, after her son Henry's marriage, Charlotte purchased an estate at Thames Ditton, where her sons lived from time to time.

This half-length portrait of Charlotte, is attributed to the German born painter Enoch Seeman and may commemorate her marriage to Digby in 1729. Seeman was a fashionable portraitist working in London; the existence of a portrait of Charlotte's brother, Stephen Fox, inscribed by Seeman and dated 1730 (private collection) suggests Seeman was working for the family at the date of Charlotte's marriage. She is shown in a painted oval, wearing a dark blue shawl over her head, with a gold diadem, in the manner of antique Roman portraits of women. A full-length portrait of Charlotte, holding a feather-arrow in her hand, was painted at around the same date, by Jonathan Richardson.

6. **Attr. Charles Philips** (1708–1747)
William 5th Lord Digby (c. 1662–1752) with the Hon Edward (d. 1746) Charlotte, (1707–1778) and the Hons Frances (d. 1788) and Catherine Digby (1704–1745)
124.5×99.5 cm
oil on canvas, 1740–1745
Provenance: Sitters, then by descent.

Sherborne Castle

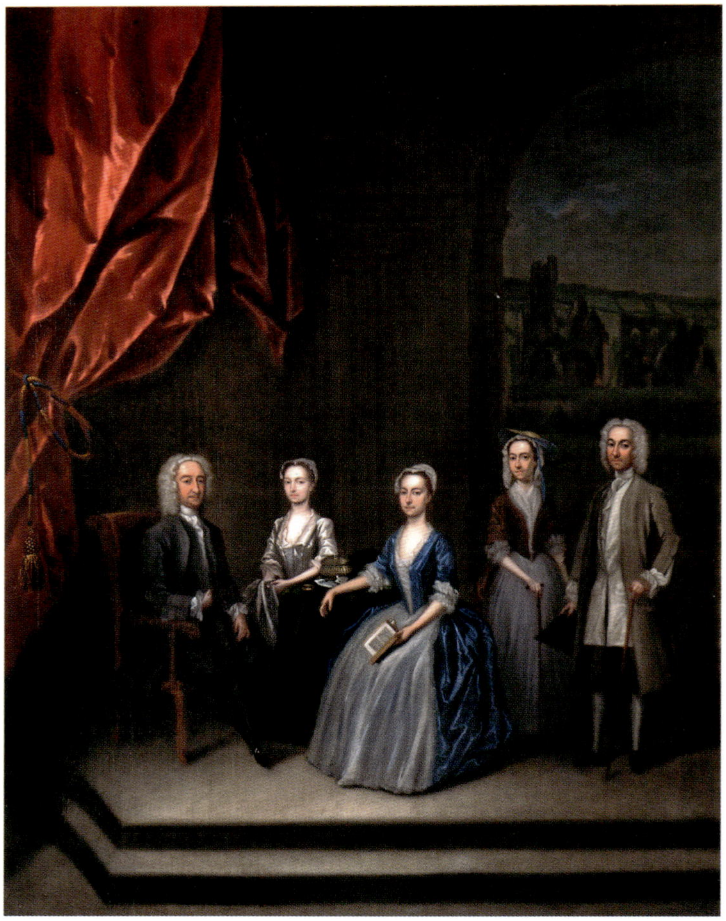

A family conversation piece set in an oak panelled room, perhaps at Sherborne Castle, with the ruins of the Old Castle visible through the window on the right. William, 5th Lord Digby of Coleshill was named 'the Good Lord Digby' in recognition of his philanthropy.[1] He married Lady Jane Noel, second daughter of the first Earl of Gainsborough, by whom he had four sons and eight daughters, residing principally at the family estate near Coleshill, Warwickshire. Alexander Pope, who visited Sherborne in 1724, wrote to Digby, 'your whole family is an example of what is almost now lost in the Nation, the Integrity of Nobility'.[2] William 5th Lord Digby is seated in front of a large red draped curtain on the left, wearing grey coat, waistcoat and breeches and black stockings. To his left two of his daughters are seated at a table. Catherine wears a blue dress and holds a book in her left hand; Frances holds a sampler in her left hand and rests her arm on the table, her workbox and papers nearby. Frances later married Lt. Col. James Cotes of Woodcote, while Catherine died unmarried aged 41, in 1745. The figures in the conversation piece are positioned on a raised dais Standing on the far right is Edward Digby, (cat. 7) the 5th Lord's oldest surviving son, with his wife Charlotte Digby née Fox (cat. 5). They turn slightly towards one another each holding walking canes; Charlotte's straw hat with unfastened blue ribbons implies they were recently walking on the estate.

Charles Philips, court painter to the Prince of Wales, was a successful portrait painter popular with the nobility. His small-scale full-length conversation pieces of doll-like groups in known interiors such as this, were very popular among the nobility throughout the 1730s. The attribution to Philips is long-standing and, given the ages of the sitters, the portrait was probably painted some time between 1740–45, by which time the vogue for such portraits was passing.

A Tory and Stuart sympathiser, Digby refused to take the oath of allegiance to William and Mary. MP for Warwick, (his Irish peerage enabled him to sit in the House of Commons), Digby was an active legislator until he retired in 1698 when he inherited the Sherborne estate from a cousin. There he settled into the life of an independent country gentleman but also carried out the charitable activities which merited his moniker, visiting Fleet Prison to settle the accounts of inmates. After the death of his wife in 1733 he endowed a school in Sherborne for thirteen poor girls. Digby outlived most of his children and was succeeded not by Edward, who died in 1746, but by his grandson Edward (cat. 8). This portrait therefore records three of his surviving children, yet in a short time two of them were also dead. William also sat for his portrait to Robert Taylor, of which several versions and an engraving are known.[3]

1 M. Kilburn, *ODNB*, Oxford, 2008. Whiston, an anti-trinitarian clergyman associate of Digby's, invented this description of Digby.
2 Ed. G. Sherburn, *The Correspondence of Alexander Pope*, Oxford, 1956, 3, p. 52. Pope was no doubt aware of Digby's Stuart leanings. During his visit Pope planted Scotch firs at Sherborne.
3 A print of *5th Lord Digby* by Robert Taylor, was engraved by John Faber in 1743.

7. **Attributed to Robert Taylor** (fl. 1737–1755)

The Hon Edward Digby (d. 1746) with three of his sons Henry (1731–1793), Robert (1732–1815), and William (1733–1788)
oil on canvas, c. 1736–1740
74.5×61 cm

Provenance: Sitters, then by descent.
Literature: Hutchins, 3rd. ed., 4, p. 280; L. M. Portman, *Catalogue of the Pictures at Sherborne Castle*, 1862, p. 106.

Sherborne Castle

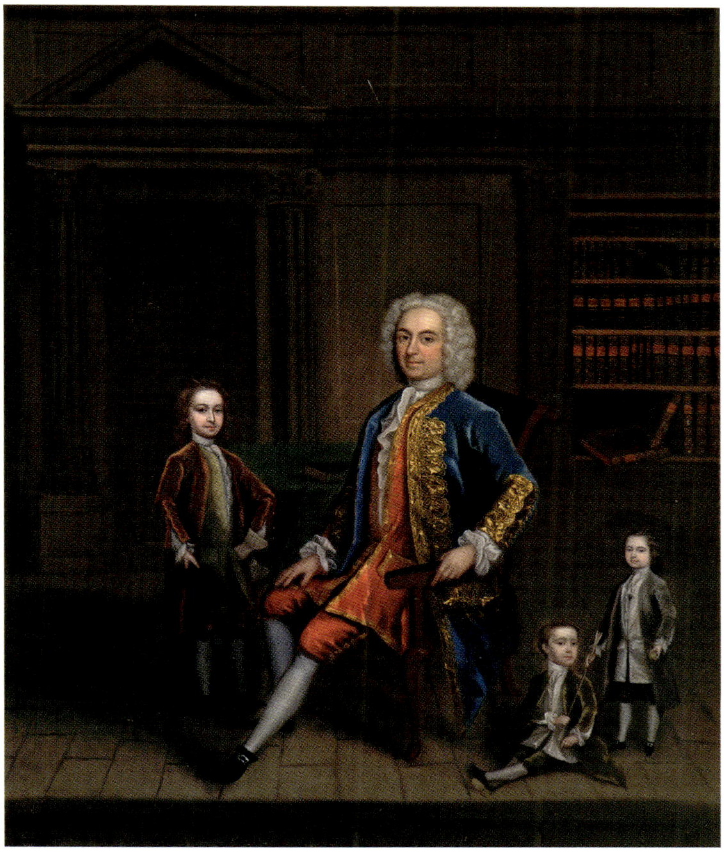

A portrait showing Edward Digby, son of 5th Lord Digby, seated with three of his older sons. It is one of a pair of group portraits probably painted between 1736 and 1740. The second portrait shows Edward's wife Charlotte (cat. 5) seated on a raised dais, with her oldest son Edward (cat. 8) standing nearby with an open book and her daughter Charlotte holding flowers. The pair of portraits are attributed to Robert Taylor, who also painted head and shoulders portraits of the 5th Lord Digby (cat. 6) and his son Wriothesley.[1] Since William Digby was opposed to the Hanoverian succession and refused to sign the oath of allegiance, it is unsurprising that he chose to employ the artist Taylor, who is understood to have had Jacobite sympathies.[2] Edward Digby, MP for Warwick, is shown seated and richly dressed. To the left Henry stands facing forwards in front of a table wearing rust velvet coat and breeches and holding his cap. On the right his brother William, wearing a green coat and breeches, is seated holding a form of bat. Standing on the far right his older brother Robert wears a grey coat and breeches, and holds the top of the bat with a ball in his left hand. The group is positioned in a panelled room, the presence of the bookcase on the right possibly signifying the old library at Sherborne Castle, and therefore a masculine space. This portrait has variously been attributed to William Hogarth and Joseph Highmore. The principal sitter in the portrait has traditionally been given as William 5th Lord Digby, however it is far more likely that on age grounds alone it shows Digby's son Edward with his sons. As such, it is one of the few known portraits of the sitter who died before inheriting the estate and title. William 5th Lord Digby also sat to Robert Taylor, of which several versions and an engraving are known.[3]

1 Bonhams, London, 9 July 2002, lots 234, 236.
2 Waterhouse, Suffolk, p. 366.
3 The print of *5th Lord Digby* by Robert Taylor, was engraved by John Faber in 1743.

The Six Digby Brothers

The respective occupations of the close-knit sons of Charlotte and Edward Digby (cats. 5, 7) of Sherborne Castle, are revealed through their portraits. They demonstrate eighteenth-century expectations dependent on position within the family, as landowner, sailor, soldier and churchman. The oldest son, Edward, aged 18 went on a Grand Tour to Italy from 1748 to 1750. His next brother Henry (cat. 9) worked as a diplomat for Sir Charles Hanbury Williams in Dresden and Vienna. Following Edward's death Henry succeeded to the title and inherited Sherborne Castle, and in the early 1760s joined his four remaining brothers in sitting to Joshua Reynolds. The next brother Robert (cat. 10) joined the navy, retiring as an admiral to Minterne, the Dorset estate he purchased; William (cat. 11) became Dean of Durham whose own son Henry inherited Minterne after Robert's death. The fifth brother Stephen (cat. 12) was a colonel in the army, became a courtier and married his cousin Lucy Fox-Strangways. The youngest son Charles (cat. 13), became rector of Kilmington, Somerset, a Fox-Strangways living; their only sister Charlotte died aged nineteen in 1753.

8. **Ranelagh Barrett** (fl. c. 1737–1768) copy after Pompeo Batoni (1708–1787)
Edward, 6th Lord Digby (1730–57)
oil on canvas, before 1760
73.5×60.5 cm
Provenance: Family commission, then by descent.

Private Collection

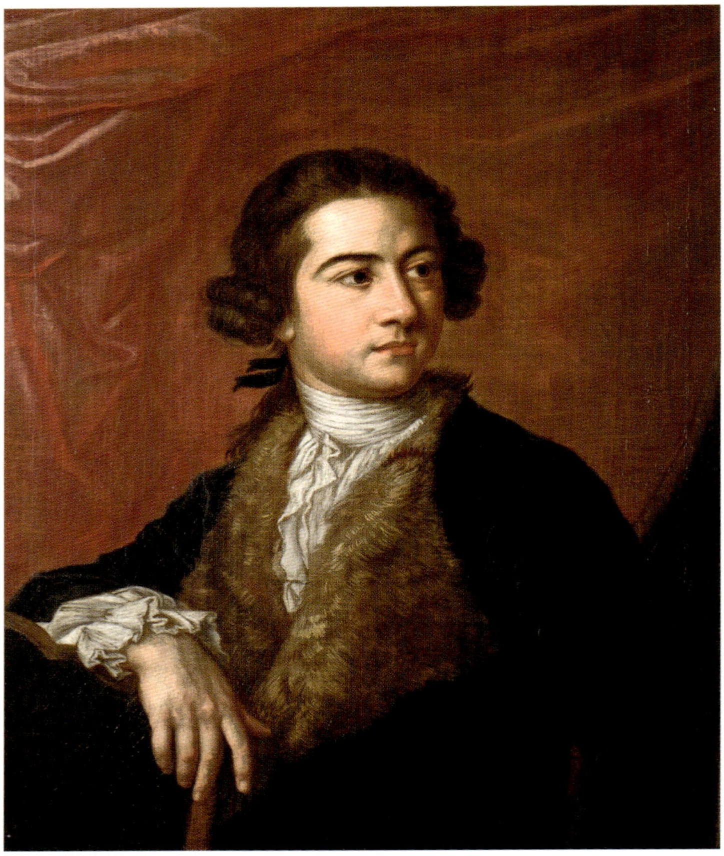

Educated at Westminster School, Edward was still at Oxford when his father died in 1746. Soon afterwards, he travelled to Italy to complete his education.[1] In 1749 he was in Rome intent on 'retaining the most beautiful passages of the Antients' (sic) whilst there he was one of the first Englishmen to sit for Pompeo Batoni.[2] On his return to Britain Edward, as future head of the family, entered politics as MP for Malmesbury in 1751; the following year he succeeded his grandfather, inheriting the Irish Barony and estates. Edward was an enthusiastic gardener, employing Capability Brown at Sherborne Castle in 1753 to create a 50-acre lake and remodel the castle grounds.[3] He emulated his grandfather by undertaking charitable work, though with great discretion. He visited Marshalsea Prison several times a year, releasing prisoners by paying their debts. Whilst visiting his estates in Ireland in November 1757 he contracted a fever and died aged only 27. As he was unmarried

Edward's title and properties passed to his oldest brother Henry (cat. 9).

This half-length copy of Batoni's portrait shows Digby in front of a red drape, dressed in a magnificent fur-lined cape. On his visit to Sherborne in 1762 Horace Walpole recorded seeing 'Edward, last Lord Digby, by Pompeio (sic); in a dark velvet with furs'.[4] While at Redlynch he mentioned a copy of the same portrait by Ranelagh Barrett set within an overmantle.[5] It is likely that the copy at Redlynch and this one were commissioned and painted in England after Edward Digby's death. Three copies of the portrait are recorded; in 1883 the Earl of Ilchester noted one at Holland House, London, there is Ranelagh Barrett's enlarged version seen by Walpole and a third at Pontypool Park.[6] This is probably the version from Holland House and is important as the earliest copy by an English artist of a portrait by Batoni.

Since Barrett left no account of his own work, a detailed reconstruction of the scope of his working practice is extremely difficult; he did not join artistic clubs or societies but mixed at the heart of a large creative community. London-based, he was given an 'office' in the Treasury by Sir Robert Walpole, paid for directly by Walpole.[7] Copyists tended to be itinerant, or attached to households and therefore removed from the centre of the London art establishment. This accounts for the difficulty of attribution. The most complete group of Barrett's works was painted for Stephen Fox; in 1741 he copied Hogarth's intimate conversation piece showing a small coterie of Fox's Whig friends.[8] The success of Barrett's Hogarth presumably prompted Fox to commission a copy of Batoni's 1749 portrait of his nephew.[9]

1 Ed. J. Ingamells, p. 299.
2 A.M. Clark, ed. E.P. Bowron, *Pompeo Batoni : A Complete Catalogue of his Works with an Introductory Text*, Oxford, 1985, cat. no. 132, pp. 303–04.
3 Edward undoubtedly knew of Brown's early work in Warwickshire not far from his seat at Coleshill. A. Smith, 'Sherborne Castle, Dorset', *Country Life*, 189, 6 July 1995, p. 62–65
4 Ed. P. Toynbee, 'Horace Walpole's Journals of visits to country seats, etc.' *Walpole Society*, 16, 1927–8, p. 44.
5 On visiting the 2nd Earl of Ilchester at Redlynch, Walpole noted the Batoni in the saloon along with a 'Copy by Barret of Queen Elizabeth's progress,' this picture, now in a private collection, was a copy of Digby's Gheeraerts, p. 44.
6 *Catalogue of Pictures Belonging to the Earl of Ilchester*, Privately printed, 1883, p. 110, no. 148. See also J. Steegman, 'Some English Portraits by Pompeo Batoni', *The Burlington Magazine*, 88, No. 516, 1946, p. 59.
7 The precise spelling of Barrett's name is contentious, Vertue calls him variously Barret, Baewick, and Barwick – the latter might be confusion with his street of residence. His sale catalogue calls him '*Ranellah Barrett*' and paintings, like the Woburn portrait of Richard Rigby are signed 'Barrett.'
8 See R. Simon, *Hogarth, France and British Art; the Rise of the Arts in 18th Century Britain*, London, 2007, pp. 234–240.
9 I am grateful to Jonathan Yarker for providing me with information about Barrett.

9. **Sir Joshua Reynolds** (1723–1792)
Henry 7th Lord and 1st Earl Digby (1731–1793)
oil on canvas, c. 1763
91.4×71.0 cm

Provenance: Sitter and by descent.
Literature: J.P. Neale, Jones's Views of the Seats of Noblemen and Gentlemen of England, Wales, Scotland and Ireland, London 1829, 2, p. 12; Graves and Cronin, 1899, 1, 250; Mannings, 2000, p. 165, (505) repr. Fig. 698.
Exhibition: *National Portraits* South Kensington 1867 (608)

Sherborne Castle

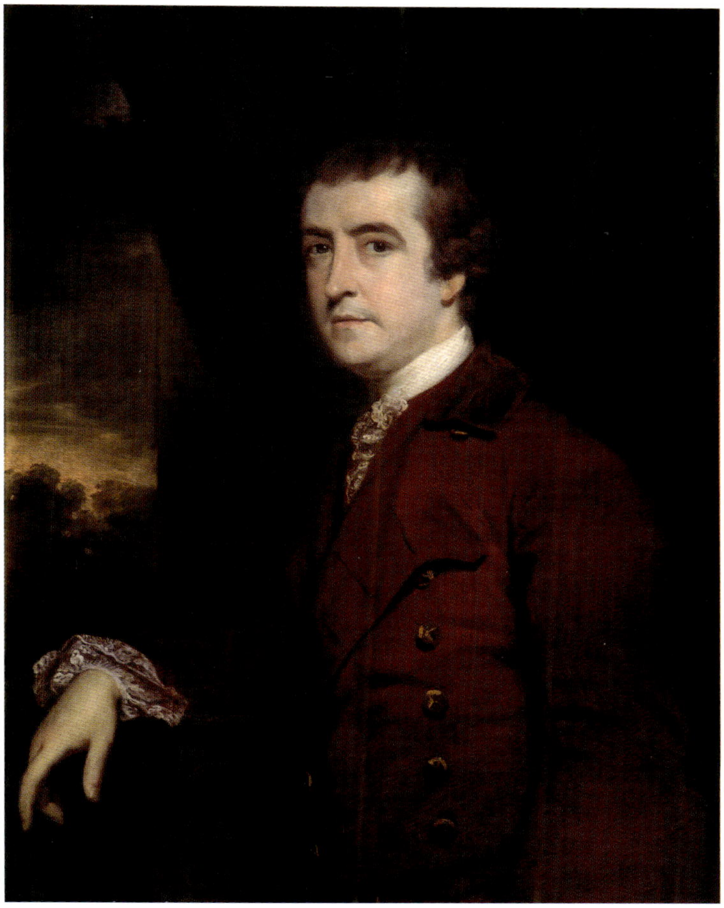

Henry Digby was the second son of Edward Digby, MP for Warwick, and Charlotte, (cat. 5) sister of Stephen Fox, 1st Earl of Ilchester (cat. 4). Like his older brother Edward (cat. 8), he was educated at Westminster, but as a second son, he was expected to follow a career, becoming in 1750 secretary to Sir Charles Hanbury Williams, ambassador to the Saxon court at Dresden. Henry travelled with him through Germany and Poland. In Vienna in 1752 Digby sat to the court artist Martin Van Meytens at the request of his mother; he had four sittings for the picture, writing 'that every body that has seen it, think it like.'[1] Following the death of his brother Edward in 1757, Henry succeeded to the family estates and Irish barony. Henry continued his late brother Edward's improvements at Sherborne, such as completing the landscaping round the lake. He employed Benjamin Bastard to build his stables in 1759, worked with Capability Brown laying out the grounds, and gothicised the Castle, in the manner of Walpole at Strawberry Hill.[2] As Lord Lieutenant between 1771 and 1793, Henry Digby was much involved with Dorset affairs, in 1789 hosting George III at Sherborne.

On Tuesday 4 August 1789 the King and Queen, Princess Royal, Princess Augusta and Princess Elizabeth visited Sherborne Castle with various attendants, including Henry's brother Colonel Digby (cat. 12). The Game Book records that after taking refreshments, they walked over the House and Upper Pleasure Ground, 'amidst the Acclamations of a Large Concourse of People assembled in the Lawn'. The royal party then rode round the park, with the King conveyed back to the house by boat, returning to dine at the Castle at 5 o' clock. They took their leave at 8 o'clock, 'leaving Lord and Lady Digby deeply impress'd with the Honour They had Received and The Very Gracious and Condescending Demeanour of their Majesties . . . .'.[3] By his second wife, Mary Knowler (cat. 14), Henry had a son Edward, who became the 8th Lord Digby.

Digby sat for this half-length portrait to Reynolds in 1763, although two appointments were also recorded in 1758. He wears his own hair, rust coat with gold buttons with lace at his neck and cuffs. His right arm rests on a plinth with a green drape behind on the right and a landscape and sky visible on the left. Mannings records that Digby paid the full price of twenty-five guineas for the portrait.[4] Other entries indicate that Digby may have paid for several further portraits, either copies of this one, of which one exists in a private collection, or perhaps he was paying for his brothers' portraits when they sat to Reynolds in the early 1760s. Henry also sat to Thomas Gainsborough in about 1778.

1 Lewis Walpole Library, Connecticut, Charles Hanbury Williams, CHW 54–10910, letters from Henry Digby, f. 136–40; 189–90; 191–92; 193–194; 200–1. I am grateful to Jonathan Yarker for this reference.
2 J. Waymark, 'Lancelot Brown (1716–83) and the Landscape Park', *Garden History*, 29, No. 1, 2001, pp. 64–81.
3 Sherborne Castle Archive, Game Book, 1784–1793.
4 Mannings, 2000, p. 165.

10. **Sir Joshua Reynolds** (1723–1792)

The Hon Robert, later Admiral, Digby (1732–1815)
oil on canvas, c. 1761–64
76.3×63.5 cm

Provenance: Sitter, then by descent.
Inscription added later on reverse: ROBERT DIGBY ESQRE, AGED 26 / CAPTAIN OF HIS MAJESTY'S SHIP 'DUNKIRK'
Literature: Graves & Cronin, 1, pp. 250–251; Mannings, 2000, p. 166, cat. no. 507.
Exhibition: South Kensington, *National Portrait,* 1868 (872).

Private Collection

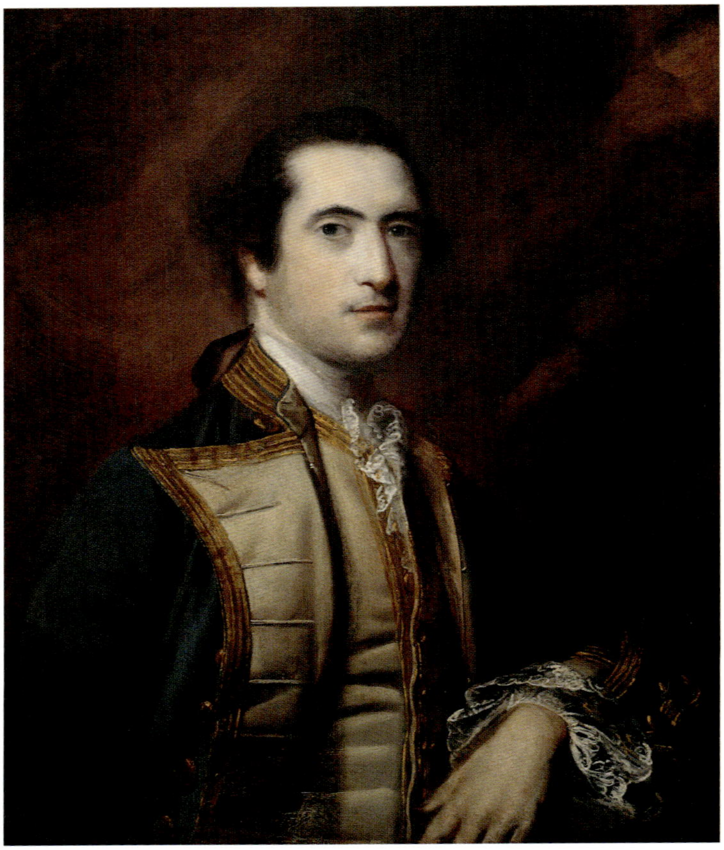

Robert Digby was the third son of Edward and Charlotte Digby. In 1744 aged twelve he entered the navy and by 1755 was a captain. Two years later he commanded the *Dunkirk* in an action off Brest. By 1766 he was unemployed, prompting his mother to write to him in October: 'Have you seen nothing in all your travels this year pretty enough to tempt you to take a wife?'[1] Digby's peripatetic life continued until 1768 when he purchased the lease of the Minterne estate, former home of General Charles Churchill, from Winchester College. By 1778 Digby was back at sea commanding the *Ramilies,* one of the leading ships in the inconclusive action between the Comte d'Orvilliers and Admiral Keppel. A rear admiral in 1779, Digby was appointed to care for Prince William Henry, Duke of Clarence (afterwards William IV) on his entering the navy on board Digby's ship the *Prince George* in 1779.[2] He was second in command in the battle off Cape St Vincent in 1780 and made Admiral of the Red.

Digby was given the command of the America Station and after the surrender of New York city in 1783, helped organise the evacuation of some 1500 United Empire Loyalists. They were relocated to the small port of Conway in Nova Scotia, transforming the tiny village into a town, which in 1787 was renamed Digby. In 1784 Robert married Eleanor Jauncey (née Elliot), eldest daughter of the Lieutenant-Governor of New York, and brought her to Minterne, near

Sherborne, where he lived in retirement after the American War ended. He was recalled to home waters in 1787, promoted to Admiral of the Blue and retired from the navy in 1794 as senior admiral of the fleet.

Reynolds painted this three-quarter-length portrait of Robert Digby between 1761–1764.[3] He is depicted in captain's undress uniform of the period and the painting was probably commissioned by his brother Henry, to celebrate his successful command of the *Dunkirk*. Although a modest portrait of a young captain, the atmospheric background suggests something of Reynolds's more ambitious portraits of naval heroes, like his 1761 portrait of Alexander Hood, 1st Viscount Bridport (private collection).[4] Digby's face now appears pale, no doubt due to Reynolds's experimentation with pigments leading to unstable colour.

Robert Digby's diaries reveal him happiest working on and improving his estate. On acquiring Minterne in 1768 he wrote, 'the valley is very bare, trees not thriving, house ill-contrived, & ill-situated'.[5] Digby's first act was to plant to break the effect of the wind, employing sailors who had served with him. He continued making modifications, planting, helping with the farms, improving his gardens, making roads or indulging "my favourite occupation" building cascades to dam the stream in the valley.[6] Robert was succeeded by his nephew Henry, son of William Digby (cat. 11).[7]

1 Minterne Digby archive, Charlotte Digby to Robert Digby, 28 Oct 1766. See H. E. Ravenhill, 'Minterne: Its connection with the Churchills and Digbys', *Proceedings of the DNH&AS*, 10, 1889, pp. 89–96.
2 Robert owned a painting of William IV as a midshipman by Benjamin West.
3 There is a portrait of Robert Digby as a young midshipman; he also sat to John Giles Eccardt, both at Sherborne Castle. For a smaller version of the Reynolds portrait of Digby, see Bonhams, 9 March 1978, lot 185.
4 Mannings, 2000, cat. no. 924.
5 Robert Digby diaries, private collection.
6 Extract from the *Salisbury & Winchester Journal*, Monday, 8 September 1788: 'WHEREAS LORD RIVERS has granted me the Deputation of the Manor of Cerne, and his Woods near Grange; I must request the favour of gentlemen and all persons whatever, not to shoot on that manor, or in those woods: and as it has been a custom for gentlemen from other counties to come to Cerne, to course upon Cerne Manor, I beg the favour of them not to course there in future. ROBERT DIGBY. Mintern,(sic) Dorset, August, 1788.'
7 Robert had two illegitimate sons, Robert Sherbourne, accomplished artist and manager of the Ravenhead plate glassworks from 1792 and Robert Murray who also had a distinguished naval career and married late. Robert's paintings of several Digby properties and those of the Ravenhead glass works are in private collections.

11. **Sir Joshua Reynolds**, (1723–1792)

The Hon Reverend William Digby (1733–1788)
oil on canvas, c. 1760
73.5×60.5 cm
Signed and dated . . . .
Inscription: *JRey . . . . pinxit 1760.*
Later addition: *Hon Wm DIGBY DEAN OF DURHAM 1733–1788*
Provenance: Sitter, then by descent.
Literature: Graves & Cronin, 1899, 1, 251; W 49 (as 1761); Mannings, 2000, p. 166, (509); E.K. Waterhouse, *Reynolds*, London, 1941, p. 49.

Private Collection

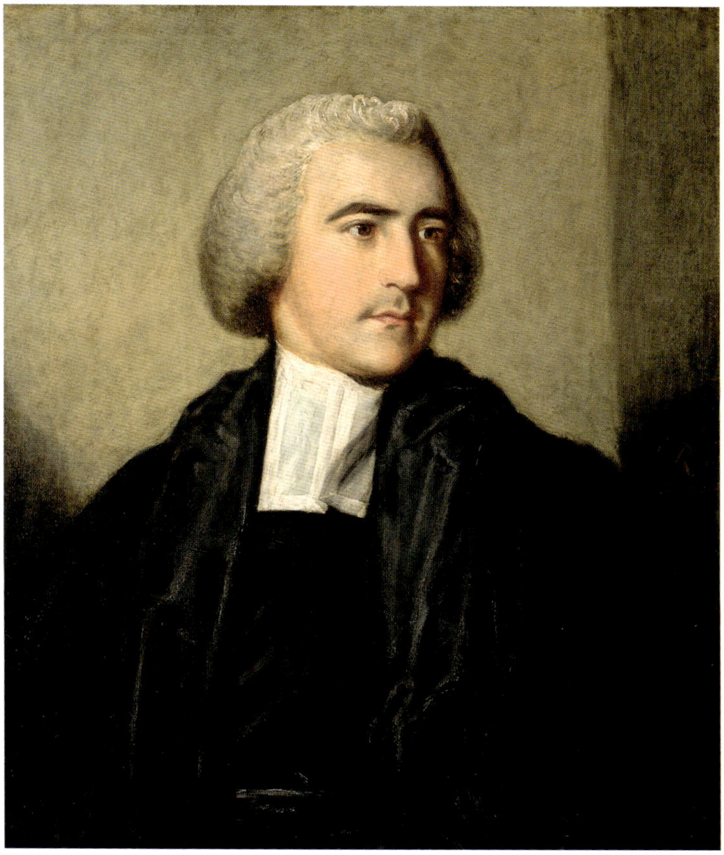

William was the fourth son of Edward Digby and Charlotte Digby (cats. 5, 7). He entered the Church and became vicar of Coleshill, a family living in Warwickshire, and Chaplain in Ordinary to George III in 1760, Dean of Worcester in 1769 and Dean of Durham in 1777. Married to Charlotte Cox in 1766, they had four sons and five daughters. Their eldest son, Henry, born in Bath in 1770, joined the Navy where his illustrious career included earning a fortune from privateering and commanding the *Africa* at Trafalgar.

Reynolds's half-length portrait of William was probably completed to celebrate his promotion as Chaplain to George III, as the painting is signed and dated 1760. Although the portrait may have been started as early as 1756, with two sittings recorded in 1758 though none for 1760. This later date may have been added by Reynolds, when it was dispatched from his studio. Digby is shown looking to the right dressed in his clerical costume, offering Reynolds the opportunity to create a delicate study in monochrome. Four versions of the portrait were made for family members, together with a mezzotint engraving by S.W. Reynolds.[1]

1 The versions are at Sherborne Castle; in a private collection; formerly in the collection of Sir Arundell Neave, Anglesey and lastly sold Sotheby's 25 November 2004, lot. 51.

12. **Sir Joshua Reynolds** (1723–1792)

Colonel the Hon. Stephen Digby (1742–1800)
oil on canvas, c. 1763
76×63.5 cm

Provenance: Sitter, then by descent.
Literature: Graves and Cronin, 1899, I, p. 250; Mannings, London, 2000, p. 166, (508) fig. 697.

Sherborne Castle

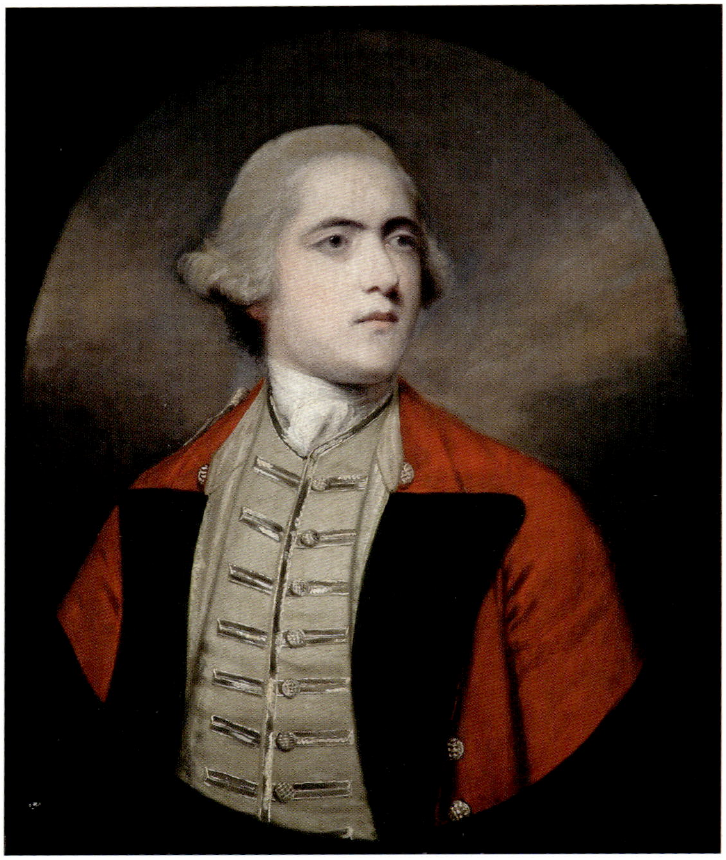

Stephen Digby was the fifth son of Edward and Charlotte Digby. He was commissioned into the army, where he served in Germany and was made captain in the 5th Regiment of Foot. He rose to the rank of colonel by 1774. He married his cousin, Lady Lucy Fox-Strangways, second daughter of the 1st Earl of Ilchester (cat. 4) in 1771. By 1782, Digby's charming personality attracted the attention of Queen Charlotte, who appointed him her vice-chamberlain. In 1788 he was master and governor of the hospital of Saint Catherine's, near the Tower of London, and also Deputy Ranger at Richmond Park, Surrey. Digby remained in court service and was one of the few people able to manage the King during his illnesses.[1] He accompanied the King to Weymouth in 1789, where his brother Henry (cat. 9) also attended as Lord Lieutenant of Dorset.

Digby's charms extended to many of the ladies at court, not least the novelist and diarist Fanny Burney, who was then one of the Queen's ladies in waiting.[2] Following the death of Digby's wife from cancer, Fanny Burney entertained hopes of marrying him. She was ultimately disappointed when in 1790, Stephen married the younger, vivacious heiress and Maid of Honour to Queen Charlotte, Charlotte Gunning. Burney vented her fury in the pages of her diary accusing him of double-dealing and lampooning Charlotte Gunning under the pseudonym 'Miss Fuzilier'.[3]

Reynold's half-length portrait places Stephen Digby in a dark oval, the face appears chalky partly due to Reynolds's experimentation with pigments, leading to unstable colours. Digby paid 25 guineas for the portrait in August 1763. Although Lady Lucy Digby also sat to Reynolds the portrait is untraced. A three-quarter length of her was sold in Reynolds's studio sale in 1796. In 1803 Digby's daughter Charlotte Elizabeth married her cousin the Reverend William Digby, son of Stephen's brother William, Dean of Durham (cat. 11).

1 S. Ayling, *George the Third,* London, 1972, p. 332.
2 Digby is disguised as Colonel Fairly in Burney's diary. See C.F. Barrett, *Diary and letters of Madam D'Arblay,* 1846–49, 3, p. 71.
3 Her comments on the couple were thought so slanderous that they were expunged from the published version of the diary.

13. **Sir Joshua Reynolds** (1723–1792)

The Reverend Charles Digby (1743–1811)
oil on canvas, c. 1761
74×62 cm

Provenance: Sitter, then by descent.

Sherborne Castle

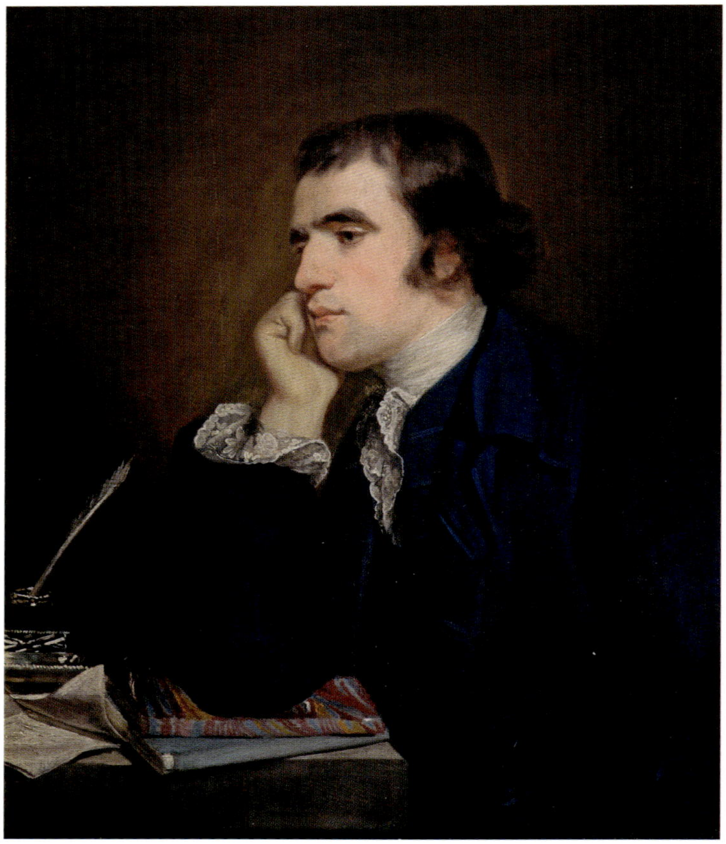

Charles Digby was the youngest of the six sons of Edward and Charlotte Digby (cats. 5, 7). He probably followed all his brothers in attending Westminster School. After Christ Church, Oxford he was given a Fox-Strangways living at Kilmington, Somerset and married Priscilla Mellior, daughter of William Mellior at Castle Cary in 1775. Later canon of Wells, Digby spent most of his life in the West Country, leading the sociable life of a rural vicar.[1]

This unpublished portrait by Reynolds probably shows Charles Digby shortly after matriculating at Christ Church in 1761. Shown with his head resting on his fist, almost in profile, with scholarly clutter on the desk in front of him, this is the most ambitious of Reynolds's portraits of the Digby brothers. Charles showed no particular aptitude as an academic, but Reynolds has captured a pensive introspection in the sitter, using a pose not dissimilar to that used in his early portrait of Sir William Hamilton (Toledo Museum, Ohio). Some confusion remains as to the precise circumstances of the commission and dating of the Digby brothers. Reynolds records Henry (cat. 9) sitting in 1758, William (cat. 11) is signed and dated 1760 and a payment by Stephen (cat. 12) of 25 guineas, the standard price for a half-length portrait, to Reynolds in August 1763 for this picture. But Reynolds's sitters' books record a series of appointments with 'Mr Digby' in 1761 and then again in 1764; these are probably not for the same portrait but for Charles in 1761, the year of his matriculation, and then for Robert Digby (cat. 10) in 1764. There is also evidence to suggest that Henry Digby (cat. 9) might have commissioned them all; his bank records show he paid Reynolds 50 guineas in 1763 and 75 guineas in 1765, enough for five half-length portraits, although this does not explain Stephen's payment to Reynolds in 1763 or the record of three payments for 25 guineas in 1765, unless they were for copies.[2]

1 A group portrait by John Hamilton Mortimer shows a hunting group of Digby with his Oxford contemporaries including the 7th Earl of Cork, Mr Bingham (of Bingham's Melcombe, Dorset) Colonel Cox and the Reverend Mr Hume. See Sotheby's, 1 July 2004, Lot. 20. Digby appears in another group portrait by Mortimer now in the Wimborne Collection, painted at Sherborne, which also includes the 2nd Earl of Ilchester.

2 For the full documentation see Mannings, 2000, p. 165–6, although the portrait of Charles is omitted.

14. **Richard Cosway** (1742–1821)

Mary, Countess Digby, neé Knowler (1745–1794)
oil on canvas, c. 1785
89.5×69.5 cm

Provenance: Sitter, then by descent.
Exhibition: National Portrait Exhibition, South Kensington Museum, London, 1867, no. 37.

Sherborne Castle

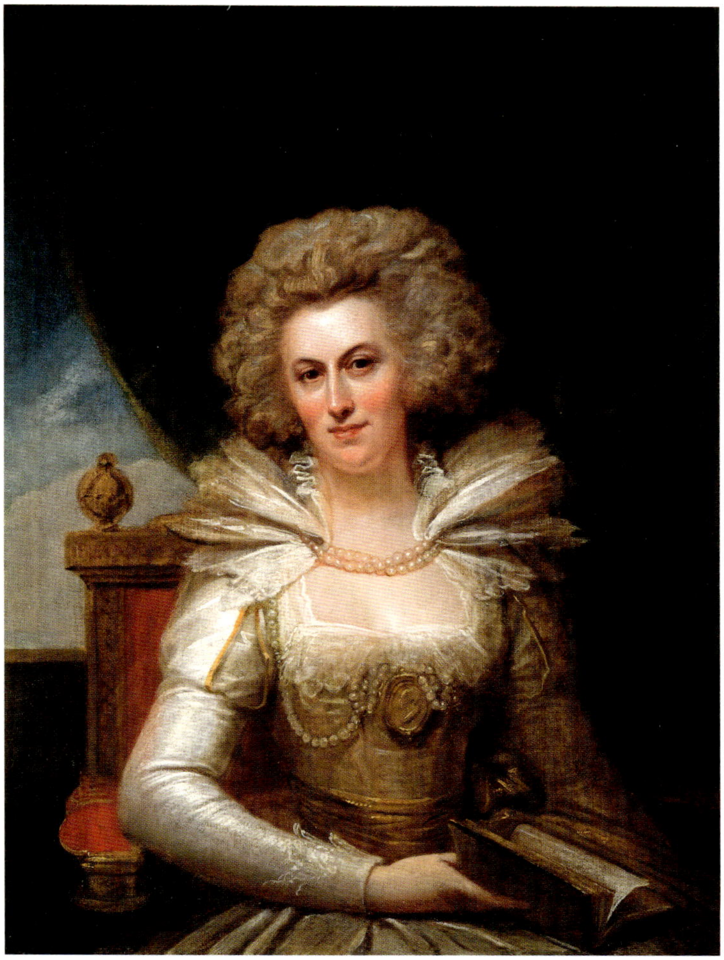

The younger daughter and co-heiress of John Knowler, barrister and Recorder of Canterbury, Mary married Henry Digby (cat. 9) in 1770.[1] Mary shared Henry's passion for Sherborne Castle, its contents, garden and landscaping the estate, taking a keen part in the redevelopment of the lake, which had been started by Henry's brother Edward. When in January 1774 the lake froze over 'Lord Stavordale, Major Digby and Captain Digby went a skating & pushed the Ladies in Chairs on the Ice'.[2] Mary was the mother of Edward, later 2nd Earl and 8th Baron Digby, three further sons and two daughters of whom only one, Charlotte, married. Mary only outlived her husband by one year and was buried with him in the Digby vault at Sherborne Abbey.

By the 1780s the Devon born Richard Cosway was a fashionable, London based portraitist; most famous for miniatures, he exhibited ambitious full-size portraits at the Royal Academy throughout the decade. Cosway has shown Mary Digby, seated in seventeenth-century costume, her hand resting on an open book. Rather than the modest, loosely Van Dyckian clothes adopted by Beach in his portrait of Rebecca Steward (cat. 39), Cosway depicts Mary in highly theatrical costume and evocative pose. Van Dyck frequently showed his mature female sitters seated in similar chairs and Cosway would undoubtedly have been aware of the Digbys' historic connection with the painter, as well as their collection of his portraits.[3] Cosway's fluid handling also suggests something of his interest in Flemish painting; Mary's loosely painted hair contrasting with her more highly finished features gives an impressive energy to the composition.

Although undated, this picture presumably shows the sitter before the death of her husband in 1793, when she spent the last few months of her life away from Sherborne Castle.[4]

1 Her elder sister Anne, married reformer Henry Penton, Esq., MP for Winchester, in 1765, who developed Islington from 1773.
2 Sherborne Castle Estate Archive, Game Book, 1771–84, 4 January 1774.
3 Van Dyck, a close friend of Sir Kenelm Digby, painted Digby and his beautiful wife Venetia on a number of occasions. Although none of the Van Dycks were in the collection at Sherborne Castle, an early eighteenth century copy of the family portrait and of Sir Kenelm were installed there as well as the copy of Van Dyck's double portrait of George Digby and his brother-in-law the Earl of Bedford, (Althorp). See S. Barnes, N. De Poorter, O. Millar and H. Vey, *Van Dyck; A Complete Catalogue of the Paintings*, New Haven and London, 2004, cat. no. IV, pp. 94–98.
4 L.M. Portman, *Catalogue of the Pictures at Sherborne Castle*, London, 1862, p. 173.

15. **Thomas Beach** (1738–1806)

Henry Thomas, 2nd Earl of Ilchester (1747–1802)
oil on canvas, 1778
73.6×62.2 cm
Signed and dated, 1778

Provenance: Sitter, then by descent.
Literature: *Catalogue of Pictures Belonging to the Earl of Ilchester*, London, 1883, no. 64; Beach, 1934, p. 64, no. 172; J. Martin, *Wives and Daughters, Women and Children in the Georgian Country House*, London, 2004, no. 9; *A Governess in the Age of Jane Austen. The Journals and Letters of Agnes Porter*, ed. J. Martin, London 1998. No. I.
Exhibition: *Dorset Artists of the Past*, Dorset County Museum, Dorchester, 1933–34.

16. **Thomas Beach** (1738–1806)

Mary Theresa, Countess of Ilchester (c. 1755–1790)
oil on canvas, 1778
73.6×62.2 cm
Signed and dated, 1778

Provenance: Sitter, then by descent.[1]
Literature: *Catalogue of Pictures Belonging to the Earl of Ilchester*, London, 1883, no. 61; E. Beach, 1934, p. 65, no. 174.

Private Collection

A pair of half-length portraits by Thomas Beach of Henry, 2nd Earl of Ilchester, and his wife Mary Theresa Grady dated 1778. Henry, the eldest son of Stephen Fox, 1st Earl of Ilchester, married Mary Theresa, third daughter of Standish Grady of Capercullen, County Limerick, in 1772. Preferring rural life to the high politics beloved of his father and cousin Charles James Fox, Henry divided his time between his estates in Somerset and Dorset.[2] After the death of Mary Theresa in 1790, following the birth of their seventh child, the Earl married his cousin Maria, third daughter of the Hon. William Digby, Dean of Durham (cat. 11). Henry died at Buxton in 1802 and was succeeded by his son Henry.

In this pair of modest portraits Beach demonstrates his debt to Reynolds. Whilst the feigned oval used to frame the sitters was markedly old fashioned by the late 1770s, the conceit of showing Mary Theresa in classicizing costume, rather than contemporary dress, accords with Reynolds's desire 'to get above all singular forms, local customs, particularities, and details of every

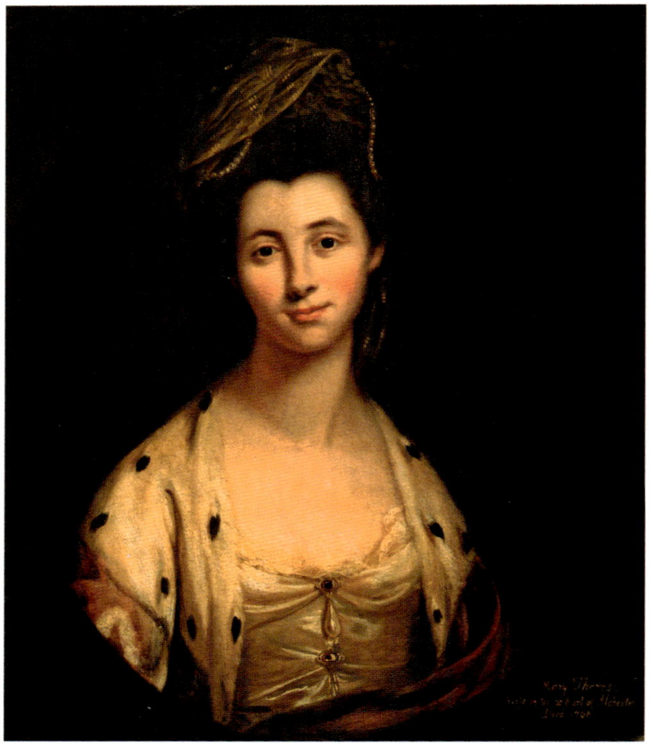

16.

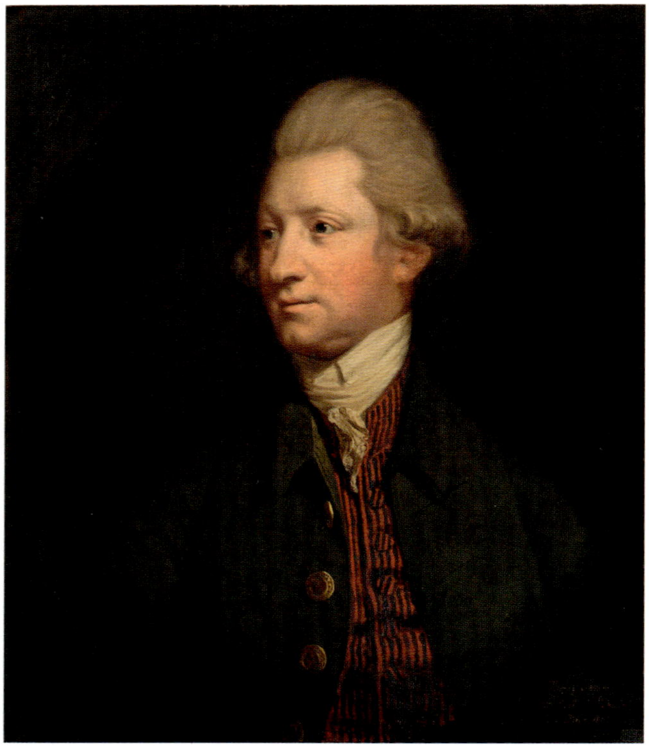

15.

kind.'[3] Indeed, it was a format he frequently adopted in his more ambitious historical portraits. The same combination of classical 'bedgown' and contemporary peeresses robes can be seen in Reynolds's portrait of *Elizabeth Gunning, Duchess of Hamilton and Argyll* (Lady Lever Art Gallery, Port Sunlight).[4] On the other hand, Beach depicts the Earl in a contemporary green jacket, with red and black striped waistcoat. This convention is repeated by Romney in his portraits of Thomas and Mary Rackett (cats. 41, 42) completed during the same decade. An unusual feature of Mary Theresa's portrait is the sprigs of shamrock woven into her hair to suggest her Irish ancestry. It is perhaps notable that Reynolds painted a full-length portrait of Lady Ilchester and two of her daughters in the same year (Bowood House, Wiltshire).[5]

The portraits were probably painted by Beach on a visit to Redlynch; in 1777 Beach painted a half-length portrait of Lady Ilchester holding a child, probably her daughter Mary (formerly at Penrice Castle) and a full-length of Lady Elizabeth Fox-Strangways and Elizabeth Kitty Acland (cat. 17). Beach continued to work for Ilchester, since at least four copies of the Earl's portrait exist.

1 A note in the *Catalogue of Pictures Belonging to the Earl of Ilchester*, 1883, states the portraits were a gift from the Earl of Limerick, although considering the number of copies of the portrait of Henry that survive, this seems unlikely.
2 For further detail about Mary Theresa's life see J. Martin, *Wives and Daughters, Women and Children in the Georgian Country House*, London, 2004; ed. J. Martin, *A Governess in the Age of Jane Austen. The Journals and Letters of Agnes Porter*, London, 1998.
3 Ed. R. Wark, *J. Reynolds, Discourses on Art*, New Haven and London, pp. 48–9.
4 Ed. N. Penny, *Reynolds*, exh. cat., London (Royal Academy of Arts), 1986, cat. 36.
5 Mannings, 2000, no. 683.

17. **Thomas Beach** (1738–1806)

Lady Elizabeth Theresa Fox-Strangways (1773–1844) and Elizabeth Kitty Acland (1772–1813)
oil on canvas, 1777
124.5×100.3 cm
Signed and dated *TB1777*
Provenance: Sitters, then by descent.
Literature: E. Beach, 1934, p. 60, No. 93.

Private Collection

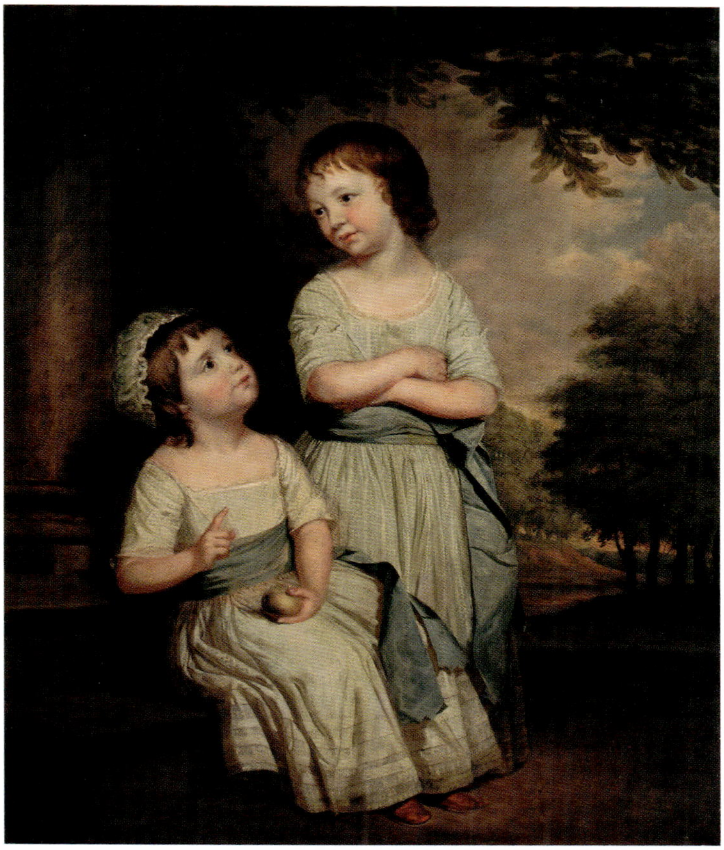

Lady Elizabeth Theresa Fox-Strangways was the eldest daughter of the 2nd Earl of Ilchester (cat. 15). She married William Davenport Talbot (c. 1770–1800) of Lacock Abbey in 1796. In 1800 their son William Henry Fox Talbot (1800–1877), the pioneer of photography, was born at Melbury.[1] Elizabeth's cousin, Elizabeth Kitty Acland, known as Kitty, was the only daughter of Colonel John Dyke Acland, best known through Reynolds's important double portrait *Colonel Acland and Lord Sydney: The Archers,* 1769 (Tate), and diarist Lady Christian Harriot Caroline Fox-Strangways, daughter of the 1st Earl of Ilchester.

Beach's portrait of the two cousins was probably painted at Redlynch in 1777 the year before his portraits of Lord and Lady Ilchester (cats. 15, 16).[2] That year he also painted a head and shoulder portrait of the 2nd Earl and one of the Countess holding a child, probably Mary Lucy (1776–1855). At this date Kitty was being cared for by the Fox-Strangways after her parents left for North America in 1776, following the outbreak of the American War of Independence.

During the expedition Lady Acland kept a famous journal of her experiences. In October 1777 Acland was wounded and captured at the battle of Bernis Heights. Determined not to be separated from him, Lady Harriot, accompanied by several servants, crossed the Hudson River in an open boat to join her husband in captivity.[3]

Beach's intimate portrait reveals his sensitive handling of children, whilst the format is similar to Joshua Reynolds's 1761 portrait of *The Ladies Amabel and Mary Jemima Yorke* 1761, (Cleveland Museum of Art) and close to Beach's own portrait of *Charles and Henry Blair* painted in 1769 (London art market) and anticipates Thomas Gainsborough's *Master John Truman-Villebois and his Brother Henry,* c. 1783, (private collection).[4] As childhood was given greater emphasis by educationalists and philosophers, so child portraiture increased in importance as a genre. Like Thomas Rackett in Romney's portrait from the previous decade (cat. 43), Beach shows Elizabeth and Kitty full of personality with Kitty declaiming to her older cousin.

1 In 1804 Elizabeth secondly married Captain Charles Feilding RN who, with the Ilchester family, assumed responsibility for managing the Lacock estate. In 1796 Kitty married Henry Herbert, Lord Porchester, later 2nd Earl of Carnarvon.
2 Beach submitted a portrait of *Mr Plomer MC at Weymouth* to the Society of Artists in 1777 so he was evidently travelling in the South West during 1776 and 1777. See A. Graves, *The Society of Artists and Great Britain 1760–1791, The Free Society of Artists, 1761–1783*, London, 1907, p. 27, no. 14.
3 The Aclands returned to England the following year and the episode was immortalized in Robert Pollard's engraving of 1784. Lady Harriot was celebrated for her outstanding heroism and loyalty.
4 With Lane Fine Art, London, 2010. See Beach, 1934, no. 23.

18. **William Hoare** (1707–1792)

The Pitt Family
oil on canvas, c. 1758–1759
138.5 × 117.5 cm
Inscribed upper left: *John Pitt / Marcia his wife Da. Of Marcus Antony Morgan/ & Wm. Morton Pitt their Son*

Provenance: Pitt Family; by descent to George Pitt; by descent from Laura Audley Gray; Christie's, 1986; Sotheby's, 1988; Collection of Evelyn Newby; Sotheby's, London, 24 November 1999 lot 48; English private collection; Holburne Museum purchase through Fergus Hall Master Paintings, 2009 by grant from independent charity, the Art Fund, MLA/V&A Purchase Grant Fund, Beecroft Bequest, Friends of the Holburne, David Posnett in memory of his mentor Harold Leger and a private donor.
Literature: *'The British Portrait'* Roy Strong, 1991, pp. 185–6, illustrated p. 198, colour plate 33.
Exhibited: The Society of Artists, 1761, no. 42; Bath, Victoria Gallery, *William Hoare of Bath*, 1990, no. 16.

The Holburne Museum of Art

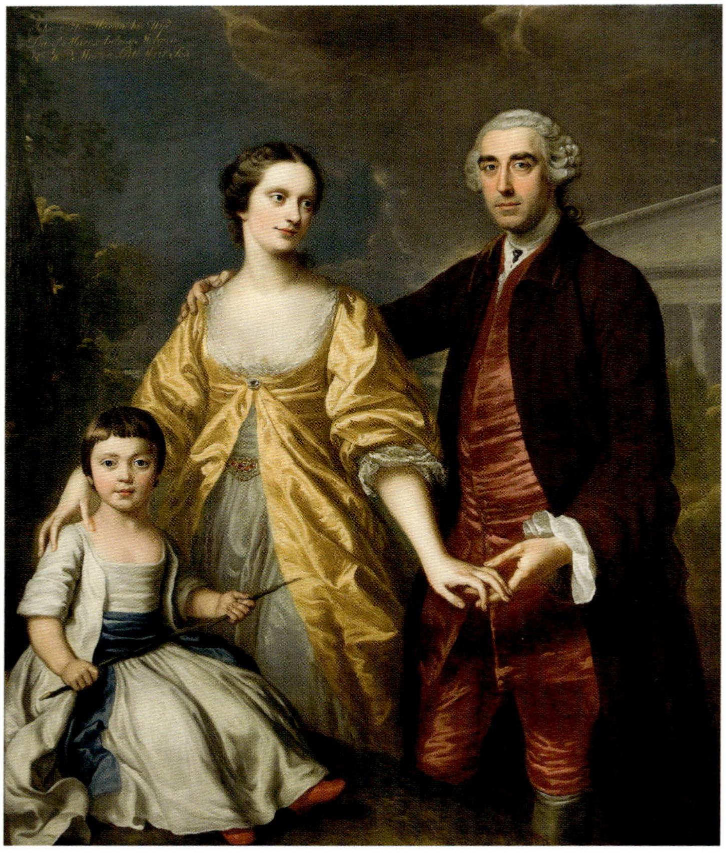

A family group portrait showing John Pitt (1704–1787) his wife Marcia (1733–c. 1818) and their son William Morton (1754–1836) aged about four or five. Pitt inherited two large Dorset estates, Encombe (fig. 26) from his father and Kingston Maurward (fig. 27) from his mother, heiress Lora Grey, who left her wealth to her sons John and William.[1]

Later known as the great 'Commoner of the West', Pitt was a man of immense fortune and considerable political influence in Dorset, which he represented as MP in four ministries between 1744–1757.[2] Pitt was one of the Lords Commissioners for Trade and Plantations, Surveyor-General to the King's Woods and Forests and Member for Wareham and Dorchester for thirty-four years. In Dorset he turned architect, building Encombe after 1734, using an architectural fusion of styles influenced by Vanbrugh, Hawksmoor and Palladio.

Close to his Prime Minister cousin William Pitt the Elder, 1st Earl of Chatham, John Pitt frequently visited him at Bath during the 1750s. Early in 1753 John Pitt married Marcia, daughter of Marcus Anthony Morgan of Cottlestown. When their son William Morton Pitt was born a year later Pitt the Elder wrote to John, 'may the boy . . . continue in perfect health and every hour add to the happiness of a man who deserves it and enjoys it'.[3] Polite society however appeared lukewarm to Marcia; Sarah Bunbury thought her manner arrogant and wrote, 'it is a little Mrs Pitts way to be uncertain . . . sometimes takes no notice of us a whole winter'.[4] Although John and Marcia had several other children, only William and their daughter Marcia survived to adulthood.

William represented Poole in Parliament for ten years from 1780, and Dorset from 1790 to 1826. He married Margaret, daughter of John Gambier, and their daughter Grace later married Henry Seymer junior (cat. 53). Although William's attempts to prevent smuggling at Encombe failed, he was an active reformer for the situation of the poor and for prisoners. He lobbied on conditions in Dorchester Gaol where, in 1798, he established a hat factory.[5] In the Dorset militia, Pitt took his cousin George Pitt's (cat. 23) part in trying to depose the Colonel of the regiment, Lord Rivers (cats. 26, 27). In 1807 William sold the entire Encombe estate, proceeded to dissipate his father's fortune and was eventually financially ruined.[6]

William Hoare painted the Pitt family portrait in Bath during 1758–1759, when at the height of his success. As the fashionable portraitist of choice for leading political, literary and society figures of the day, he dominated Bath's market for oil paintings in the third quarter of the 18th-century. His studio continued to prosper even after the arrival of the younger and

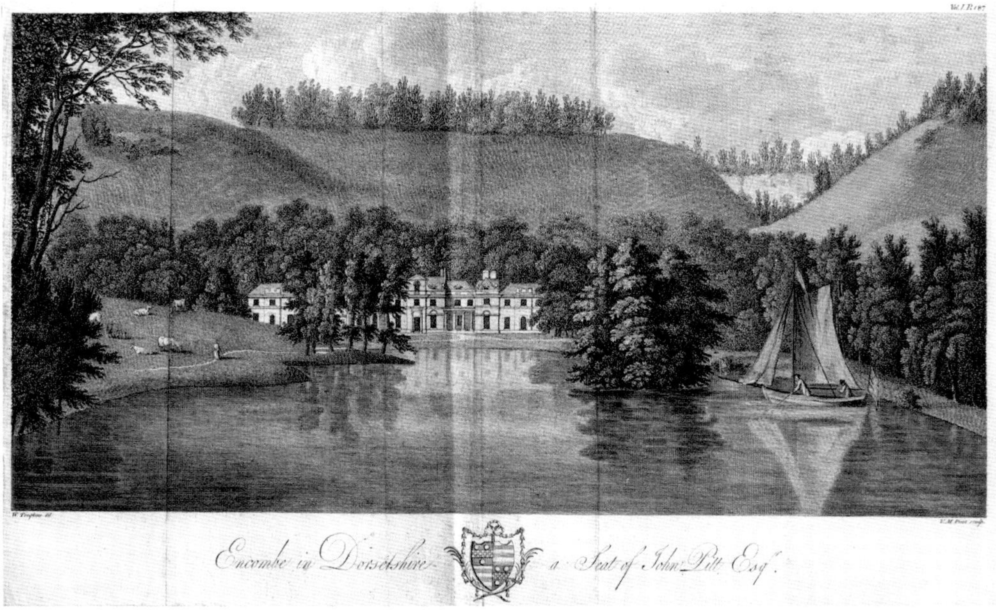

Fig. 26. *Encombe in Dorsethshire a Seat of John Pitt Esq,* folded after W. Tompkins by V.M. Picot, Hutchins ed.1, 1 p. 187, 1774.

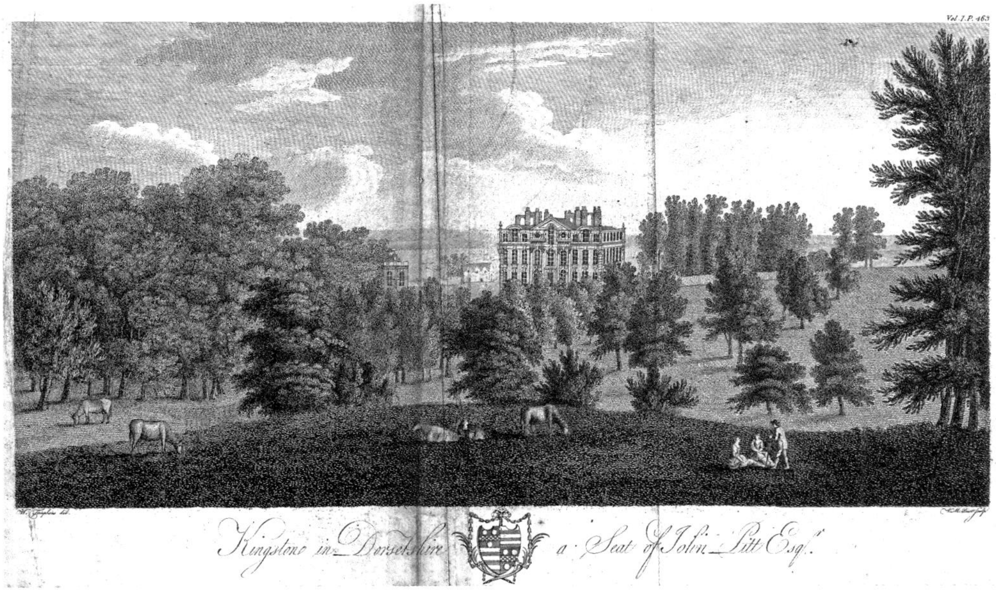

Fig. 27. *Kingston in Dorsetshire A Seat of John Pitt Esq,* folded after W. Tompkins by V.M. Picot, Hutchins ed.1, 1 p. 463, 1774.

more innovative Gainsborough in the late 1750s. Hoare's portrait presents the Pitt family in a close circle of tender familial love and affection. The graceful arrangement of the figures presents husband and wife united like a couple of dancers. John Pitt, three-quarter length, stands on the right wearing a contemporary brown coat, red waistcoat and breeches; Marcia wears a classicizing informal yellow gown, loosely laced with the hem of her skirt pinned up by a jewel to reveal her white underdress, an unusual arrangement which may suggest she is pregnant.[7] Holding a stick in both hands, William is seated, possibly on a stone-wall, wearing a white infant's dress, blue sash, a white outer gown and red shoes. A worked-up drawing for the composition (British Museum) (fig. 28), reveals him seated, perhaps on a balustrade. John Pitt stands in front of a classical porticoed building on the far right, which may allude to his interest in architecture. The classical allusions are more apparent in the drawing, setting Pitt against a classical urn.

Regarded as one of Hoare's best portraits, in 1761 it was the first he submitted to the Society of Artists, of which he was a founder member, with the title *A family; a gentleman, his lady and child.*[8] Hoare's style

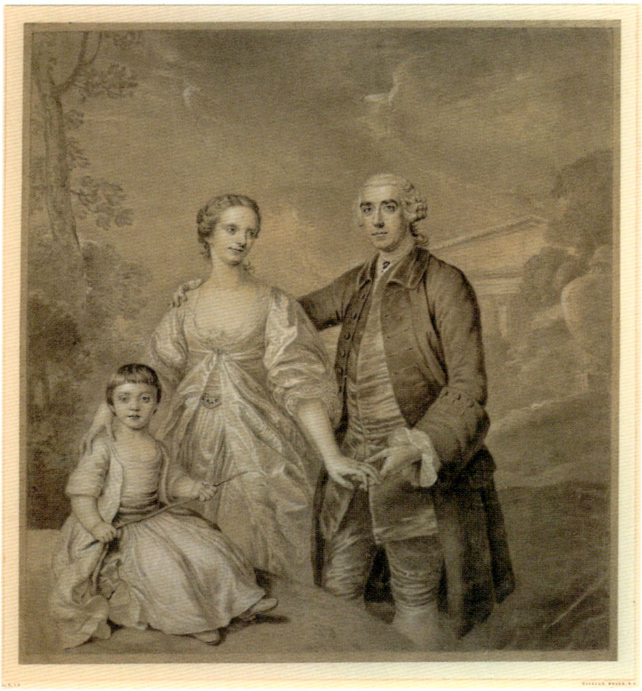

Fig. 28. *The Pitt Family*, Black chalk and stump, heightened with white, on grey paper, squared for transfer, William Hoare, c. 1758–59.

and use of strong bright colours is indebted to his prolonged sojourn in Italy, influenced by Francesco Imperiali, Pompeo Batoni and Rosalba Carriera and references the work of Van Dyck.[9] Hoare made several preparatory studies for the portrait, a composition oil study (Holburne Museum) is attributed to him as is the fully worked up black chalk drawing on grey paper (fig. 28) where Hoare has squared his drawing for transfer to the prepared canvas. This drawing is more satisfactory than the final composition, with better-positioned figures and associated features such as an urn and the apex of the roof of the building on the right.

1 In 1734 George Pitt purchased Encombe for John who also inherited Kingston Maurward after the death of his brother William in 1774.

2 In 1765 Pitt spoke in Parliament in support of West Country merchants concerned at French encroachments at Newfoundland.

3 See T. Lever, *The House of Pitt*, London, 1947, p. 112, William Pitt to John Pitt, Bath, 18 May 1754.

4 T. Lever, *The House of Pitt*, London, 1947, p. 101, Lady Sarah Bunbury to Lady Sarah O'Brien, Castletown, 6 July 1775.

5 *The Reports of the Society for Bettering the Condition and Increasing the Comforts of the Poor*, 1798, 1, 446, p. 5; pp. 47–54, contains an extract from an account of the gaol and house of correction at Dorchester by Wm. Morton Pitt, Esq.

6 It seems likely that the classical portico visible to the right-hand side in the present painting represents Encombe before 1870. See T. Lever, *The House of Pitt. A Family Chronicle*, London, 1947, p. 363.

7 Perhaps with her daughter Marcia, born 1759.

8 Lewis Walpole Library, 49.3885.2.v.1, *Catalogue of the Pictures, Sculptures, Models, Drawings, Prints &c. Exhibited by the Society of Artists of Great-Britain, At the Great Room in Spring-Garden, Charing Cross, May the 9th 1761*, p. 6, no. 42, Horace Walpole annotated his copy next to the title and in his hand added, *Mr John Pitt &c.*

9 Hoare would almost certainly have seen Van Dyck's celebrated portrait of the Herbert family at Wilton House.

19. **British School c. 1799**

Lady Caroline Damer (1752–1829)
oil on canvas
28.9×23.4 cm

Provenance: Sitter, then by descent to Ireland; Christie's sale, Castletown House, Co Kilkenny, Ireland, 7–8 October 1991, lot 224.

Private Collection

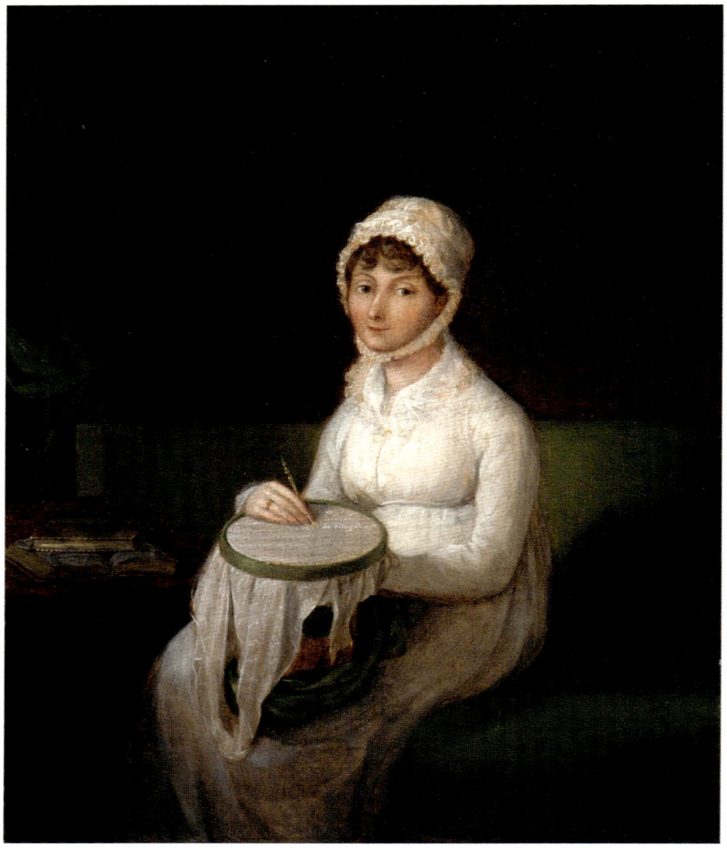

Lady Caroline Damer was the only daughter of Joseph Damer, (fig. 14) first Earl of Dorchester and Caroline Sackville, daughter of the first Duke of Dorset of Milton Abbey.[1] Caroline's three brothers all died without issue during her lifetime, leaving unmarried Caroline the eventual heiress.[2] The Damer family was frequently at Weymouth with the royal family or visited by them, and Lady Caroline developed a friendship with the royal princesses. Mary Frampton's journal records 'the royal family were much attached to her' and Lady Caroline 'was on terms of intimacy with the princesses at the end of her life'.[3] On the death of her brothers, Lady Caroline inherited several estates in England and Ireland; in London she lived at Dorchester House, Park Lane, and in Dorset she established a school at Milton Abbas for twelve poor children who were clothed and taught to read.

The small intimate portrait reveals the image of a highly accomplished woman in the late eighteenth century. Previously attributed to miniaturist and portraitist Richard Cosway, Lady Caroline is shown seated on a green settle.[4] She is engaged in tambourwork, a form of embroidery worked in white thread creating fine chain stitch upon muslin stretched tightly over a circular hoop – hence tambour. She holds the hoop in her left hand and a gold tambour hook in her right, the stitches she is working on clearly visible. Tambourwork was a fashionable activity for an aristocratic woman at leisure. It was used to ornament dresses, curtains, caps, borders and all varieties of white trimmings. The painting intentionally reveals the elegance of her wrist as she punches the stitches through the muslin.

1 When Caroline Damer's mother died in 1775, her father Joseph Damer commissioned Italian sculptor Agostino Carlini to create a tomb to her memory in Milton Abbey Church, designed by Robert Adam. After her father died his effigy was added to the monument.
2 In 1776 her brother John had committed suicide leaving a widow, the sculptress Ann Damer. Lionel, Caroline's youngest brother, was an officer in the Dorset Volunteer Rangers and MP for Peterborough. He lived at Came House near Dorchester where George III visited him; he died in 1807. With the death of Caroline's unmarried brother George (cat. 28) in 1808 the title became extinct.
3 Frampton, 1885, p. 24.
4 Private communication with Stephen Lloyd confirms the portrait was not painted by Richard Cosway.

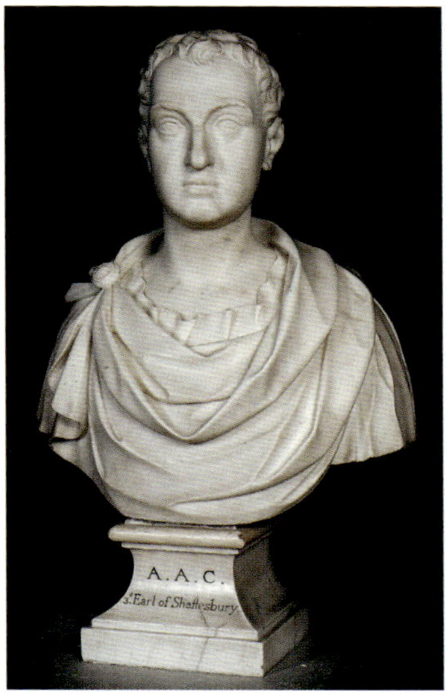

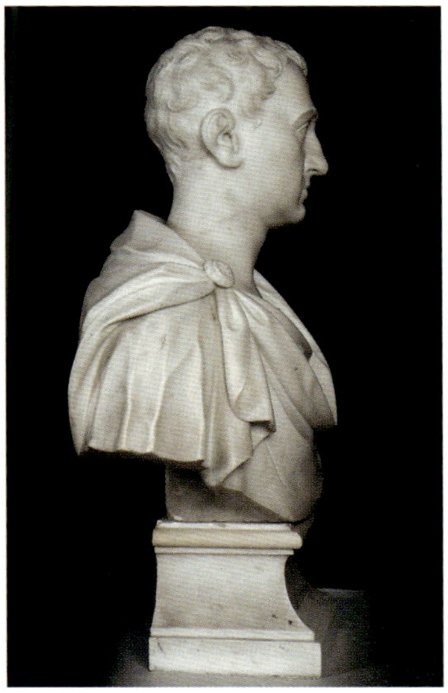

20.

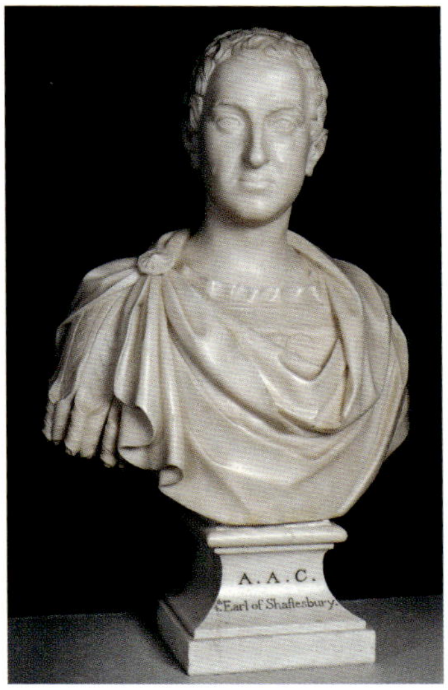

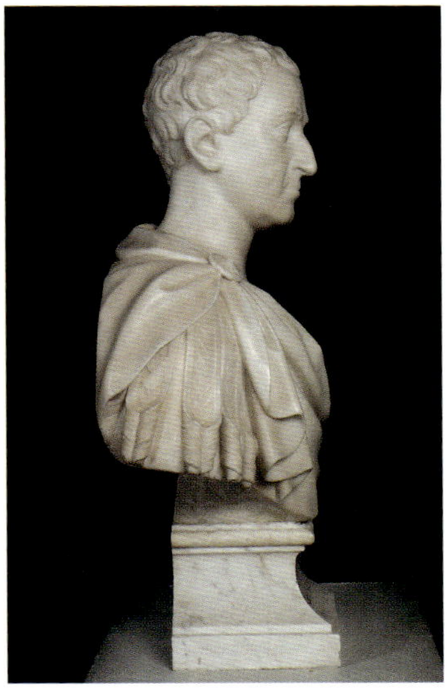

21.

20. **Peter Gaspar Scheemakers** (1691–1781)
Anthony Ashley Cooper, 3rd Earl of Shaftesbury (1671–1713)
marble, 1766
72.5 cm high
Inscribed on socle: *A.A.C. 3rd Earl of Shaftesbury*
Provenance: Sitter, then by descent; purchased by DNH&AS, Christie's, London, 26 June 1980, Lot. 11, with the aid of the Art Fund and V&A Purchase Fund.
Literature: R. Gunnis, *Dictionary of British Sculpture 1660–1851*, London, 1968, p. 343.

21. **Peter Gaspar Scheemakers** (1691–1781)
Anthony Ashley Cooper, 4th Earl of Shaftesbury (1711–1771)
marble, 1766
81 cm high
Inscribed on socle: *A.A.C. 4th Earl of Shaftesbury*
Provenance: Sitter, then by descent; purchased by DNH&AS, Christie's, London, 26 June 1980, Lot. 12, with the aid of the Art Fund and V&A Purchase Fund.
Literature: R. Gunnis, *Dictionary of British Sculpture 1660–1851*, London, 1968, p. 343.

Dorset Natural History and Archaeological Society

In 1766 Anthony Ashley Cooper, 4th Earl of Shaftesbury, commissioned busts of himself and his dead father, the celebrated philosopher and 3rd Earl of Shaftesbury, from the sculptor Peter Scheemakers. The imposing portrait busts show father and son fashionably dressed in Roman costume, the 4th Earl presenting himself as the intellectual heir to his father.

The Ashley Coopers were a powerful Whig family. The 1st Earl, an influential politician during the Restoration, managed the early upbringing of his grandson, Anthony, later 3rd Earl of Shaftesbury, placing him under the tuition of the great philosopher John Locke. On the death of his father in 1699 he became 3rd Earl, working tirelessly on behalf of West Country Whig candidates in the Lords (fig. 29). Aged thirty, ill health curtailed his political career, after which he concentrated most of his energies on philosophical and literary writing. Following the lead of Locke, the 3rd Earl became an important writer on human behaviour and aesthetics, advocating in his 1711 *Characteristics of Men, Manners, Opinions, Times* the foundation of an academy of art based on continental models and the benefits of a national school of history painting. Retiring and reflective, his Neo-Platonist beliefs promoted a politeness; his sharp observations of human nature

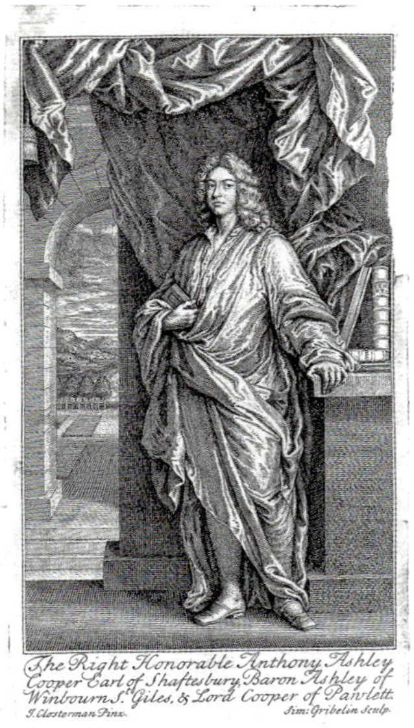

Fig. 29. *3rd Earl of Shaftesbury*, after John Closterman, line engraving by Simon Gribelin, 1723.

parallelled his belief that all things belonged to a harmonious cosmic order and that virtue promoted the good of all humankind. Shaftesbury's approach to aesthetics was highly influential throughout the eighteenth and nineteenth centuries in Britain and Europe.[1]

Shaftesbury regulated his own image carefully, believing the artist to be a mere mechanic, executing the superior inventions of the patron. It is therefore striking that his son should have commissioned two portraits characteristic of Scheemakers's style which show little evidence of the earl's personal taste.[2] Scheemakers frequently showed contemporary sitters in antique costume, eighteenth century patrons keen to see themselves as the heirs to the philosopher statesmen of the Augustan age.

The 4th Earl wrote a biography of his father in which it is clear that although his father died when he was two years old, he was an ardent defender of his father's reputation. Married at the age of fourteen to Lady Susannah Noel, their Dorset home was St. Giles House near Wimborne, built by the 1st Earl in 1650. As a powerful landowner and peer the 4th Earl was politically active both nationally and locally in Dorset, which he served for many years as Lord Lieutenant.

However, his great love was the arts; in the early 1740s the 4th Earl employed architect Henry Flitcroft to make extensive alterations to St. Giles, including the interior.[3] The Earl was an important patron of George Frideric Handel, who sometimes stayed with the Shaftesburys in Dorset. The 4th Earl died on 27 May 1771 aged 60 and was buried in the family church; his memorial there was made by Peter Scheemakers's son Thomas.[4]

1 See L. E. Klein, *Anthony Ashley Cooper Shaftesbury (Earl of), Characteristics of Men, Manners, Opinions, Times*, Cambridge, 1999.

2 I. Roscoe, 'Peter Scheemakers', *The Walpole Society*, London, 1999, 61, cat. no. 178, includes a similar bust by Scheemakers of *John Leveson-Gower, 1st Earl Gower.*

3 Between 1742 and 1744 the planned re-decoration included the White Hall, Dining Room, Tapestry Room and Large Drawing Room. Executed in the manner of William Kent, this evolved into the rococo by the middle of the century.

4 Peter Scheemakers worked on two memorial sculptures in Dorset, at Mapperton for Richard Broadrepp c. 1740 and for George Strode at St. Mary's, Beaminster in 1753. See J. Newman and N. Pevsner, *Dorset*, London, 1972, pp. 30 and 85.

22. **Attributed to Christopher Hewetson**

(1739–1798)

Peter Beckford, (1740–1811)

marble, c. 1766

57 cm high

Provenance: Presumably sitter, then by descent.

Private Collection

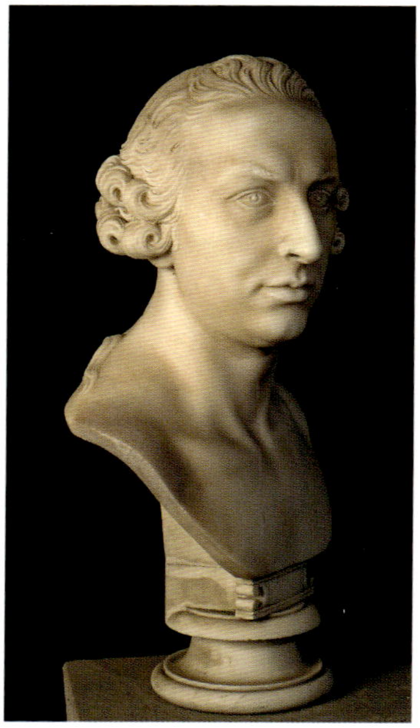

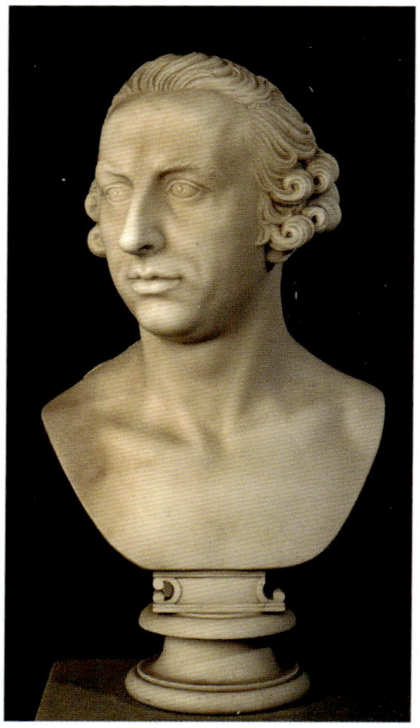

Traveller, sportsman and man of letters, Peter Beckford, descended from a family of sugar planters in Jamaica, inherited his Dorset estate, Iwerne Stepleton near Blandford, from his father Julines in 1765. The family wealth was vested in the West Indies, but Peter Beckford never visited, preferring the cultural attractions of the Continent and domestic pleasures of Dorset. In 1773 Beckford married Louisa Pitt, daughter of George Pitt of Stratfield Saye (cats. 26, 27) and sister of George Pitt, 2nd Lord Rivers (cat. no. 23). They lived initially in London but Beckford preferred life at Stepleton, and it was in Dorset that he bred his famous pack of fox-hounds. Beckford is chiefly remembered for writing two important works on field sports, the 1781 *Thoughts upon Hare and Fox Hunting* and *Essays on Hunting* which were early and unprecedentedly detailed manuals on the sport. In 1772 he sat to Thomas Beach wearing the livery of the Beckford Hunt (location unknown), and in 1785 commissioned Francis Sartorius to paint portraits of his dogs set in the park at Stepleton (Upton House).[1] Beckford was also a Ranger of Cranborne Chase with magisterial duties to enforce Forest Laws.[2]

In 1783 Louisa was diagnosed with tuberculosis, prompting the Beckfords to move to the warmer climate of Italy.[3] It was possible during the sixteen years he spent living in Florence that Beckford sat for this white marble bust. Although not signed or dated, the bust is stylistically similar to the work of the Irish sculptor Christopher Hewetson, who was resident in Rome from 1765 until his death in 1798. The socle, bare torso and queue visible on the left shoulder are all elements associated with Hewetson's work, and in composition and character the bust is close to a signed bust of an unknown man (formerly collection of Mrs R. Blacknel).[4] The bust appears to be associated with the similar portrait of Beckford's brother-in-law, George Pitt (cat. 23), although there are differences in handling. This might be explained by a difference in date, Beckford's bust could have been completed during his first trip to Italy in 1766 and it is not unlike Hewetson's early, documented bust of Charles Townley (British Museum).[5]

Beckford remained in Florence until 1799 when he returned to Dorset with his children to an estate depleted by debt.[6]

1 The Beach portrait was known to be with the Seymer family in the early nineteenth century.
2 For the fullest account of Beckford's life see A. Higginson, *Peter Beckford*, London, 1937.
3 Louisa died, 30 April 1791, in Florence, attended by her mother Lady Rivers, and was buried in Leghorn, see J. Ingamells, *A Dictionary of British and Irish Travellers in Italy, 1701–1800*, 1997, London, pp. 70–71.
4 B. de Breffny, 'Christopher Hewetson', *Irish Arts Review*, 3, p. 60, cat. no. 35.
5 Beckford seems similar in age to his portrait by Pompeo Batoni of 1766, now in Copenhagen (Statens Museum for Kunst). An export licence for his property issued August 1767 mentions 'un Ritratto moderno' which might refer to either a marble bust or painting. See I. Bignamini and C. Hornsby, *Digging and Dealing in Eighteenth Century Rome*, New Haven and London, 2010, 1, p. 238.
6 In 1807 Beckford's daughter Harriet married Henry Ker Seymer, descendant of Henry Seymer (cat. 53) and close friend of her family. Horace William Pitt-Rivers, son of Peter and Louisa Beckford, succeeded his uncle as third Baron Rivers and Lord of Cranborne Chase.

23. **Attributed to Christopher Hewetson** (1739–1798)

George Pitt, 2nd Lord Rivers (1751–1828)
marble, c. 1772
58 cm high
Provenance: Sitter, then by descent.

Private Collection

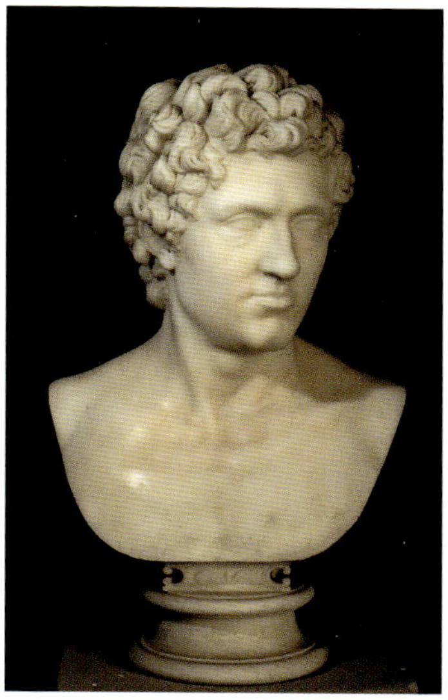

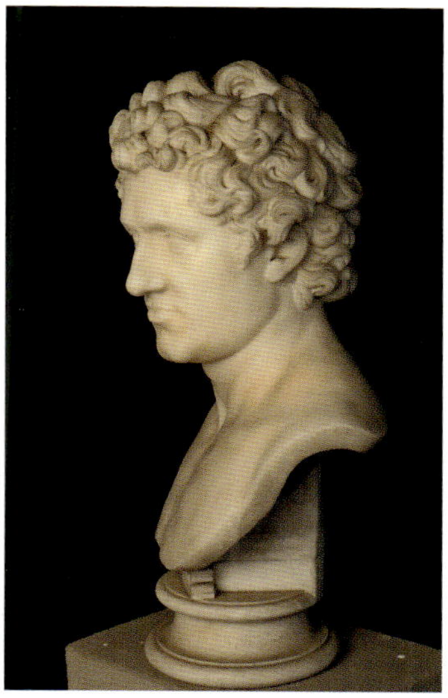

Only son of the first Lord Rivers, (cats. 26, 27) George Pitt was born at Angiers, France and lived on the Continent in his youth. In 1774 his father stood down as MP for Dorset, enabling him to represent the county in Parliament with Humphrey Sturt (fig. 6) and Francis Browne.[1] He was very fond of his sisters Penelope Ligonier, Louisa Beckford and Marcia Pitt, with whom he had shared a difficult home life; their father was described by Walpole as brutal and half-mad, who drove their mother to exile in Italy.[2] George's obituary in the *Gentleman's Magazine* observed as a young man he was 'a shining member of the fashionable world .... much addicted to field sports for which he had a predilection,' a passion he shared with his brother-in-law, Peter Beckford.[3] Unmarried, Pitt sold his Hampshire estate, Stratfield Saye, to the nation in 1817 for Arthur Wellesley, 1st Duke of Wellington.

The unsigned portrait bust of Pitt, appears to be by the same hand as that of Peter Beckford and is here attributed to the Irish sculptor Christopher Hewetson, who was based in Rome until his death in 1798. Although Pitt is not recorded in the Brinsley Ford archive as having travelled to Italy, it is likely he is the George Pitt recorded in Rome in 1772 by Patrick Home, who confided in his notebook: 'a sensible worthy man ... Mr Geo Pitt. Handsome Figure – Good natured – much addicted to low women'.[4] The bust shows Pitt looking to the left, in a pose loosely based on the famous bust of Caracalla in the Capitoline, with bare shoulders, a format Hewetson used in his signed and dated bust of John Campbell, 1st Baron Cawdor (Cawdor Castle) dated 1785.[5] The socle is also characteristic of Hewetson, being based on one originally used by the Italian sculptor Bartolomeo Cavaceppi.

Despite the dearth of records, Pitt probably visited Italy again between 1783 and 1791 when the Beckfords were resident in Florence. Considering its similarity to the bust of Peter Beckford (cat. 22), it might well have been completed on an unrecorded trip to Italy during the 1780s. The bust presumably passed to Pitt's heir, William Beckford, but is first recorded in the nineteenth century.

1 He stood at two further elections, 1780 and 1784, before following the family tradition by resigning in favour of his cousin William Morton Pitt in 1790 (cat. 18).
2 Thomas Gooch's painting showing the Hon. Marcia and the Hon. George Pitt, riding in the park of Stratfield Saye House, 1782, Paul Mellon Centre, New Haven.
3 The *Gentleman's Magazine*, 1828, 97, p. 463.
4 J. Ingamells, *A Dictionary of British and Irish Travellers in Italy, 1701–1800*, 1997, London, pp. 1772–773.
5 B. de Breffny, 'Christopher Hewetson', *Irish Arts Review*, 3, no. 3, 1986, cat. no. 3.

24. **Attributed to William Hoare** (1707–1792)

Sir (George) Edward Wilmot (1693–1786)
pastel on paper, c. 1740s
60×45 cm

Provenance: Sitter, then by descent.
Literature: Hutchins, ed. 3. Vol. 2, p. 528

Private Collection

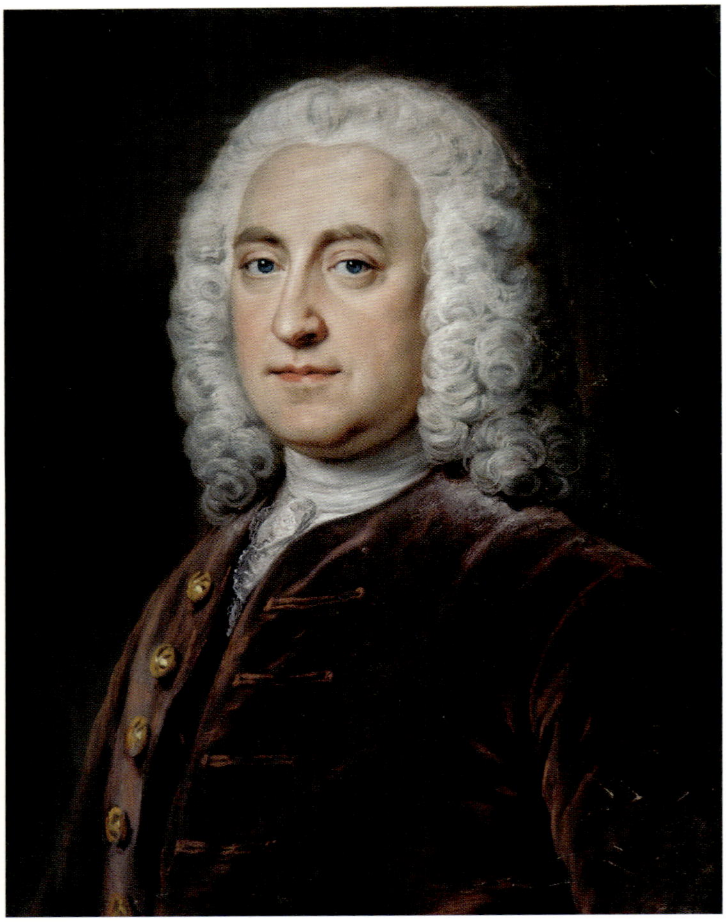

Edward Wilmot was the second son of Robert Wilmot of Chaddesdon, Derbyshire and Joyce Sacheverell. He practised as a physician from 1725, working at St Thomas's Hospital, and was elected FRS 29 January 1730 and Harveian orator in 1735. Wilmot's introduction to the royal household followed his marriage to Sarah Marsh Meade (1702–1785), daughter of the great Richard Meade, physician to King George II. Wilmot was some-time Physician General to the Army, and Physician in Ordinary to Queen Caroline, Frederick, Prince of Wales and King George II. Wilmot was created a baronet on 15 February 1759, became physician-in-ordinary to George III (cat. 1) in 1760 and both retired from practice and left London the next year. When his daughter Jane married Thomas Williams of Herringston, Dorset, Edward also moved there until his death aged 94.

It is highly probable that Wilmot sat to his head and shoulders portrait, almost certainly by William Hoare, in Bath. Despite the nineteenth century label on the frame the portrait is not by Reynolds, but by a fine pastellist of the calibre of Hoare. Pastel portraits gained popularity through the influence of the Venetian Rosalba Carriera. Eminently more portable than oils, layers of thick colour could be rapidly built up, resulting in both an intensity of colour and a lustrous finish, particularly for costumes.

In his *History*, Hutchins referred to the 'fine picture of the late Sir Edward Wilmot', in the dining-parlour of Herringston, 'expressive of that mildness and goodness of heart, by which he was eminently distinguished through a long and exemplary life'.[1] Although Wilmot had died by the time George III spent his summers in Dorset, the King, on one of his frequent visits to the house, commented on the portrait, expressing his pleasure at being so reminded of his physician.

1 Hutchins, ed. 3, 2, p. 528.

25. **Pompeo Batoni** (1708–1787)

Henry Bankes (1757–1834)
oil on canvas, 1779
96.5×71 cm
signed and dated: *POMPEO BATO[NI] / PINX. ROM. 1779*

Provenance: Sitter, then by descent to Ralph Bankes who presented it to the National Trust, together with the estates of Corfe Castle and Kingston Lacy and its entire contents in 1981.
Literature: J. Steegman, 'Some English Portraits by Pompeo Batoni', *The Burlington Magazine,* vol. 88, No. 516, 1946, p. 55–63 and A. Clark, ed. P. Bowron, *Pompeo Batoni: Complete Catalogue*, Oxford, 1985, no. 418, p. 349–50.

National Trust, Kingston Lacy

Henry Bankes was the only surviving son of Henry Bankes and Margaret, daughter of John Wynne, Bishop of Bath and Wells. He attended Fountayne's Academy, a fashionable private boarding-school in Marylebone Park, where he forged a life-long friendship with fellow pupil Thomas Rackett (cat. 43).[1] From there he went to Westminster School and Trinity Hall, Cambridge, succeeding to his father's extensive Dorset estates, including Kingston Hall and Corfe Castle, in 1776. Bankes embarked on a four-year 'Grand Tour' of Italy in 1778 and recorded his tour in a travel diary and correspondence sent to his mother Margaret in Dorset.[2] It was whilst in Rome that Bankes sat to Batoni for his portrait.

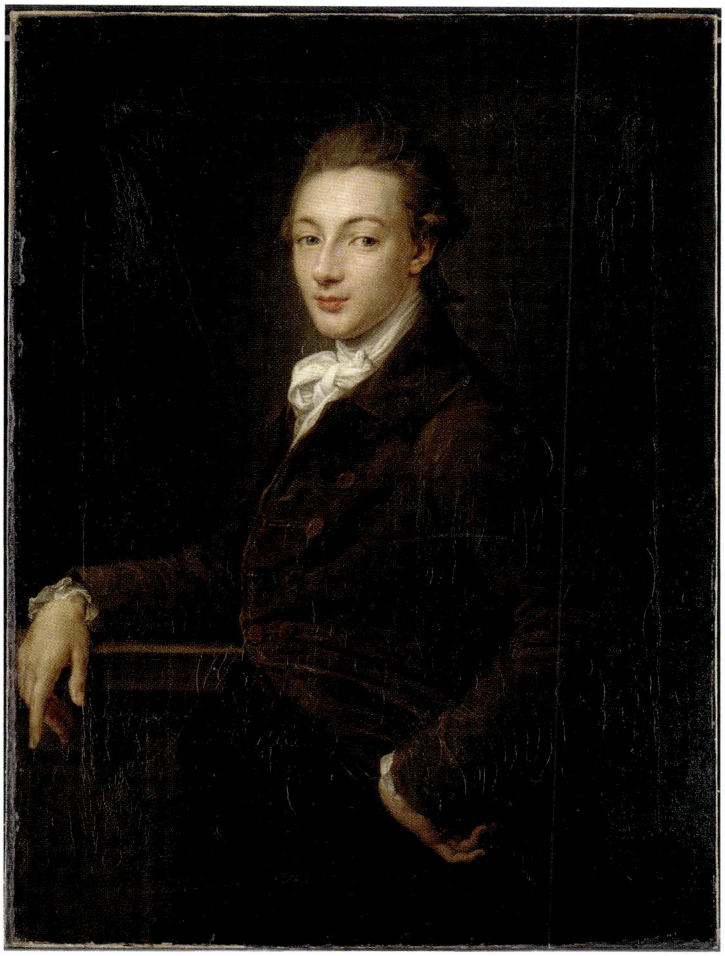

The commission is remarkably well documented in a series of six letters Bankes dispatched from Rome to his mother in Dorset, not only giving us an accurate account of the chronology of the painting and the logistics dispatching it home but, most unusually, the sitter's negative opinion. By the late 1770s Lucchese Batoni had been the principal portraitist in Rome for almost twenty years, patronized by a stream of European visitors to the city. The commission seems to have originated with Margaret Bankes; Henry wrote in August 1779 'you desire me to have my Picture painted. The most famous artist is Pompeo Battoni (sic); but to speak without prejudice I do not think his portraits equal to those of Reynolds: if you wish to have my likeness from Rome I would rather have it cut in cameo or Intaglio'.[3] Despite his antipathy towards Batoni, Henry acquiesced to his mother's request, observing 'I am not sorry otherwise to do it as I have been several times at his house to hear his daughters sing, one of whom is indeed an uncommonly fine singer . . . his colours stand much better than Sir Joshuais [sic] tho for taste and everything else I do not think him equal to him'.[4] Bankes wrote to his mother to inform her the portrait was finished in the November. He then described the painting observing 'It is certainly like me, but without any sort of Taste or good painting I have had the greatest difficulty in making him keep it quite simple in a dark coat the right arm resting against one of those pedestals which are so often found in painting & never anywhere else. The size is three quarters and a strong shade comes upon the lower part of it'.[5] The painting is notably sober for Batoni, clearly the result of Bankes's influence. Bankes was aware of Batoni's notorious dilatoriness, observing the artist's poor financial situation had prompted the swift completion of the painting. But in May 1780 Bankes wrote to his mother: 'my picture is again in Battoni's (sic) hands on account of some little alterations when he will let it go I know not, as I have unfortunately paid him'.[6] Bankes was eventually able to inform his mother in September 1780 that the painting was en route to Ostend, having been dispatched by the principal British dealer in Rome, Thomas Jenkins.[7] In his last letter from Rome Bankes offers a final damning assessment of the portrait: 'I think it but a melancholy cold picture whose only merit is being simple and having nothing offensive'.

In 1784 Bankes married Francis Woodley and seems never to have had his portrait painted again. He is notable by his absence from the series of Beach portraits of the officers of the Dorset Volunteer Rangers commissioned by the first Lord Milton in 1794. On Henry Bankes's death in 1834, his estate was inherited by his elder surviving son, the infamous William John Bankes, when the Batoni portrait was hung in the Billiard Room.[8]

1 The school was on the present site of Devonshire Mews. Handel was a friend of the founder, Dr Fountayne, and performed for the boys.
2 J. Ingamells, *A Dictionary of British and Irish Travellers in Italy, 1701–1800,* London and New Haven, 1997, p. 47; DHC, D/BKL Box 8C/67 Folder 2, series of letters between Henry Bankes from Italy to his mother Margaret Bankes in Dorset.
3 DHC, 6/1, Henry Bankes to Margaret Bankes, Rome, 14 August, 1779. Henry Digby wrote from Vienna in 1751 that his mother, Charlotte Digby 'desires if there is an extreme good painter here that I would have my picture done' he eventually sits to the court painter Martin Van Meytens (private collection). Lewis Walpole Library, Connecticut, Henry Digby to Charles Hanbury Williams, Vienna, 24 December, 1751, CHW 54–10910 f. 189–90. I am grateful to Jonathan Yarker for this reference.
4 DHC, 6/2, Henry Bankes to Margaret Bankes, Rome, 28 September, 1779.
5 DHC, 6/3, Henry Bankes to Margaret Bankes, Rome, 24 November, 1779.
6 DHC, 6/4, Henry Bankes to Margaret Bankes, Rome, 6 May, 1780. In the same letter Bankes refers to the British artists in Rome working for the notorious Earl Bishop of Derry, observing that he thought the Irish painter Jacob More 'is really excellent and preferred by some people to Hackert'.
7 DHC, 6/6, Henry Bankes to Margaret Bankes, Rome, 23 September, 1780. Bankes observed to his mother 'I hear Angelica [Kauffman] has left England and is coming here this winter & if she should paint portraits Battoni (sic) would find in her a very considerable rival'.
8 *Inventory and valuation of Furniture, Paintings, Wine, Plate, Horses, Harness &c &c. at Kingston Hall 1835*, DHC, Box D/BKL 8 C/58, p. 58: 'Paintings in Billiard Room. H. Bankes Esq[re]'.

26. **Thomas Gooch** (1750–1802)

George Pitt, First Lord Rivers (1721–1803) as Colonel of the Dorset Militia
oil on canvas, 1782
66.5×61.2 cm
signed and dated
Provenance: Sitter, then by descent.

Private Collection

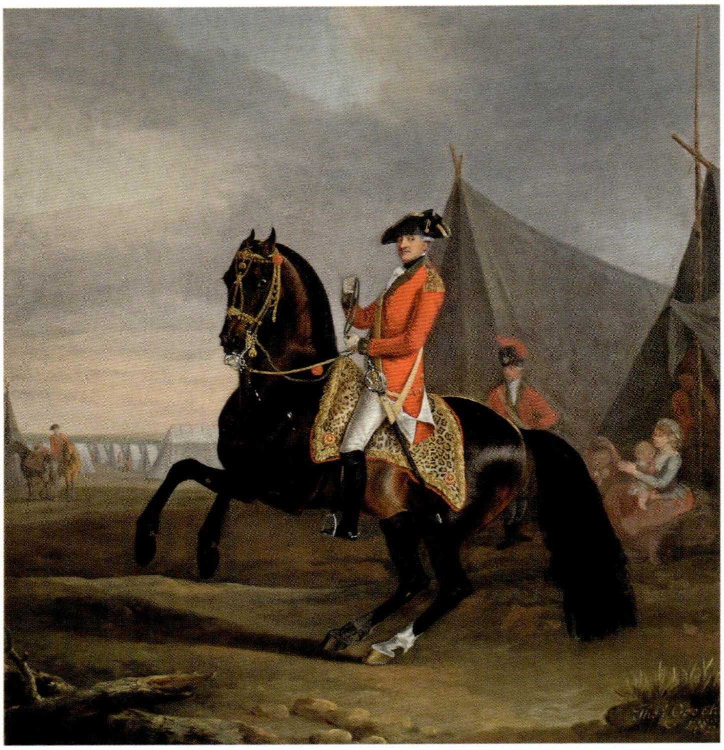

Born in Geneva, Pitt was the eldest son of George Pitt, of Stratfield Saye. Between 1740–1742 Pitt travelled to Italy, where he sat to Rosalba Carriera in Venice. He married Penelope Atkins in 1746; they had three daughters and a son.[1] Though Pitt was the largest landowner in Dorset he chiefly lived at his 900-acre Stratfield Saye estate complete with his ménage. He was MP for Shaftesbury and Dorset between 1747 and 1774, and created Baron Rivers of Stratfield Saye in 1776. In the year Pitt sat to Gooch for his portrait he became a lord of the bedchamber and appointed Lord Lieutenant for Dorset in 1793.

On the formation of the Dorset militia in 1757, Pitt was appointed its Colonel, and in Gooch's portrait he is shown wearing his colonel's uniform. This was an office he held with immense pride and consequently wished his portrait to proclaim his role with the militia. In 1759 his wife wrote, 'my husband is gone with his Regiment to Quarters and is not a little pleased with his new employment. I'm told he is an excellent officer, and this, his Regiment, is the flower of the Militia'.[2] The first camp took place two miles west of Dorchester on Bradford Heath in 1757 and may be the site of the camp shown in Gooch's portrait.[3] Under Pitt, the Dorset Militia frequently moved around the south of England; the *Morning Post* for 28 March 1781 reported that at Southampton 'his Lordship ordered four concerts for the amusement of the polite circle, every fortnight, one to be performed by the band of the regiment, assisted by some Gentlemen of Salisbury Cathedral'.[4]

The Colonel for 40 years, Pitt's authority was challenged in 1793 by his son George Pitt (cat. 23), a major in the corps, together with other officers of the regiment, concerned at his treatment of a junior officer.[5] Accusing his father of being 'suspicious, uncandid and unjust', the son sought to replace his father as Colonel with Lord Milton – who sensibly declined. The ensuing row lasted four years, resulting in Rivers publishing the correspondence in a private volume, both to clear his name and demonstrate his loyalty to the crown.[6] The letters reveal Rivers's pleasure in serving in the militia, 'a corps with which he has passed the pleasantest and most happy of his years'.[7] This family dispute was an unwelcome distraction as it took place against the backdrop of the increasing threat of invasion.

A celebrated horseman, Gooch's portrait shows Rivers demonstrating his horsemanship in managing his horse, with the control manifest in the handling of the reins. Dressage, a highly prized skill, reached its peak in the eighteenth century. Rivers dominates the image, affirming his power and control, his hauteur manifest as he and the horse, both aristocratic thoroughbreds, stare out of the picture space. Rivers was given a horse by the King and his remarkable horsemanship was commemorated in these lines:

'Paw, curvet, champ and prance
And to the Music of the Band
In justest Measure dance'.[8]

Rivers is positioned in front of lines of camp tents, soldiers, female camp followers and their children with the Dorset downs in the distance, offering a rare glimpse of Dorset life in a military camp. His splendid uniform of red coat with moss green lapels and cuffs, decorative buttons, gold epaulettes and trim is emphasised by the horse's luxurious leopard coat. Gooch adds other touches of red to the painting in the hat, sword, plume, and the woman's dress. There are four known portraits of Rivers as Colonel of the Dorset Militia, most importantly the full-length by Gainsborough who stayed at Stratfield Saye whilst working on the portrait and with whom he was on close terms. Gooch produced two versions of the Rivers portrait and Thomas Beach a miniature (cat. 27). In Gainsborough's powerful and penetrating portrait of Lord Rivers 1768–69 (Cleveland Museum of Art) he wears the uniform of the Dorset militia complete with military greatcoat, but is not mounted. A description of George Pitt collected by Dr William Cuming (fig. 24) reveals that the elderly Pitt's graceful carriage and amorous chat charmed the ladies of Dorchester leading to an ode, *The doleful Lamentation of the Single Women of Dorchester on the Departure of Colonel Pitt* sung to a mournful tune.[9]

Gooch's portrait is a smaller variance of his *Portrait of a nobleman on a managed horse (Lord Rivers)* exhibited at the Royal Academy in 1782.[10] Rivers was an early patron of Thomas Gooch who was essentially a sporting painter. The same year that Gooch exhibited Lord Rivers's picture he painted the portrait of Rivers's son and daughter, Marcia and George, riding in the park of Stratfield Saye House.[11]

1 Horace Walpole accused George Pitt of cruelty towards his wife; the couple separated in 1764. Lady Rivers spent a great deal of time living abroad.
2 W. Talbot, 'Thomas Gainsborough: George Pitt, First Lord Rivers', *The Bulletin of the Cleveland Museum of Art,* 58, No. 9, 1971, p. 258–268.
3 Isaac Taylor's 1765 map of Dorset, (endpaper) shows the site of the camp.
4 *Morning Post and Daily Advertiser,* 28 March 1781.
5 The officers challenging Rivers were Colonel Michel, Captain Bingham, Sir George Glynn, Major George Pitt (cat. 23), W. M. Pitt (cat. 18), E. M. Pleydell, John Bastard and Walter Hodges.
6 *The Present State of the Dorsetshire Militia set forth in a series of letters between the Colonel and some of the Principal Officers of That Regiment From September 1793 to this time,* London, Parts I & II, 1797, Part II, p. 84.
7 W. Talbot, 'Thomas Gainsborough: George Pitt, First Lord Rivers', *The Bulletin of the Cleveland Museum of Art,* 58, No. 9, 1971, p. ix.
8 W. Boswell Stone, 'William Cuming, M. D., 1714–1787', *Proceedings Dorset Natural History and Antiquarian Field Club,* 24, 1903, p. 42.
9 W. Boswell Stone, 'William Cuming, M. D., 1714–1787', *Proceedings Dorset Natural History and Antiquarian Field Club,* 24, 1903, p. 34–55.
10 Exhibited in the Royal Academy, no. 183, now at Bramham Park. The focus of this larger portrait is mostly on the sitter with several soldiers standing close behind him, and tents in the distance, but no followers are included.
11 Probably *Portraits of a young nobleman and his sister on horseback,* showing Stratfield Saye in the distance, exhibited at the Royal Academy, 1783, No. 116, (collection, Yale Centre for British Art).

27. **Thomas Beach** (1738–1806)

George Pitt, First Lord Rivers (1721–1803) as Colonel of the Dorset Militia
oil on canvas, 1779
34.5×27 cm
Provenance: Thomas Beach by descent to Capt. J.H.P. Brain; Sotheby's 18 December 1974; Christie's 1975, purchased by The Keep, Dorchester via the Army Ogilby Trust
Literature: Beach, 1934, p. 69, No. 24.
Exhibition: Society of Artists, 1780

The Keep Military Museum, Dorchester

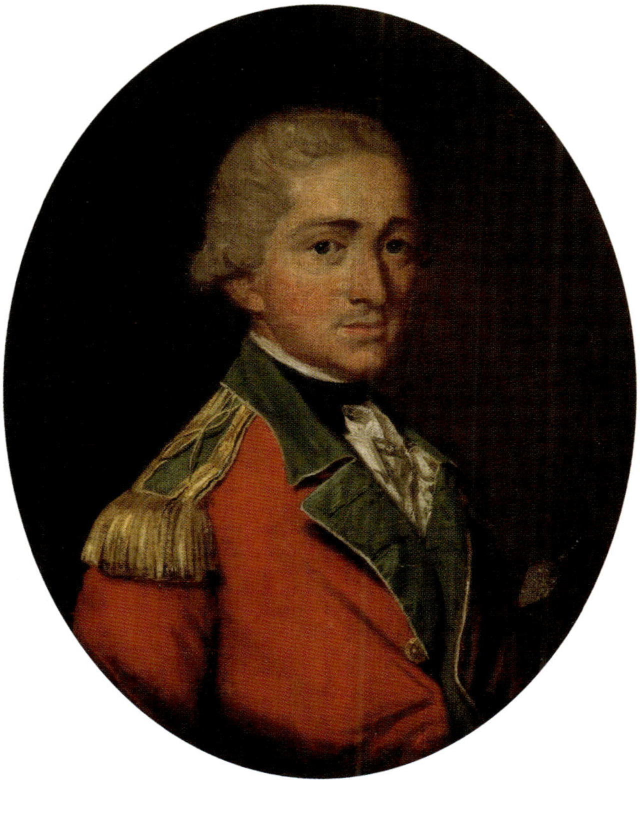

A miniature head and shoulders portrait set in an oval of Lord Rivers. He is shown as Colonel of the Dorset Militia wearing red coat with green facings and gold epaulettes. Rivers could have sat to Beach in Bath but it is more likely to have been executed in Dorset when Rivers was at his Cranborne Chase home Rushmore Lodge, which Beach was known to have visited. The miniature did not result in any other commissions for Beach, and remained in his possession at his death in 1806.

Portraits of the Dorset Volunteer Rangers

Beach's portraits of the officers of the Dorset Volunteer Rangers were commissioned by the 1st Earl of Dorchester (fig. 14), for display in the library at Milton Abbey. Lord Dorchester undoubtedly initiated the project because his son, George, was Colonel of the Rangers. Beach, the portraitist working in Dorset, was the logical choice for this local commission particularly as Lord Dorchester was his long-standing supporter.[1] The Rangers were a corps of light cavalry, founded by George Damer (cat. 28) in 1794, to defend the county against the renewed threat of invasion (fig. 30). Dorset was divided into divisions (initially called troops), with each officer responsible for raising their own troop to defend allocated areas and be prepared to put down 'Riots and Tumults'.[2]

Between 1794 and 1799, thirteen of its officers sat to Beach apparently for Lord Dorchester, these canvases survive along with a number of copies.[3] Its membership initially consisted of George Damer's friends, but this changed over the next decade as more troops were formed and areas of responsibility reassessed. In each

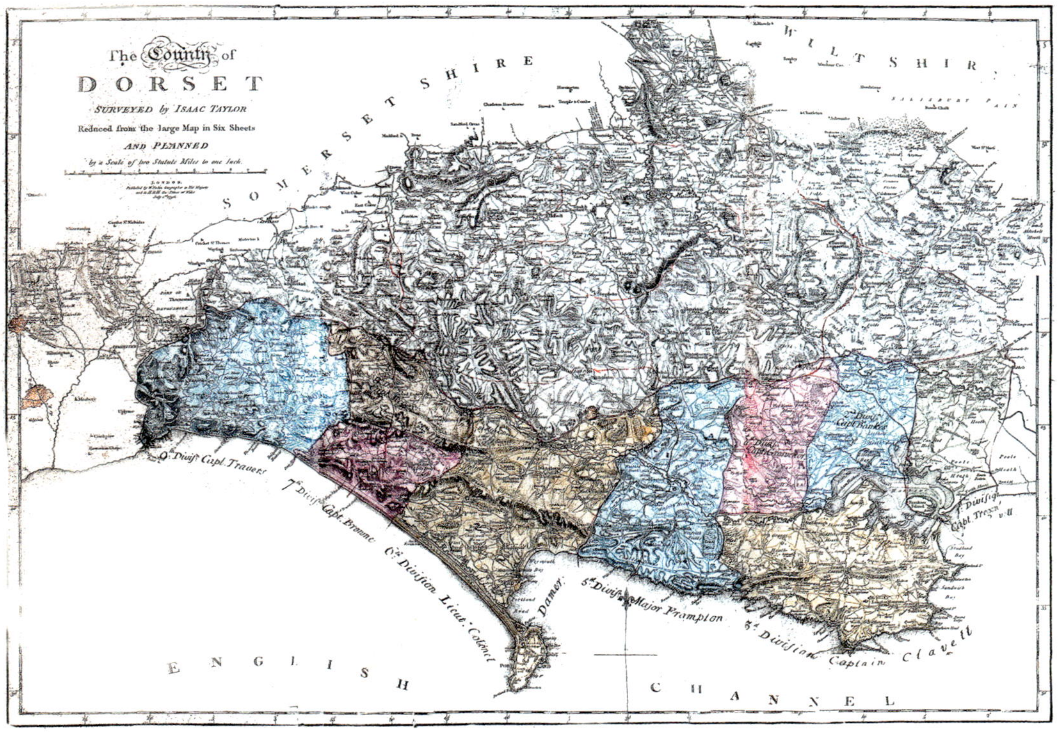

Fig. 30. *Map of Dorset showing the coastal areas of responsibilty of the Dorset Volunteer Ranger officers*, Isaac Taylor, 1798.

portrait Beach included landscape details relevant to the individual; William Clavell of Smedmore stands against a backdrop of the cliffs close to his house and the area under his command, while the last portrait in the series positions John Wyldbore Smith in front of his house at Sydling St Nicholas.[4] Portraits commemorating the sitters' affiliation with certain organizations or membership of club, regiment or hunts were not without precedent in the eighteenth century, although Beach's Dorset Volunteer Rangers represent perhaps the fullest though least documented of the period. In the 1660s Sir Peter Lely had supplied paintings of the Flagmen of Lowestoft, showing the Admirals who had fought at the battle of Lowestoft for James, Duke of York. Kneller had painted members of the Kit-Kat club and George Knapton members of the Society of Dilettanti. On a more local level Joseph Wright of Derby who, as his name suggests, worked principally in Derby, painted members of the Markeaton Hunt in hunt livery in 1762–63.[5] But Beach's portraits, in showing a self-regulating, volunteer force, are unusual.

The portraits of the sitters are three-quarter length, shown standing wearing the uniform of the corps created by Lord Milton: black velvet collar and cuffs on a green jacket with gold buttons inscribed *D.V.R.*, gilt epaulettes, white leather breeches and a crimson sash. They adopt a range of attitudes holding swords, wearing or holding their elaborate headdress of black bearskin with white plume with a dash of red, peaked in front, with a leopard-skin band round it and inscribed in gilt letters on the front *'Dorset Rangers'*.

List of Officers in Dorset Volunteer Rangers.

Engaged to serve in Case of Riots and Tumults, in any of the adjoining Counties; and in Case of Invasion, in any Part of Great Britain. 4th June, 1801.

Ranks.	*Names.*	*Residence.*	*No. in each Troop.*
Colonel....	Earl of Dorchester	Milton Abbey.....	-
Lt. Colonel	Hon. Lionel Damer	Came..............	68
Major......	James Frampton...	Moreton...........	68
	R. E. D. Grosvenor	Charborough......	75
	F. J. Browne.......	Frampton..........	44
	R. Travers..........	Up Loders.........	56
	Thos. Meggs.......	Piddlehinton......	42
Captains	L. D. G. Tregonwell	Cranborne.........	40
	W. Clavell..........	Smedmore.........	43
	T. B. Bower........	Iwerne Minster...	64
	Henry Bankes......	Kingston-Hall....	33
	George Snow.......	Langton............	-
	George Churchill..	Dorchester.........	-
	Nicholas Ingram...	Weymouth.........	-
	J. H. Browne......	Weymouth.........	-
	Richard Austen....	Wimborne.........	-
Lieuts.	St. Barbe Tregonwell	Cranborne.........	-
	E. B. Portman.....	Bryanston..........	-
	E. Dally............	Bridport...........	-
	C. B. Wollaston...	Dorchester........	-
	J. Barker...........	Wareham..........	-
	H. C. Haines......	Tincleton.........	-
	Tho. Stillingfleet..	Cranborne.........	-
	W. Whitaker......	Shaston............	-
	Joseph Weld.......	Lullworth Castle,	-
	J. W. Smith.......	Forston............	-
Cornets	Thos. Weld........	Lullworth Castle.	-
	Thos. Pickard.....	Bloxworth.........	-
	T. H. Bastard......	Charlton...........	-
	F. A. Hayter.......	Wareham..........	-
	J. G. Harris........	Bailie..............	-
Adjutant...	T. B. Bower........	Iwerne Minster...	-
Surgeon....	Christ. Arden.....	Dorchester........	-
		Total	533

Fig. 31. *List of Officers in Dorset Volunteer Rangers*, 4 June 1801.

George Damer wore a different bearskin with green plumage, to distinguish him as the commanding officer. The portraits represent an almost complete account of the field officers and commanders, although one surprising omission is Henry Bankes, the only captain in the field who did not sit to Beach (cat. 25).[6]

Beach first painted the Colonel, George Damer, in 1794.[7] The following year Beach painted portraits of seven of the officers; amongst them was Thomas Weld shown wearing his captain's uniform with the coast of Dorset visible behind him, probably Lulworth Cove.[8] However George III did not sign Weld's commission because he was a Roman Catholic, nor was the Lord Lieutenant, Lord Rivers (cats. 26, 27), permitted to sign on his behalf.[9] Family tradition suggests that Weld may have continued in an honorary capacity, which perhaps enabled Beach to paint Weld's portrait wearing the uniform of the DVR.[10] It is likely that Beach stayed at Lulworth to work on Weld's Ranger portrait, producing portraits of Weld and his wife Mary (cats. 31, 32) at the same date.[11]

In 1798 three more troops were formed, prompting Beach to paint four more Ranger portraits, having received, according to his diary, a draft for £50 from George Damer 2nd Earl of Dorchester, his father having died in January 1798. Beach stayed with each of the officers while painting their portraits. His 1798 diary reveals that while painting the officers he was based with Lord Dorchester at Milton Abbey, where he was very much at home. Beach was at Milton Abbey between 14 September and 30 October working on the Ranger portraits, particularly the swords and sashes. This included a copy of Lord Dorchester commissioned by Tregonwell (cat. 30) on which he worked for 17 days. Beach borrowed the housekeeper, Mrs Woodward, to sit in for George Damer, who was not in residence.[12] The portrait was eventually dispatched to Tregonwell on 21 October. Beach briefly left Milton Abbey to stay with the other sitters, at a time of mounting activity amongst the Rangers, and by Friday 7 December he was back at Milton Abbey, where he visited the troops in exercise on the downs and records showing one of the sitters, Mr. Bower of Iwerne, around Milton Abbas. The next day he framed and hung the recently painted Dorset yeomanry pictures in the library. They remained at Milton Abbey until the house was sold to Lord Hambro in 1852, when they briefly moved to Came House, and are now elsewhere in a private collection.[13]

The officers presented a captive audience for Beach, eager to be shown in the splendour of their uniforms. Beach, as a successful and efficient portraitist, was the obvious person to portray the Rangers for Milton, whose large house had walls to be filled. It is a matter of speculation that this created a mutually beneficial scheme for Lord Milton, celebrating his son's achievement in forming the Rangers and for Beach painting their portraits. Instead of paying for a number of expensive portraits, perhaps a deal was struck in which Beach agreed to paint the portrait of each officer for Lord Milton, for a small fee. This was in anticipation of Beach earning money from potential copies of the sitters, for which Beach would charge the correct amount, thus making the project commercially viable for Beach. This is perhaps evinced by the number of copies of Lord Milton's portrait which were made. It is estimated that at least three were made, as several of Beach's sitters wished to hang Milton's portrait together with their own. Additionally, in 1795, Beach produced an engraving of Lord Milton, which, with the help of his cousin Bill Beach in Dorchester, he was able to sell to the officers and interested people. The diary records Dr Richard Pulteney (cat. 54) buying a proof in 1798. Collectively these portraits form a remarkable group of pictures, revealing the response of the Dorset aristocracy and gentry to the threat of invasion.

1 Beach had already painted in 1789 portraits of two officers of the East Riding Gentlemen and Yeomanry Cavalry.

2 DHC, D/FRA/X3, manuscript by J. Frampton, *Account of the Origin and proceedings of the Dorset Yeomanry Cavalry from 1793–1814*, p. 13.

3 The known DVR portraits by Beach are *George Damer, Viscount Milton*, Colonel, 1794 and copies 1795, 1798; *Captain Thomas Weld*, Lulworth Castle, 1795 and copy; *Captain William Churchill*, 1795; *Captain the Hon. Lionel Damer*, 1795; *Major James Frampton*, 1795 and copy; *Captain Richard Erle Drax Grosvenor*, 1795 and copy; *Captain Richard Travers*, 1795; *Captain Francis John Browne*, 1795; *Captain Thomas Meggs*, 1798; *Captain L.D.G. Tregonwell*, 1798; *Captain Bowyer Bower*, 1798; *Captain William Clavell*, 1798 and copy; *Cornet John W. Smith*, 1799. Beach was also commissioned by the 1st Earl of Dorchester c. 1798 to paint a portrait of the Prince of Wales to hang in his library with the DVR officers, however he was not dressed in their uniform, and his precise status in relation to the DVR is therefore unclear. Beach's portrait of the Reverend William Chafin of Chettle House, Chaplain to the Rangers, also hung in the library (whereabouts unknown), see Hutchins, ed.3, 4, p. 395.

4 William Richards of Smedmore was born at Winfrith Newburgh and succeeded his uncle George Clavell and assumed the name and arms of Clavell.

5 J. Egerton, *Wright of Derby*, exh. cat., London (Tate), 1990, pp. 38–41, cat. nos. 5–8.

6 According to Frampton the first to enrol were, Captains: William Churchill, Henbury; Lionel Damer, Came; Thomas Weld Senr, Lulworth Castle; James Frampton, Moreton; Richard Erle Drax Grosvenor, Charborough Park; Francis John Browne, Frampton; Lieutenants : George Churchill, Dorchester; Lewis Dymock Grosvenor Tregonwell, Cranborne; William Churchill, Colliton; Thomas Meggs, Piddlehinton; William Walter Yea, Forston; George Mon, Langton; Cornets: Thomas Weld Jnr., Lulworth Castle; William Richards Jnr., Warmwell; Richard Austin, Wimborne; John Herbert Browne, Weymouth and George Gould, Upwey. When more troops were formed in 1798 their commanders also sat to Beach, see (fig. 31).

7 By 1798 when Beach painted the second batch of officers, George Damer had become Lord Milton 2nd Earl of Dorchester, as his father had died in January 1798.

8 The family version was destroyed in a fire.

9 DHC, D/FRA/X3, manuscript by J. Frampton, *Account of the Origin and proceedings of the Dorset Yeomanry Cavalry from 1793–1814*, pp. 20–21.

10 I am indebted to David Clammer for information relating to the Dorset Volunteer Rangers. Major James Frampton took over Weld's responsibilities, though Weld's sons continued to serve as cornets.

11 Beach remained on good terms with Weld, no doubt hopeful of further commissions, his diary records that on 14 September 1798 he called at Lulworth on his way from Smedmore to Milton Abbas.

12 By this date Lord Milton was also Colonel of the Dorset militia and away on duty in Ireland.

13 Beach, 1934, p. 36, suggests the collection of portraits was once offered to the town of Dorchester on condition that a public gallery should be prepared, but it was turned down. Beach's portrait of Tregonwell did not stay with the others, but is in a private collection (fig. 33), with copies at the Town Hall, Bournemouth, and the Russell-Cotes Art Gallery and Museum (cat. 30).

28. **Thomas Beach** (1738–1806)

George Damer, Viscount Milton (1746–1808) as Colonel of the Dorset Volunteer Rangers
oil on canvas, 1794
125×100 cm
signed and dated
Provenance: Sitter, then by descent.

Private Collection

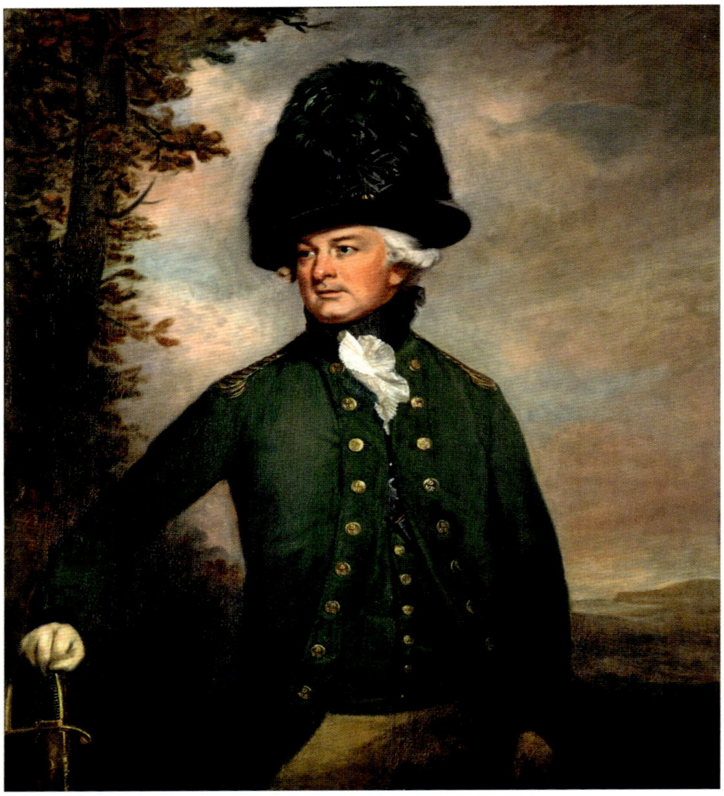

George Damer, second son of Joseph Damer, 1st Earl of Dorchester (fig. 14), served in the army under Lord Cornwallis during the American War of Independence. Damer was MP for Dorchester between 1780 and 1791 when he was unseated on petition in favour of Cropley Ashley Cooper, later 6th Earl of Shaftesbury. On the death of his father in 1798, Damer succeeded to the earldom since his eldest brother had killed himself in 1776, leaving a widow, the sculptress Ann Seymour Damer (1749–1828).[1]

The portrait shows George Damer, standing almost three-quarter length facing forwards, looking to left. As commanding officer of the Dorset Volunteer Rangers his uniform differs from that of the other officers in the troop. He wears a longer green jacket with gold buttons distinctively inscribed *DVR*, and lacks the crimson sash worn by the other officers. Damer's elaborate, rimmed black bearskin headdress with a black cockade, gold button and green feathers, is also unique. Damer stands in a landscape with a silver birch tree on the left and the Dorset coastline opening up in the distance behind on the right.[2] This coastline probably implies the area of Weymouth and Portland for which his brother Lieutenant Colonel Lionel Damer, as commander of the 6th division, was responsible from Ringstead Bay to Abbotsbury. As commanding officer with overall responsibility for Dorset, Damer had a wider brief.

This portrait is probably the original commissioned by George Damer's father, with a second more finished version forming part of the series for the library at Milton Abbey, and may have passed to a cadet branch of the Damer family. Beach worked on a third version at Milton Abbey during the last part of 1798. His diary reveals it was commissioned by Lewis Tregonwell (cat. 30) and started by Beach on 31 August 1798. Damer was not available to sit for the Tregonwell version, as he was dealing with affairs following the death of his father earlier in the year, so the Milton Abbey housekeeper, Mrs Woodward, sat in his place for Beach four times. Beach probably used the second version of the portrait, already at Milton Abbey, for likeness whilst working on that third version. The Tregonwell copy was finished on 3 October, having taken 16 days, during which time Beach was also working on other DVR officers' portraits. He finally sent the portrait to Tregonwell on 21 October.[3] Beach's diary reveals that back in Bath, on 22 December, he was working on another copy of Lord Milton's portrait. A mezzotint of Viscount Milton's portrait after Beach, was produced in 1795 by I. Jones.[4] From Beach's diary we know he was distributing copies of the prints in Dorset to order, probably from his cousin Bill Beach's shop in Dorchester, since he ordered six prints of Lord Milton on 4 October. A later diary entry records Beach sending Richard Pulteney (cat. 54) a proof of *Lord Milton* on Thursday 8 November 1798.

1 Damer shot himself at a tavern at Covent Garden, in 1776. His suicide may have been provoked by the refusal of his father, Lord Milton, to discharge his debts. Horace Walpole bequeathed the widow, Anne Damer, Strawberry Hill as his executor and residuary legatee where she lived from 1797 to 1811.

2 George Damer's younger brother, the Hon. Lionel Damer, of Came House near Dorchester, was also an officer in the corps.

3 There is another version now in the Art Gallery of New South Wales purchased in 1951 from Agnew's, which probably came from a sale by Admiral Sir Reginald Erle Drax, of Charborough Park.

4 Print produced after George Damer succeeded to the title, with the heading *The Right Honourable Lord Viscount Milton as Colonel of the Dorsetshire Volunteer Rangers.*

29. **Thomas Beach** (1738–1806)

Major James Frampton (1769–1855) of the Dorset Volunteer Rangers
oil on canvas, 1795–97
125.5 × 100 cm
Inscribed: *JAMES FRAMPTON Esq MORETON*
Provenance: Sitter, then by descent.

Private Collection

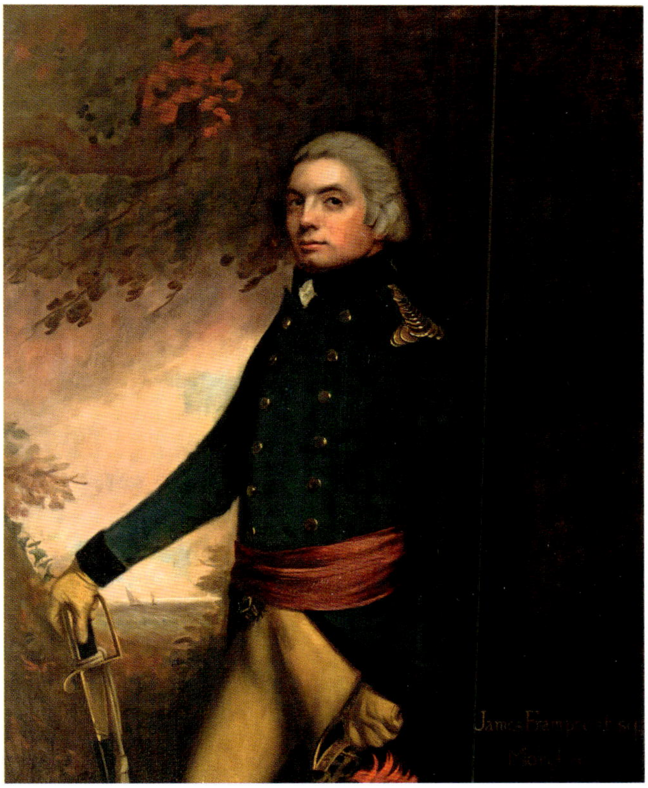

James Frampton was a founding officer of the Dorset Volunteer Rangers and, as the major, one of eight officers who sat to Beach in 1795. James Frampton claimed 'I thought it highly proper for everybody to shew themselves in such times as these and ready to do their utmost to defend their own property and the County at large from all innovations the followers of the French system might try to introduce'.[1] His fear is understandable; he had witnessed the French revolution at first hand. In 1808 Frampton commanded the 5th Division with responsibility for Milborne St Andrew, Bere Regis and Wool and the coastal area between Worbarrow Bay and Ringstead (fig. 32). This included the area around Lulworth as Thomas Weld, a Catholic, was not permitted to command a troop. Frampton is shown standing three-quarter length facing front in the Rangers' uniform of black velvet collar and cuffs on a green jacket with gold buttons, gilt epaulettes, white leather breeches and a crimson sash.[2] In his gloved hand he holds his elaborate headdress of black bearskin peaked in front, showing a dash of red plume and gilt letters *DORS* standing for Dorset, clearly visible. Frampton is shown standing in front of a stone plinth under the large oak tree framing the image. In the far distance on the left the boats, shoreline and sea suggest his area of defensive responsibility with his troop of 68 men. The portrait is one of two versions of Frampton by Beach, the other hung in the library at Milton Abbey.

Frampton became a Lieutenant Colonel in the reformed Corps in 1808 until the threat of invasion had passed and it was finally disbanded in 1814. He inherited the Moreton estate from his father in 1784, and continued the improvements started by his father. In 1799 he married the third daughter of the 2nd Earl of Ilchester, Lady Harriot Fox-Strangways (cat. 64).

1 DHC, D/FRA/X3, manuscript by J. Frampton, *Account of the Origin and proceedings of the Dorset Yeomanry Cavalry from 1793–1814*, p. 1. See too H. F. Finberg, 'Thomas Beach, Portrait Painter,' *The Connoisseur*, No. 203, July 1918, p. 147.
2 For his series of yeomanry portraits for Milton Abbey, Beach generally inscribed the buttons *DVR* in what can be assumed to be the primary versions.

30. **After Thomas Beach** (1738–1806)

Captain Lewis Dymock Grosvenor Tregonwell (1758–1832) of the Dorset Volunteer Rangers
oil on canvas, c. 1800
44.5 × 33.7 cm
Inscribed: *Lewis Tregonwell Esq Cranbourn Lodge*
Provenance: Russell-Cotes Art Gallery and Museum, purchase from Mrs Inglis, 1969.

Russell-Cotes Art Gallery and Museum

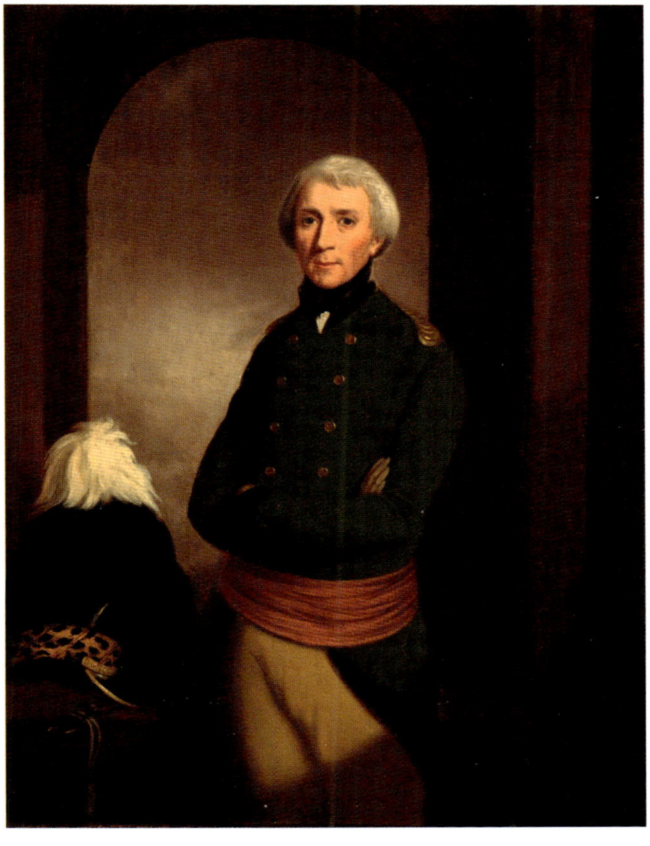

Lewis Tregonwell is acknowledged as the founder of Bournemouth.[1] As a captain in the Dorset Volunteer Rangers, he led cliff top patrols in the area from Bourne Heath to Poole Harbour (fig. 32). Tregonwell was responsible for the easternmost region, keeping watch for smugglers and French invaders.[2] By 1801 he was commanding the 1st Division of the Volunteers, responsible for Bourne Bottom and Bourne Chine (the site of what was to become Bournemouth) along North Shore to Poole Harbour as far as and including Branksea (sic) Island Battery on North shore and on the Studland Common side. He later became a Justice of the Peace and Deputy Lieutenant for the county.

Tregonwell is shown three-quarter length standing facing forward with arms folded. He wears the Ranger uniform of the green jacket with black velvet collar and cuffs, gold buttons marked DVR, crimson sash, white leather trousers and his own hair. He stands under an arch referred to by Beach in his diary. His headdress of black bearskin rests on a table on the left with a cascade of a white plume and the gilt letters *DORSET* readily visible on the badge. The tip of the hanger of his sword is on the far left.

Although this miniature is attributed to Beach it has neither the subtlety of the facial features of the original (fig. 33), in a private collection, nor the definition of architectural detailing. We know from his diary that Beach stayed with Tregonwell at Cranborne Lodge near Blandford Forum in 1798. He started the primary version on Monday 20 August, by dead colouring the whole. On Thursday 23rd he recorded going onto the Down to see the Troop, returning to the lodge to paint the architectural background. He worked on the face, drapery and figure of the portrait for six days, before returning to his base, Milton Abbey, on Tuesday

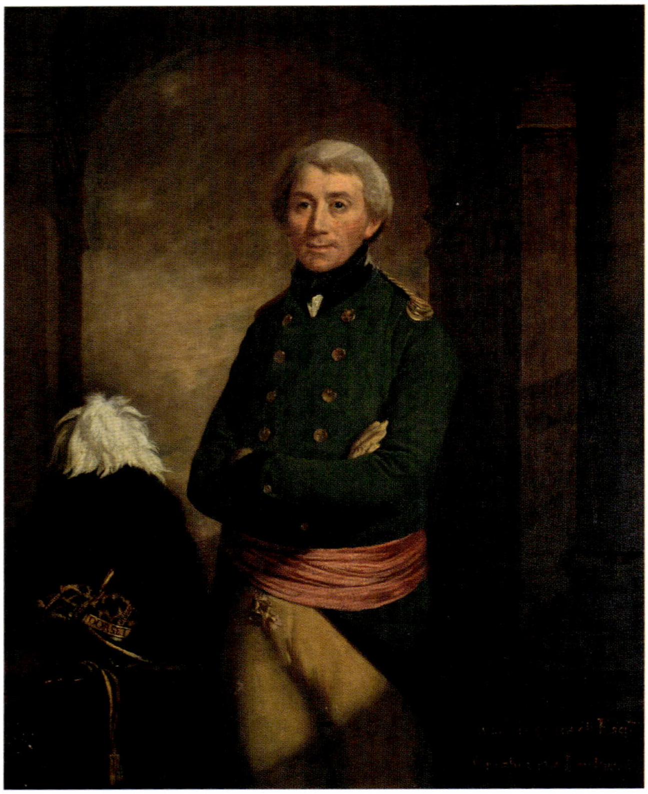

Fig. 33. *Lewis Dymock Grosvenor Tregonwell (1758–1832),* oil on canvas, Thomas Beach, 1798.

28th. He did not work on the portrait again until Wednesday 26 September, finishing it on 13 November having worked on it for twelve days. Beach again used a member of the Milton Abbey staff, Mr Bridge, to sit in place of Tregonwell. He was also working simultaneously on portraits of other Ranger officers, Clavel, Meggs and Bower, as well as a copy of Lord Dorchester for Tregonwell. Hutchins records that the portrait was at Milton Abbey but it does not seem to have remained with the rest of the portraits and only one version is known in a private collection.[3] Two later copies of the Tregonwell portrait after Beach were made, one full-size is in the Mayor's Parlour in Bournemouth, and the other is this miniature version at the Russell-Cotes Art Gallery and Museum, both indicating the sitter's importance to the town.

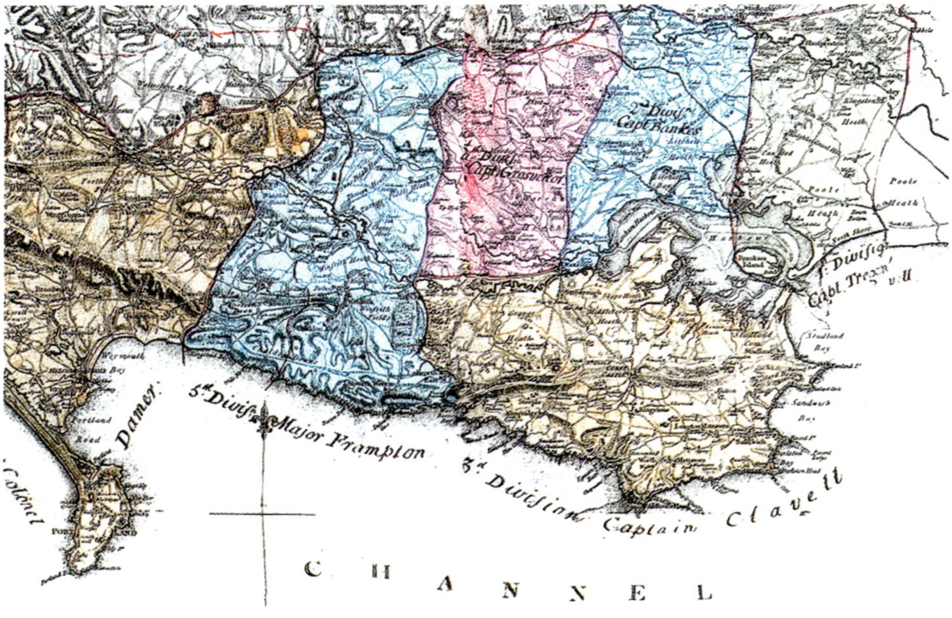

Fig. 32. *Detail of Map of Dorset showing the coastal areas of responsibilty of the Dorset Volunteer Ranger officers,* Isaac Taylor, 1798.

1 After visiting the mouth of the River Bourne in 1810, Tregonwell built a house nearby in 1812; when others followed this grew into Bournemouth.
2 DHC, D1721/3/1, *1799–1804*.
3 Hutchins, ed. 3, 4, p. 395.

31. **Thomas Beach** (1738–1806)
Thomas Bartholomew Weld (1750–1810)
oil on canvas, 1795
124.5×99 cm
signed and dated: *Beach pinxit 1795*
Provenance: Sitter, then by descent.
Literature: E. Beach, 1934, p. 74, No. 298.
R. Legg, *Dorset Families,* Devon, 2002, p. 82.

32. **Thomas Beach** (1738–1806)
Mary Weld (1752–1830)
oil on canvas, 1795
124×99 cm
signed and dated: *Beach pinxit 1795*
Provenance: Sitter, then by descent.
Literature: E. Beach, 1934, p. 74, No. 297

Private Collection

Thomas Weld succeeded to the Lulworth estate on the death of his older brother Edward following a riding accident, and added to it through purchases and inheritance.[1] Immensely wealthy, he married Mary Massey-Stanley in 1772; they had fifteen children of whom most survived to adulthood. Thomas continued his brother Edward's 1750s redevelopment of the castle (fig. 34).

A devout Catholic, Thomas was actively involved in the move towards emancipation. When in 1778 the Relief Act removed some of the obstacles imposed on Catholics by the Penal Laws, they were allowed to celebrate Mass.[2] As a result in 1786 Thomas Weld engaged the architect John Tasker to build a chapel, the first free-standing Catholic church to be built in England since the Reformation. According to family tradition George III gave Thomas permission to build the Chapel which was completed in 1786, and the first mass was held at Candlemas.[3] Set in the parkland Weld created, Tasker's fine chapel was of such enormous importance to Weld that he is shown holding its plans in his portrait. These plans were also published in the second and third editions of Hutchins (fig. 35).

In 1789 George III, Queen Charlotte and three of the princesses first visited Lulworth Castle by sea from Weymouth. They viewed the chapel, were shown the priests' rich robes and expressed their approval. Fanny Burney recorded the event in detail, observing the chapel 'ornamented with immense expense and richness'.[4] This included an altar dispatched from Rome by the great Quarenghi. Anxious to demonstrate his allegiance to the monarch, Weld went to great expense serving his royal guests on new gold and silver plates inscribed 'Long Live the King'.[5] Like Francis Fane at Spetisbury, Weld gave sanctuary to Roman Catholic religious fleeing from the effects of the French Revolution, particularly Franciscan nuns and Trappists who established a monastery in the grounds of Lulworth. Weld gave Stonyhurst College, with thirty acres of land, to exiled Jesuits and entirely

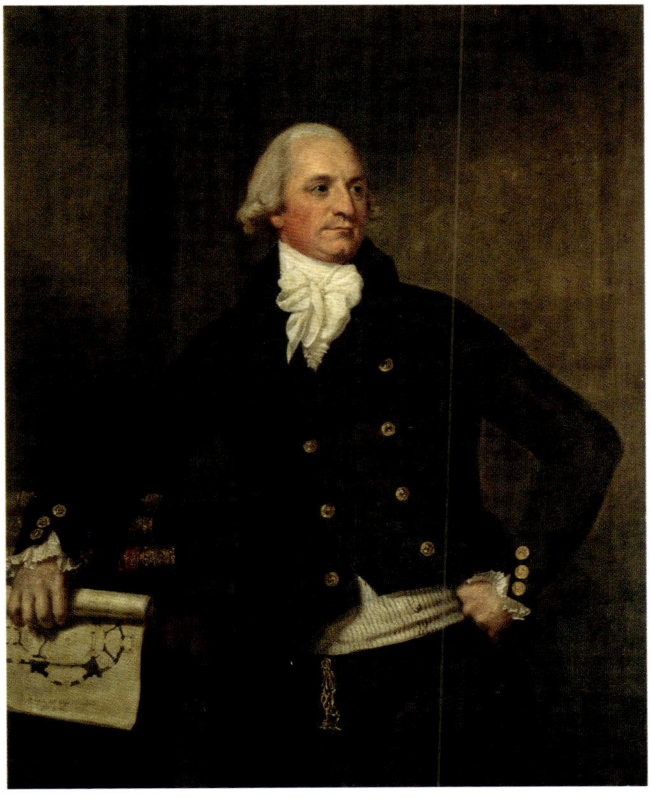

31.

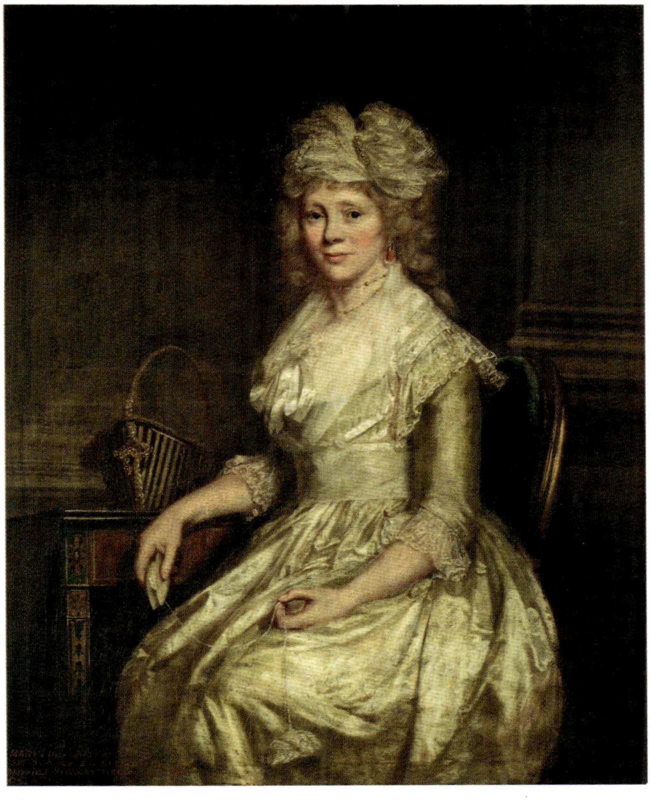

32.

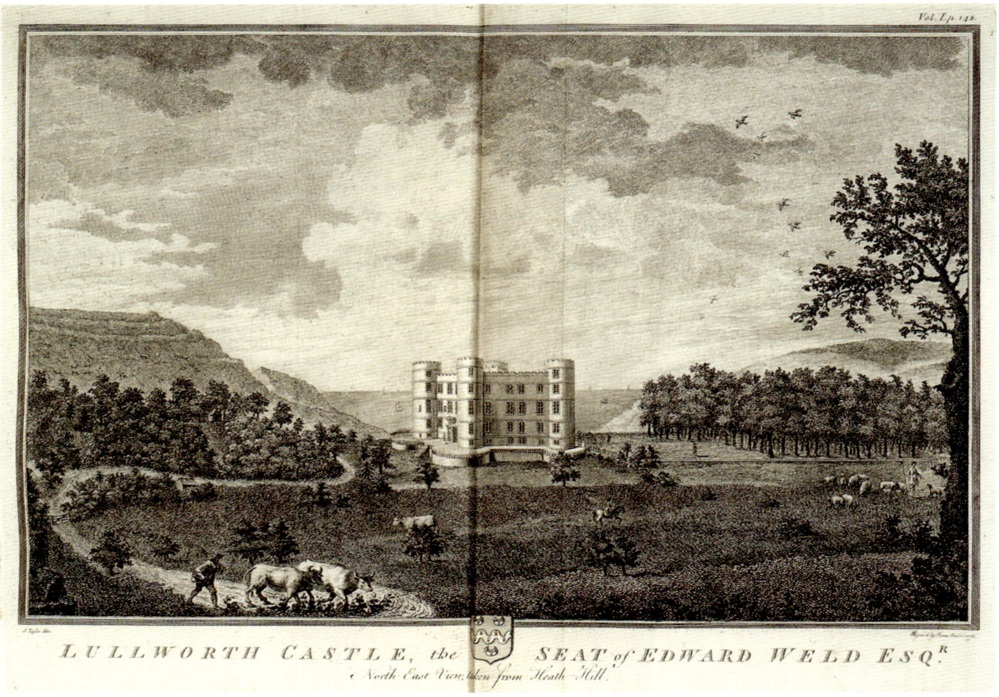

Fig. 34. *Lullworth (sic) Castle the Seat of Edward Weld Esq. N.E. View from Heath Hill*, folded after Isaac Taylor by James Basire, Hutchins ed.2, 1, p. 227.

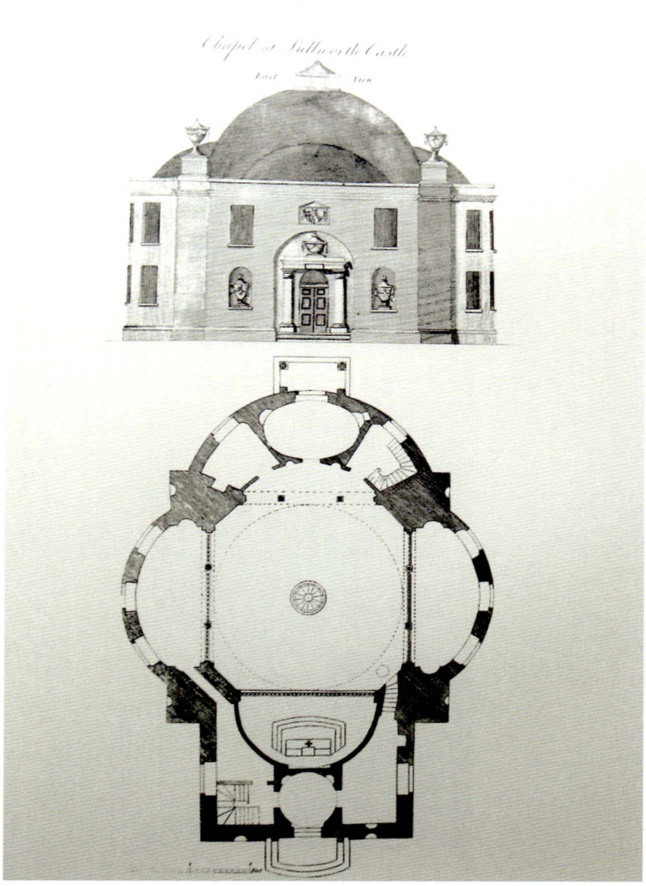

Fig. 35. *Lulworth Chapel*, Hutchins, ed.3, 1 opp. p. 376.

supported the English Poor Clares who had fled from Gravelines and in whose order his sister Mary was a nun (cats. 59, 60).[6]

Weld volunteered as a captain when the Dorset Volunteer Rangers were formed in 1794 and sat for Beach in 1795 wearing the DVR officer's uniform (fig. 36). However, George III refused to sign Weld's commission because he was a Roman Catholic and ensured the Lord Lieutenant did not endorse it, forcing Weld to resign, disband his troop and James Frampton then assumed responsibility for the protection of the Lulworth coastal area. In his manuscript account of the formation of the DVR Frampton wrote:

'In the Spring of 1795 the Commissions were signed omitting Mr Weld and his son who were obliged to retire from the improbability of having persons of their persuasion in the Corps. They were much regretted by all of us as they were very active and eager in their business. Some few of Mr Weld's troop retired, but the rest, at least by far the greater part of them, joined my Troop.'[7]

Weld, a generous benefactor to the project, continued to serve in an honorary capacity (fig. 31). He probably sat to Beach in the summer of 1795, and at the same time commissioned him to paint the pair of three-quarter length portraits of Thomas and Mary Weld (cats. 31, 32).

In Beach's portrait Thomas Weld is shown, wearing wig, brown breeches and coat with gold double breasted buttons, striped waistcoat, full neckcloth tied in a bow and lace at his cuffs. His right arms leans on a pile of books resting on a table and he holds a partly rolled up plan of the Chapel in his hand.[8] A copy of this portrait was made in 1900 for Stonyhurst College, which Weld founded.

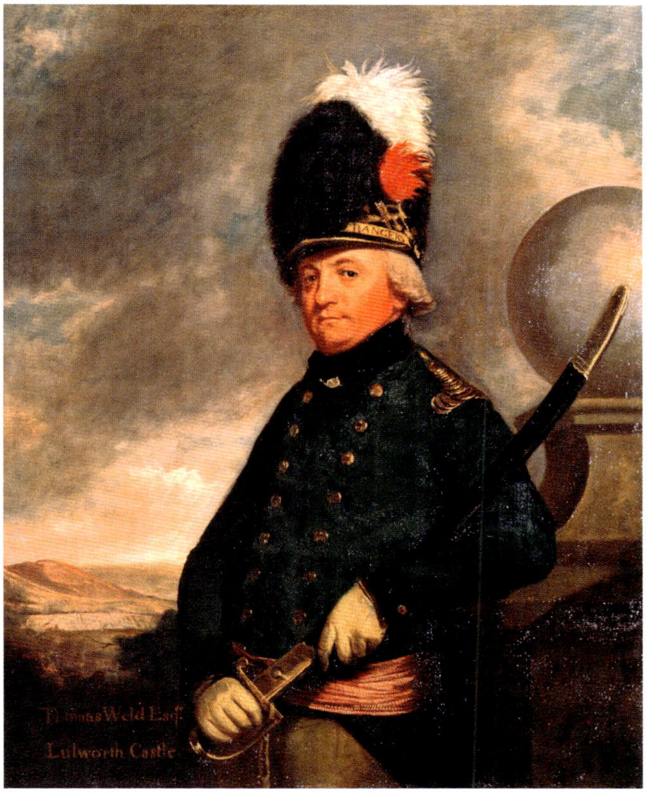

Fig. 36. *Thomas Weld as a captain in the Dorset Volunteer Rangers*, oil on canvas, Thomas Beach, 1795.

In the pendant portrait to Thomas Weld, Mary, daughter of Sir John Stanley-Massey-Stanley of Hooton, Cheshire, is shown seated to left and facing forwards. She wears a yellow dress, tied in at the waist, her long hair cascades onto her shoulders and is swathed in gauze with gold thread and threaded pearls. She wears a delicate necklace and large drop earrings and a sweet demeanour. She rests her right arm on an occasional table banded with green and holds a skein of wool in her right hand. In her left is a ball of wool she is winding. A green and gilt porcelain basket sits on the table, and hanging on the wall behind her there may be a tapestry. The portrait contrasts with that of her husband and highlights the domesticity of Mary's role.

1 Edward Weld was briefly married in 1775 to Mary Anne Smythe, later Mrs Thomas Fitzherbert, who secretly married George, Prince of Wales in December 1785.
2 The Welds experienced restrictions on travel, firearms and the ownership of horses.
3 D. Watkin, *George III. The Architect King* London, 2004, p. 142, family tradition suggests that when Thomas Weld approached George III about building a chapel, the King apparently replied, 'Build a family mausoleum and you can furnish the inside as a Catholic chapel if you wish'. The previous family mausoleum in the parish church had been demolished.
4 See *Diary and Letters of Madame D'Arblay*, 4, p. 308, Fanny Burney observed the castle '*abounds in pictures of priests, saints, monks and nuns, and is decorated with crosses and Roman Catholic devices without end*'.
5 The royal party made two further visits in 1791 and 1792.
6 Weld's son Thomas became a Cardinal and went to live in Rome.
7 DHC, D/FRA/X3, manuscript by J. Frampton, *Account of the Origin and proceedings of the Dorset Yeomanry Cavalry from 1793–1814*, p. 21. Frampton's account makes clear that the exclusion of Weld and his son, a Cornet, was a cause for concern to the other officers who were reluctant to accept their commissions without the Welds.
8 See J. Manco & F. Kelly, 'Lulworth Castle from 1700', *Architectural History*, 1991, 34, pp. 145–170.

33. **Godfrey Kneller** (1646–1723)

John Bond (1678–1744)
oil on canvas, 1723
74×62 cm
signed and dated: *G Kneller 1723*
Provenance: Sitter, then by descent.

Private Collection

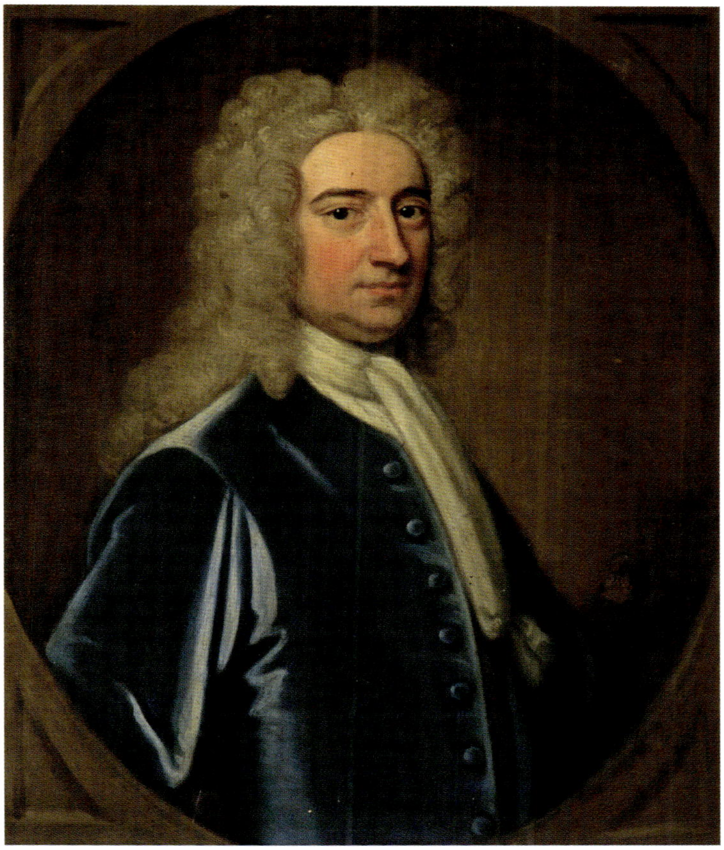

The Bond family, originally involved in trade, increasingly assumed public positions. They became Dorset county squires and in the words of Martin Bond, had 'eased off' by the nineteenth century.[1] Studious from childhood, John Bond, son of Nathaniel Bond, was learned, sober and honest unlike his effervescent brother Denis Bond (fig. 37). The brothers represented a colourful and ambitious generation of the Bond family. John lived at Tyneham, traditionally the home of younger sons of the Bond family. The urbane John was a member of the Inner Temple, and a Barrister between 1721–1744, becoming MP for Corfe Castle from 1720 until 1741. He married Margaret Williams (1688–1775), third daughter of John Williams of Herringston, an able woman of strong character.[2] John was buried at Steeple in 1744 and his oldest son John (cat. 34) inherited the family's primary residence, Creech Grange, from his uncle.

John was two years younger than his brother Denis (1676–1746). Also a lawyer, he sat to Godfrey Kneller in

34. **British School 18th Century**

John Bond (1717–1784)
oil on canvas, c. 1750
52×42 cm
Provenance: Sitter, then by descent

35. **Allan Ramsay** (1713–1784)

Mary Bond, neé Dummer (1717–1787)
oil on canvas, before 1749
74.9×63.5 cm
Provenance: Sitter, then by descent.
Literature: A. Smart ed. J. Ingamells, *Allan Ramsay; A Complete Catalogue of his Paintings,* New Haven and London, 1999, cat. no. 51, p. 880.

Private Collection

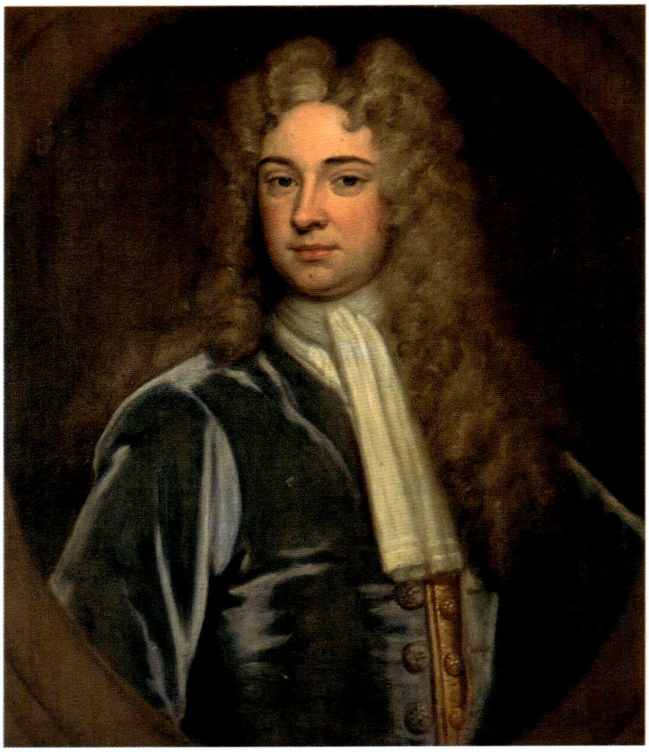

Fig. 37. *Denis Bond (1676–1746),* oil on canvas, Godfrey Kneller, 1714.

1714 (fig. 37). John's sober life in Dorset was in marked contrast to that of his brother Denis who spent much time in London. Between 1709 and 1732 Denis was variously MP for Dorchester, Corfe Castle and Poole but was expelled from Parliament when some dubious financial transactions came to light.

Denis retained the Recorderships of Dorchester, Weymouth, Poole and Wareham. He lived at Creech Grange where his improvements included building the south front, and a folly on the hill above the house; still a landmark today. In 1729 he married Leonora Sophia Colt, formerly wife of Edward Dummer, and became step-father to her three children. In the absence of any direct heirs Denis left his property to three of his brother John's children, the principal estate went to the eldest, John Bond (cats. 34, 35), married to his uncle John's step-daughter Mary.

The head and shoulders portrait, previously unpublished, shows John Bond in an oval to right and facing forwards. He wears a full-bottomed wig, blue velvet jacket and white cravat. As the leading society portrait painter in England, it was inevitable that both brothers chose to sit to Kneller in London.[3]

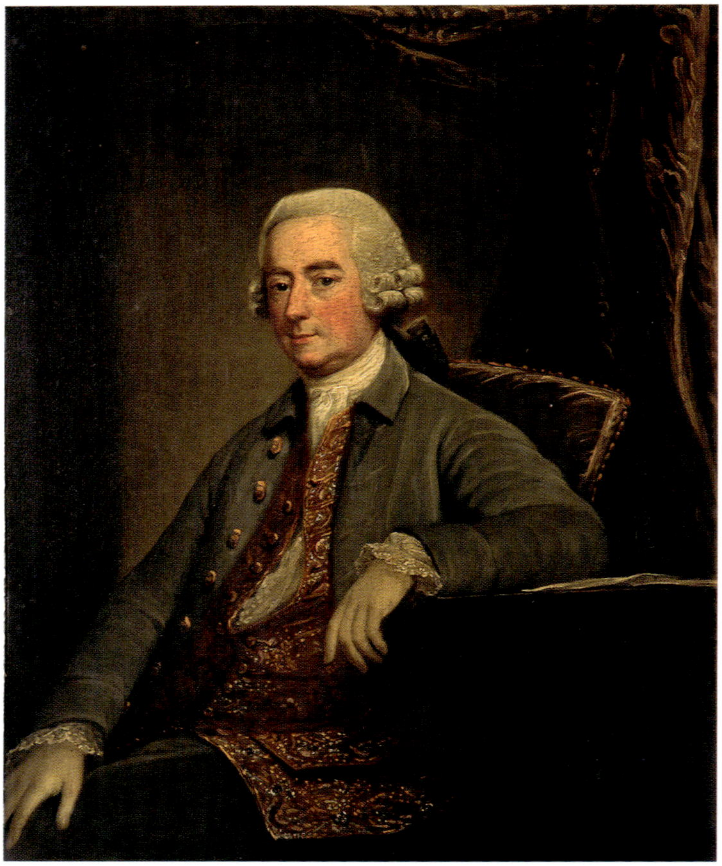

John Bond studied law but on inheriting the considerable estate of Creech from his uncle Denis (fig. 37) he retired to Dorset. He was Recorder for Wareham in 1746 and for Dorchester in 1756, and like his father was MP for Corfe Castle (cat. 33) from 1747–61 and again from 1764 until 1780.[1] John married Mary Dummer, eldest daughter and co-heir of Edmund Dummer of Swaythling, in 1749. Mary's widowed mother, Leonora Colt, had married Denis Bond, so she grew up at Creech.[2] The union was apparently a happy one and they had eight children.

1 For a full account of the Bond family see M. Bond, *A Dorset Family, A Brief History of the Bonds*, Dorset, undated, privately published.

2 Family papers reveal Margaret enabled her nephew Robert Williams to train as a cabinet-maker in Dorchester. He made a great deal of furniture for John Bond at Creech Grange. M. Bond, *A Dorset Family, A Brief History of the Bonds*, Dorset, privately published. p. 15.

3 There is no reference to the portrait in J. Stewart, *Godfrey Kneller and the English Portrait,* Oxford, 1983.

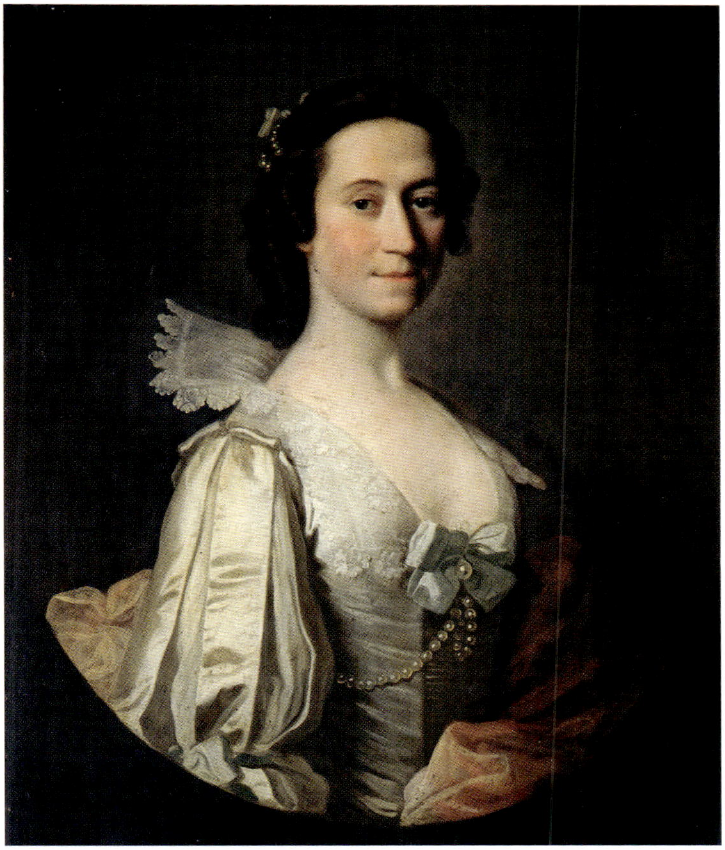

John remained devoted to family life at Creech, and also maintained a lively interest in local affairs, corresponding with Sir Peter Thompson (cat. 47) over the intricacies of Poole elections.

Both portraits were probably painted around the time of their marriage and whilst John is shown seated, in a modest portrait by an unidentified hand, Mary was painted by one of the most fashionable painters of the mid-century, Allan Ramsay. The half-length portrait shows Mary in a painted oval wearing a Van Dyckian dress of cream silk with slashed sleeves, lace collar and blue silk bow at the bodice attached by an asymmetrical string of pearls. Seventeenth century costumes, poses and compositions were extremely popular amongst portraitists from the 1740s. Based in London, Ramsay produced a large number of portraits before returning to his native Edinburgh in 1754. To assist production, Ramsay employed the most famous drapery painter of the period, the Flemish-born Joseph Van Aken. A chalk study by Van Aken of the pose and costume of Mary Bond survives in Edinburgh.[3]

1 Hutchins, ed. 3, 2, p. 362.
2 Mary's grandmother owned Kenton Hall, Suffolk, which Mary sold on inheriting.
3 The drawing is in the National Gallery of Scotland, Edinburgh. See A. Ribeiro, 'Some Evidence of the Influence of the Dress of the Seventeenth Century on Costume in Eighteenth-Century Female Portraiture', *The Burlington Magazine*, 119, no. 897, 1977, pp. 832–834 for a discussion on Joseph Van Aken who made a series of drawings of versions of Van Dyck dress, now in Edinburgh.

36. **Thomas Hudson** (1701–1779)

Sir John Browne (1696–1750)
oil on canvas laid on board, 1740s
126×100 cm

Provenance: Sitter, then by descent; private purchase 1950s; Sotheby's British Paintings 1500–1800, 18 November, 1992, Lot 36; purchased by DNH&AS, 1993.

Dorset Natural History and Archaeological Society

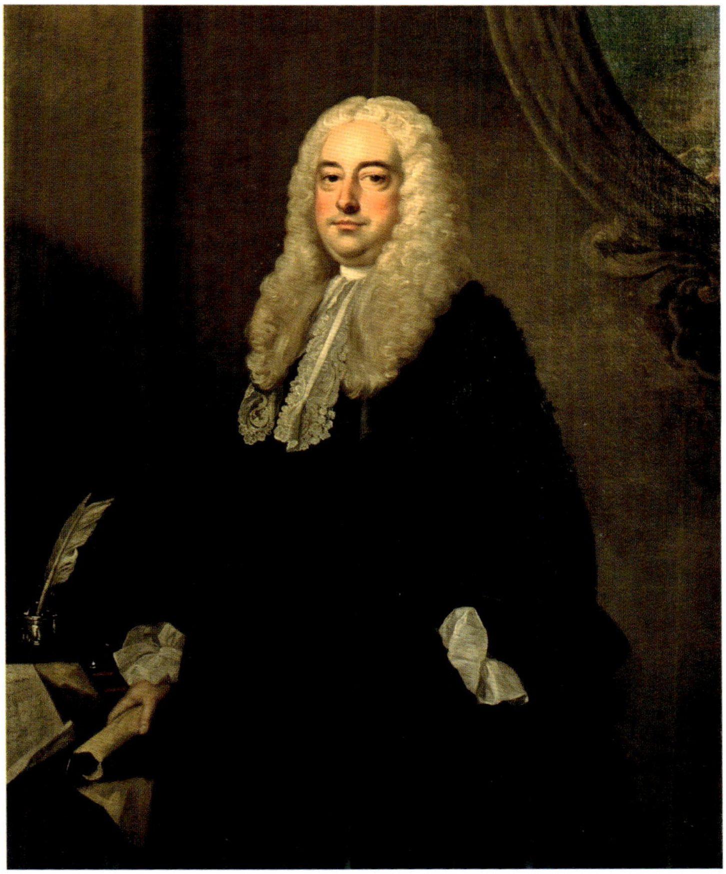

A three-quarter length portrait showing Sir John Browne standing by a table, wearing legal robes and holding a scroll in his right hand. The sitter was the son of Robert Browne of Frampton and Forston. He was born at Blandford St Mary, educated at Hart Hall, Oxford, and trained at Lincoln's Inn. He was called to the Bar in 1727 and was MP for Dorchester from that date until his death.

Browne was one of the most eminent chancery lawyers of the period, standing counsel for the East India Company. A Tory, he spoke out against the Seamen's Bill in 1741. Although he did not live in Dorset, he was one of King's Counsel and recorder of Dorchester, which he also represented in four successive parliaments from 1727 to his death in 1750. Through his legal practice he acquired a great fortune which, unmarried, he left to his brother George. In grateful thanks his brother erected a monument in Frampton Church eulogizing his achievements.

37. **John Downman** (1750–1824)

The Reverend John Richards (1740–1803)
oil on copper, 1778
22×18 cm

Literature: G.C. Williamson, *John Downman, ARA, His Life and Works*, London; J. Munro, *John Downman 1750–1824; Landscape, figure studies and portraits of 'Distinguished persons'*, Cambridge.

Long Bredy Parochial Church Council

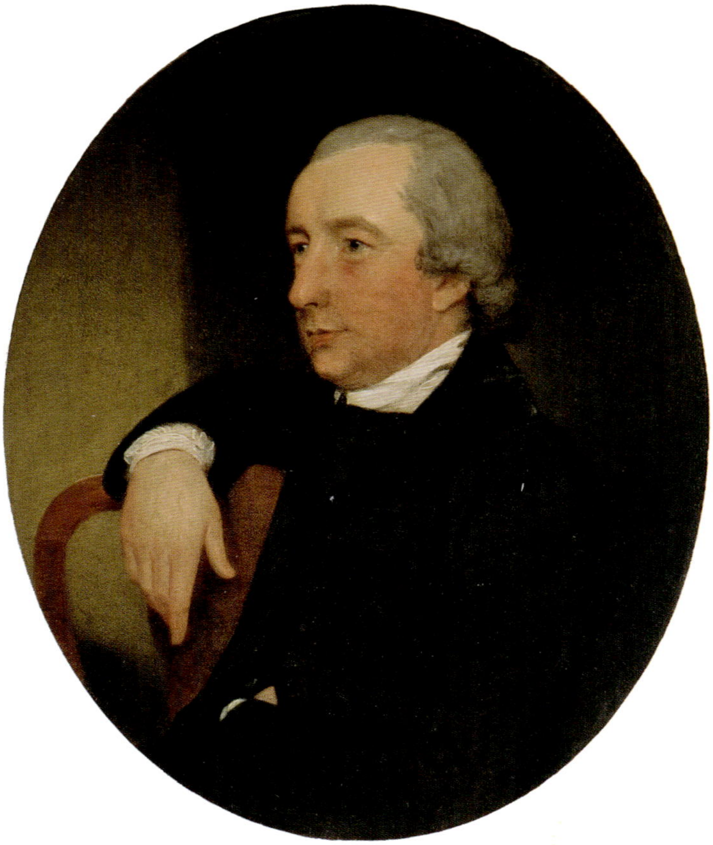

The Reverend John Richards was the son of George Richards (d. 1746), MP for Bridport. His grandfather George was a Spanish merchant dealing in wool and sherry, and High Sheriff of Dorset in 1710. John Richards owned the manor of Long Bredy together with other land and farms in West Dorset and lived at Long Bredy in the house built by his father in 1740.[1] Like the Reverend Thomas Rackett (cat. 43) he was a wealthy country parson, who lived well and enjoyed country pursuits.

Portraitist Downman enjoyed success through the speed with which he worked and the highly finished likenesses of his sitters. His portrait of Richards, one of a pair with his wife Mary, (private collection) described as 'the celebrated daughter of Dr. Moisey of Bath', is a relatively early portrait painted in 1778.[2] During this year Downman was staying in Exeter, having married the daughter of the cathedral's organist, William Jackson, Thomas Gainsborough's friend.

Typical of Downman's early oil portraits, the small oval portrait of Richards is painted on copper.[3] Half-length, Richards is shown seated in profile facing left. In black clerical clothing he wears his own hair with his left hand tucked into his waistcoat; his right arm rests on the back of a chair. Downman complimented Richards on 'the finest manor for game in England'. He was staying with Richards in Dorset while painting the portraits, an established practice followed by Thomas Beach, also in Dorset at the same time.[4] Mrs Richards sat to Downman at the same time for which there is a red and black chalk sketch in the British Museum. Whilst with the Richards, Downman's portrait of Francis John Browne of Frampton, 'on a visit at Longbreddy House', attests to the speed of his likenesses.[5] Based in London, Downman periodically returned to the West Country over the next thirty years. He was back at Long Bredy in 1790 to paint the portrait of Miss Richards (whereabouts unknown). She later married Francis John Browne, one of Downman's other Dorset sitters, and his charcoal and red chalk sketch of Miss Richards's portrait is now in the British Museum. The two families remained close since Richards appointed a member of the Browne family as an executor. 1790 was also the year Downman painted his only other known Dorset commission, that of the three children of Edmund Pleydell.

1 See Hutchins's *History*, ed.2, 2, pp. 706, 749; See also the *Proceedings* of the DNH&AS, 28, pp. 30–49; 39, pp. 20–28; 65, pp. 112–122.
2 G. Williamson, *John Downman, ARA, His Life and Works*, London, p.liii. During his retirement Downman systematically assembled albums of studies for portraits of 'Distinguished Persons'. They are now divided between the Fitzwilliam Museum, Cambridge and the British Museum.
3 Downman painted Mrs Richards's portrait in 1778 (private collection). There are three black, red and white chalk portrait sketches on brown paper of the Richards family in the Fitzwilliam Museum, relating to this visit by Downman. One shows the Reverend Richards mounted in the 2nd Series, 3, No. 25, and two of his wife.
4 G.C. Williamson, *John Downman, ARA, His Life and Works*, London, pp. xviii; J. Munro, *John Downman 1750–1824; Landscape, figure studies and portraits of 'Distinguished persons'*, Fitzwilliam Museum, Cambridge, 1996, p. 45, the Reverend Richards is reproduced and his wife referred to, see p. 89.
5 Browne's portrait is also referred to in G.C. Williamson, *John Downman, ARA, His Life and Works*, London, p. iiii; J. Munro, *John Downman 1750–1824; Landscape, figure studies and portraits of 'Distinguished persons'*, Fitzwilliam Museum, Cambridge, 1996, p. 44, 2nd Series, 3, No. 28.

38. **Thomas Gainsborough** (1727–1788)

John Bragge (1741–1786)
oil on canvas, 1767
74×61.5 cm

Provenance: Sitter's family until 1909; bought by Knoedler, 1909: Walter Lewisohn, New York, 1912: Anon. sale, New York, 20 February 1930 (92); bt. Picchetto; purchased from the Leger Gallery with the assistance of the National Art Collections Fund, the Victoria & Albert Museum Purchase Grant Fund and Miss Eleanor Bragge, 1982.
Literature: E. Waterhouse, *Gainsborough*, London, 1958, p. 55, No 79.

Dorset Natural History and Archaeological Society

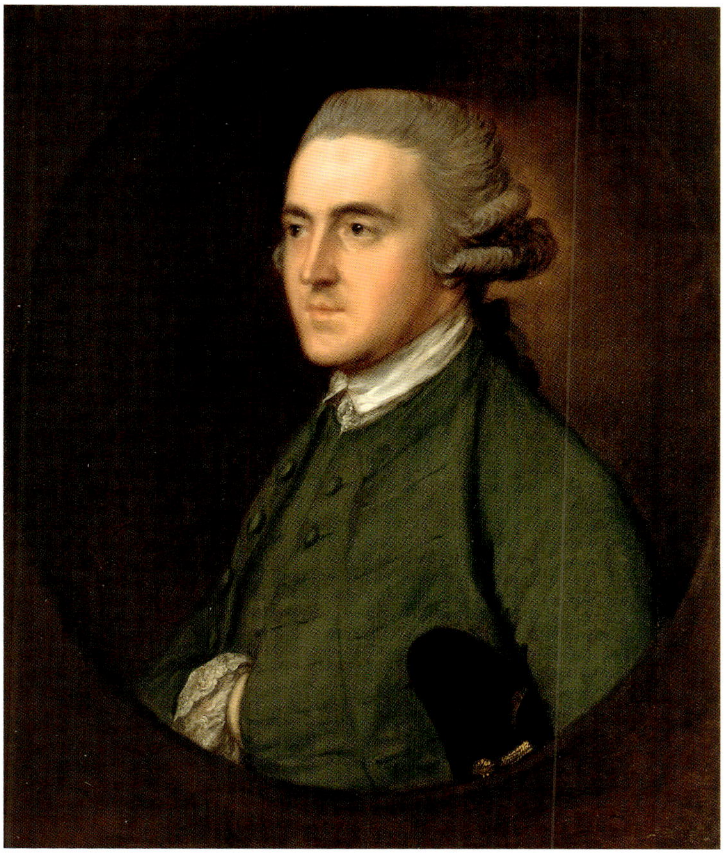

John Bragge, born at Sadborow, was a member of the family who had lived there since 1650.[1] He was the only son and heir of John Bragge (1692–1745) and his second wife Lucy, daughter of Lovelace Hayne whom he married in 1737.[2] The Hayne family, wealthy Berkshire landowners, also owned considerable amounts of land in Bath as it was developing as a fashionable resort and spa. Only four when his father died, John's neighbour Francis Gwyn of Forde Abbey became his guardian. He matriculated at Magdalen College, Oxford in 1758 and by 1761 was a student of Lincoln's Inn. The following year Bragge married a local girl, Elizabeth daughter of Benjamin Adney of Pymore near Loders in Dorset; presumably through their Hayne connections they were married at fashionable Bath Abbey. In 1767 John and Elizabeth were again in Bath, where they sat to Gainsborough for a pair of half-length portraits. Between 1773 and 1775 John Bragge rebuilt the Sadborow family mansion that had fallen into disrepair during his long minority; he became a Justice of the Peace and Deputy Lieutenant for the county in 1776.

Gainsborough has placed Bragge in a painted oval with a plain background. The half-length portrait shows him wearing a green jacket and waistcoat, white collar and cuffs trimmed with lace. The portrait reveals a man of substance and standing; Bragge's clearly delineated features accentuated by strong lighting of the head and firmness of modelling, are characteristic of Gainsborough's portraiture in his first decade at Bath. The portrait of Elizabeth Bragge, now in America, shows her wearing a white dress with pink ribbons and a lace bonnet with pink bows. The Sadborow papers show Gainsborough was paid 40 guineas for the pair, the going rate for portraits of the period before Gainsborough moved to London in 1774.[3]

1 Until the Dissolution Sadborow belonged to Forde Abbey. Sadborow, Thorncombe, was a detached part of Devon surrounded by Dorset, which in 1844 was transferred to Dorset. Consequently Hutchins paid scant attention to the Bragges. The Third Edition includes an account of Thorncombe and a very sketchy account of the Bragges. See 'The Bragge Family of Sadborow and Their Muniments' by G D Squibb, *The Proceedings of the DNH&AS,* 1942, pp. 58–68.

2 Lucy's brother Charles Hayne was a Newbury solicitor who played a large part in administering the family estates and responsible for the development of the Bath estates. The Hayne estates were later added to the Bragge's Devon and Dorset property.

3 See Devizes Record Office, Sadborow Papers, 8339, f. *50 ap.*

39. **Thomas Beach** (1738–1806)

Rebecca Steward (1766–1859)
oil on canvas, 1783
74.8×62 cm
Signed and dated: *TBeachpinxt.1783*

Provenance: Christie's (July 4, 1930, Lot. 151); Daniel H. Farr & Co New York; Sothebys (New York 25 November 1981, Lot. 51); purchased Dorset Natural History and Archaeological Society with the assistance of the National Art Collections Fund and the V&A Museum Purchase Grant Fund, 1984.
Literature: Beach, 1934, p. 71 (269).

Dorset Natural History and Archaeological Society.

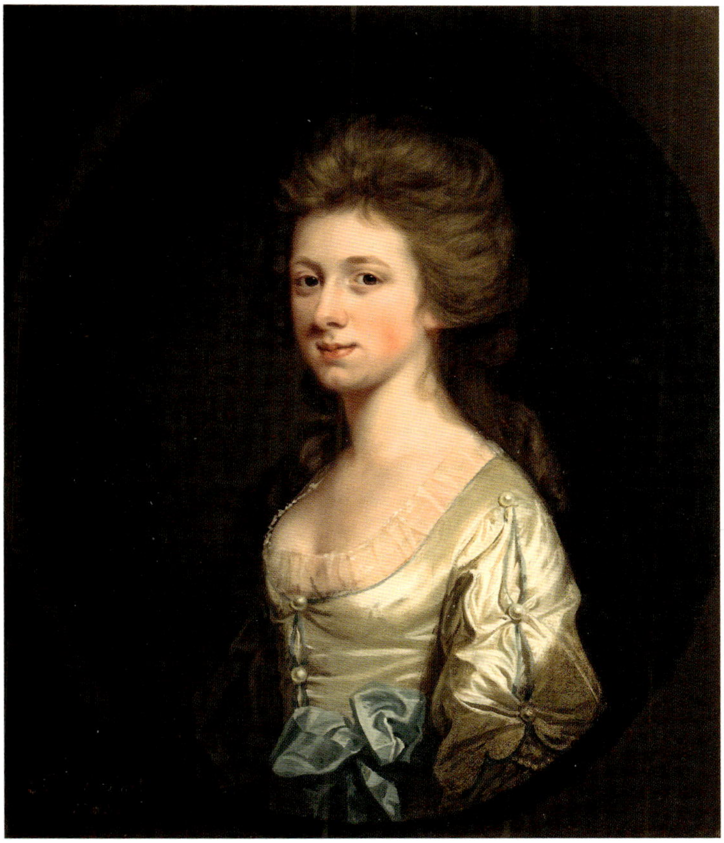

Rebecca Steward was the oldest of the seven children born to Gabriel Steward, MP for Weymouth from 1778 to 1788. The Stewards were a large powerful Dorset family who had settled in and around Weymouth in the eighteenth century, having come from St. Helena.[1] Gabriel had close ties with the East India Company and Portland quarrying. At his death in 1792 John Trenchard (cat. 40) wrote to the artist Ozias Humphry: 'old Gabriel Steward . . . was attended by a Long Procession of Aldermen and Burghers, the Church was amazingly crowded. Old Gab has left a very respectable family his widow and children are [truly] amiable.'[2]

In 1783 Beach was in Weymouth painting the portrait of Francis Steward (William A. Rudd, Cincinnati), probably commemorating his second period as mayor, when Gabriel Steward took the opportunity to commission Beach to paint the portraits of his two eldest children, Rebecca and Gabriel.[3] In the portrait of seventeen-year old Rebecca, Beach uses a fairly outdated format for the 1780s, showing the sitter in a painted oval frame, dressed in loosely Van Dyckian costume, similar to that employed by Allan Ramsay in his portrait of Mary Bond (cat. 35) some thirty years earlier. Beach's use of a *retardataire* formula was probably prompted by the provincial status of his sitter, but he achieved a remarkably effective and charming portrait. Rebecca was recorded living in South Walks, Dorchester in 1852.[4] She died aged 92 in 1859, unmarried, and was buried at the Civic Cemetery in Dorchester.

1 The Steward family papers are lodged at the Bodleian Library, Oxford.
2 Letter in the Library of the Royal Academy, HU/4/62, John Trenchard to Ozias Humphry, Warmwell, 17 Jan 1792.
3 Fifteen year-old Gabriel was later MP for Weymouth and a land tax commissioner. His portrait, dated 1783, was listed by Beach, 1934, as no. 269, p. 71. It sold at Christie's, 4 July 4 1930, Lot. 152, the whereabouts of this portrait is not known.
4 'Nobility, Gentry and Clergy. Dorchester with Fordington', *Slaters Directory*, 1852–53.

40. **Thomas Beach** (1738–1806)

John Trenchard (1736–1819)
oil on canvas, 1793
74.5×61.5 cm
signed and dated: *T. Beach Pinxit 1793*
Provenance: Sitter, then by descent.

Private Collection

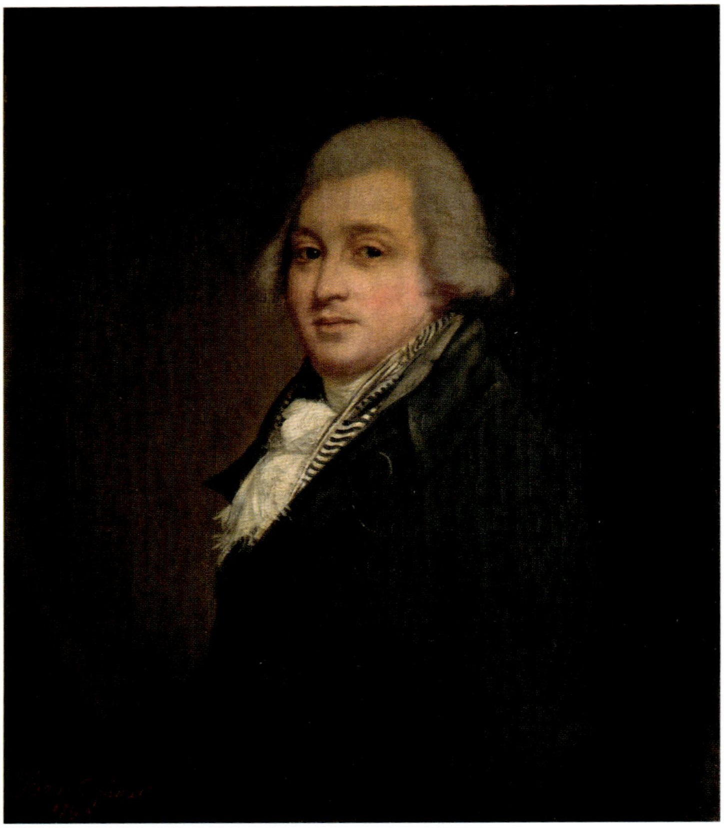

The Trenchard family owned extensive land in Dorset for over 350 years, from the beginning of the sixteenth to the early nineteenth centuries.[1] They augmented their estates through purchase and judicious marriages to heiresses. Like the Bonds (cats. 33–35), whilst earlier generations had taken part in public life, by the eighteenth century the Trenchards had settled into a comfortable life as country gentlemen fulfilling local rôles as magistrates and MPs.

John Trenchard was the third son of George and Mary Trenchard and as such had received the manors of Poxwell and Sturminster Marshall in 1752.[2] Appointed Commissioner of Taxes in 1756 he lived comfortably in Welbeck Street, London, and never married. John was interested in family history and contributed to the second edition of Hutchins's *History*. His correspondence with the artist Ozias Humphry gives a glimpse of his lifestyle. In September 1790 he writes having had 'a very good journey into Dorsetshire' that he is 'enjoying myself much with my Dogs and guns.'[3] The following year Humphry is instructed to purchase 'a brown cloth frock coat and Breeches and an Embroidered wastcote [sic]' from 'Mr[s] Knight in the Strand', reminding Humphry to buy flannel lined breaches 'or I shall catch my Death.'[4]

Beach shows Trenchard as an elegant country gentlemen in this hitherto undocumented portrait, dated 1793. The format typifies the formula Beach had developed for half-length portraits by the end of his career, placing the sitter in a feigned oval to the left and facing forwards. The portrait was almost certainly painted during one of Beach's summer visits to Dorset.

1 Private family papers reveal that the Trenchard estate was widely dispersed across the county. The principal areas of their estates were at Hammoon in the north, Wolfeton near Dorchester in the south and Bloxworth and Lytchett in the east.
2 Trenchard inherited the old Lychett Matravers manor house from his father.
3 Royal Academy Library, HU/4/60; John Trenchard, to Ozias Humphry, Dorset, 1 September 1790.
4 Royal Academy Library, HU/4/60, John Trenchard to Ozias Humphry, Warmwell, 2 December 1791.

41. **George Romney (1734–1802)**

Thomas Rackett the Elder (c. 1725–1799)
oil on canvas, 1775–1776
74.9×62.2 cm

42. **George Romney (1734–1802)**

Mary Rackett née Caillouel (c. 1734–1800)
oil on canvas, 1775–1776
74.9×62.2 cm

Provenance: Sitters and by descent. Purchased by Dorset Natural History and Archaeological Society 2008 with the assistance of the National Art Collections Fund, the Heritage Lottery Fund S.W. and local fundraising.

Literature: G. Yarker, 'Three Rackett Family Portraits by George Romney', *Transactions of the Romney Society*, vol. 13, 2008, pp. 4–15

Dorset Natural History and Archaeological Society

Thomas and Mary Rackett lived with their only child Thomas (cat. 43) in a farmhouse at Wandsworth and at King Street, Covent Garden, where Rackett maintained his business as a tailor.[1] He attended Milton Abbas Grammar School in the 1730s, forging Dorset friendships and connections which sustained him throughout his life.[2] In 1756 the *Public Advertiser* described Rackett as a 'Master Taylor of King Street' living amongst fellow mercers, drapers and lacemen.[3] Increasingly wealthy, Rackett served on the Master Taylors committee from 1770. His wife Mary, née Caillouel (cat. 42), was from a Huguenot merchant family who settled in England in 1685, maintaining significant family and commercial connections with Boston, trading in cloth, and owning property in Normandy. Mary's family wealth undoubtedly contributed to their comfortable lifestyle amongst such notable people as the actor David Garrick, George Romney and Thomas Arne.

George Romney moved south from Cumbria in 1762, to establish a painting practice. By 1767 he lived near Covent Garden in Great Newport Street, close to the Racketts, enjoying a prolific and financially successful several years spent working in Italy. Thomas Rackett senior commissioned Romney to paint the magnificent full-length portrait of his son (cat. 43) in 1768 and bust-length portraits of himself and his wife in 1775–76 in London.[4]

Rackett the Elder is shown seated in a green chair, with hands folded into his arms; compared with the exuberance of his son's portrait, Thomas Rackett is shown as severe and sober. His magnificently ornate brocaded blue-green silk waistcoat edged in silk and gold thread suggests his trade; the elegant manner shows the sitter as urbane, confident, affluent and at ease. Mary Rackett is shown seated in a red chair, in front of a drape, holding a small brown volume and wearing a neo-classical, cross-over blue silk dress with a crimson sash, a typical Romney invention of the 1770s, and blue silk ribbons and pearls threaded through her fashionably piled-up hair. The portrait conveys a strong personality which we know from her correspondence was both sociable and lively and who

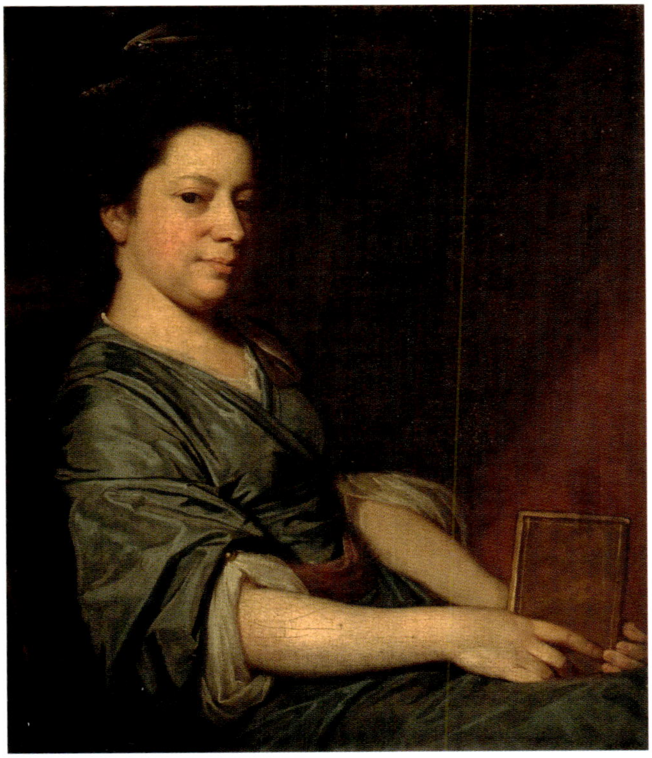

42.

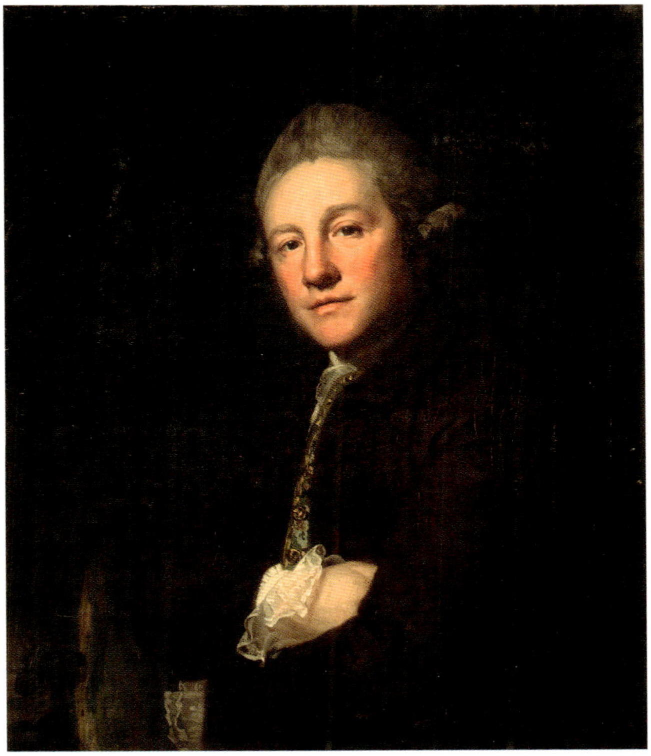

41.

enjoyed a close friendship with Mrs David Garrick over many years.[5]

1 The 40-acre Wandsworth farm was sold in 1791. Despite the Rackett archive deposited at the Dorset History Centre, Mary and Thomas's early lives are unclear; they married at the controversial New Chapel, Mayfair, on 15 February 1754.
2 From private family papers, a footnote to a letter from the Reverend W. Chafin (fig. 9) to F.T. Browne, 27 July 1816.
3 Classified Advertisement, *Public Advertiser*, 18 October 1756.
4 Private communication with Professor Aileen Ribeiro confirmed the wig's style dates the portrait to about 1775–76.
5 See the Rackett archive, DHC, Mary Rackett's sole surviving journals, 1797 and 1799 reveal her numerous contacts, intimate friendship with Mrs David Garrick and close family life.

43. **George Romney** (1734–1802)

Thomas Rackett the Younger (1756–1840)
oil on canvas, c. 1768
183 × 120 cm

Provenance; Sitter, then by descent, purchased by Dorset Natural History and Archaeological Society 2008 with the assistance of the National Art Collections Fund, the Heritage Lottery Fund S.W. and local fundraising.
Literature: Ed. H.S.L. Dewar, *The Thomas Rackett Papers, 17–19th Centuries,* Dorset Record Society, Dorchester, 1965; F. D. Neale, *A History of the Reverend Thomas Rackett, 1756–1840, Rector of Spetisbury, Dorset,* Poole, 2000; G. Yarker, 'Three Rackett Family Portraits by George Romney,' *Transactions of the Romney Society*, Volume 13, 2008, pp. 4–15.

Dorset Natural History and Archaeological Society

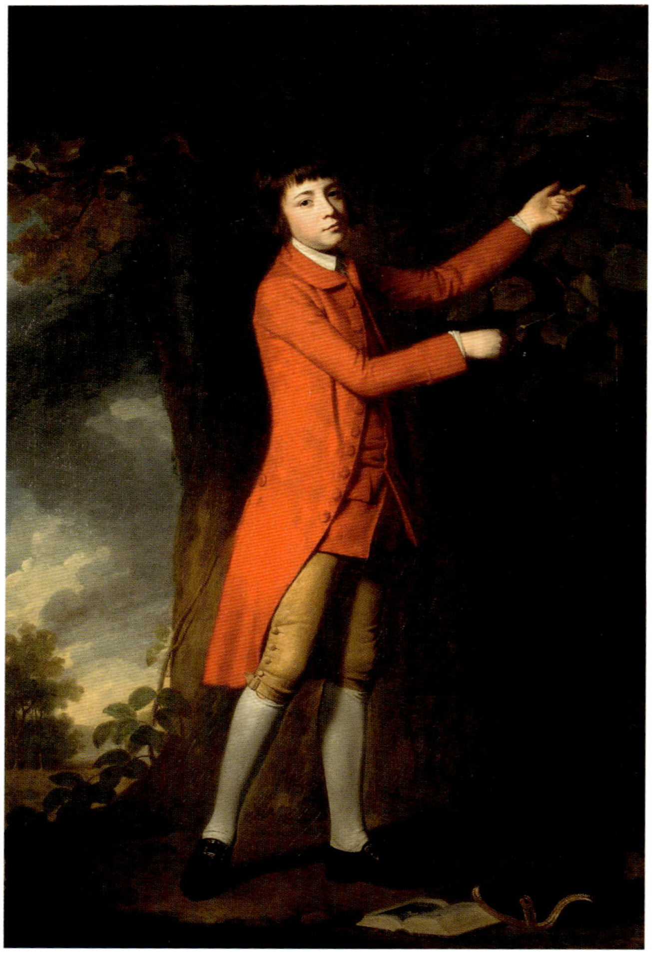

The elegant full-length portrait of twelve year-old Thomas Rackett the Younger dates from Romney's first years in London. His sensitive treatment of the boy, poised between boyhood and manhood is an important full-length portrait of an adolescent by Romney. Master Rackett, only surviving child of Thomas and Mary Rackett (cats. 41, 42), stands facing forwards, wearing his own hair with an up-to-date fringe, red woollen frock coat and matching waistcoat.[1] Resting on the ground his upturned three-cornered beaver fur hat trimmed with gold thread, props open a book. Rackett stands in front of an oak tree with a smaller hazel tree to the right. He points towards the hazel nut sprig he will cut down with the pruners he holds in his right hand, revealing his interest in natural history. Influenced by physician and botanist Dr Richard Pulteney (cat. 54) since the age of ten, at the time of the portrait Rackett was tutored by surgeon, naturalist and empiricist, John Hunter. Through this sharply observed portrait Rackett's parents wished to present their precocious only child as a boy of learning, promoting scholarship as a high ideal.[2]

Thomas attended Fountayne's fashionable private boarding school with Henry Bankes (cat. 25) and Charles Hatchett, who both remained lifelong friends. Highly musical, Rackett played the piano and studied drawing with Theodosius Forrest (1728–1784) and the Sandby brothers. From 1773 he was at University College, Oxford as a pupil of John Baptist Malchair (1729–1812), and in 1780 was ordained deacon at the Chapel Royal in St James's Palace, and priest at Duke Street Chapel on 24 December 1780.[3] Two days later 25-year old Thomas Rackett (fig. 38) was admitted to the living at Spetisbury and Charlton Marshall, near Blandford, presented by his father who secured the major patronage of the living through his friendship with Francis Fane, M.P. for Dorchester, who lived at Spetisbury.

In July 1781 Rackett married Dorothy Tattersall (c. 1751–1835).[4] The handsome Spetisbury living came with a finely proportioned Rectory and land where they lived for the rest of their lives.

At Spetisbury Rackett pursued his natural history interests, planting unusual specimen trees in the rectory grounds. Though rector there for 59 years, he spent at least three months each year at his London house, visiting friends, the theatre and actively involved with various learned societies and charitable activities.[5] A Fellow of the Linnean Society by 1795 and the Royal Society in 1803, Rackett was also a Fellow of the Society of Antiquaries.

Though Rackett never travelled abroad he corresponded widely. A contributor to scientific debate, Rackett knew Joseph Banks, Humphry Davy, Tiberius Cavallo (cat. 55), William Maton, Charles Hatchett and Michael Faraday. His West Country circle of savants included Aylmer Bourke Lambert, Henry Seymer

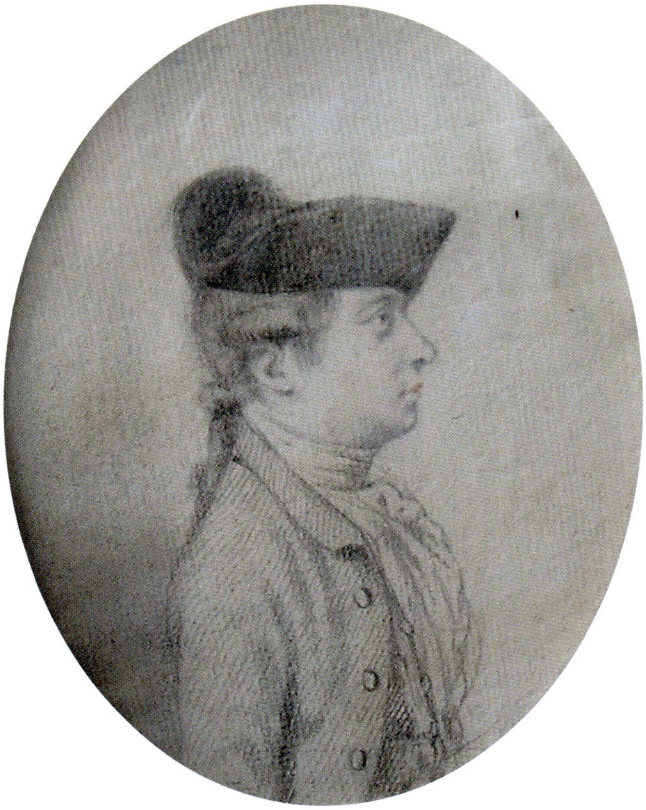

Fig. 38. *Thomas Rackett,* pencil, artist unknown, c. 1780.

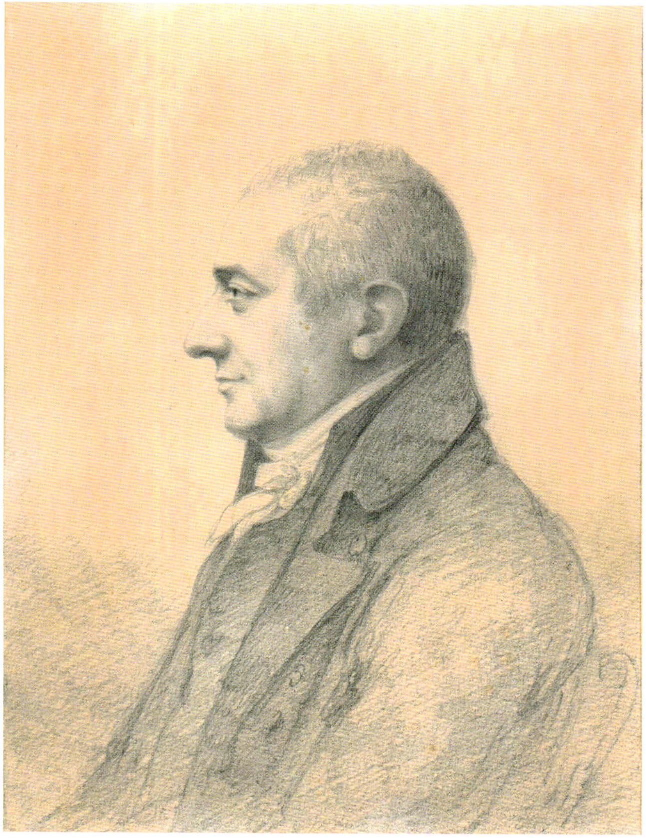

Fig. 39. *Thomas Rackett,* pencil, John George Wood, 1811.

(cat. 53) and Dr Richard Pulteney, with whom he collaborated on an essay on Dorset shells for the Second Edition of Hutchins which also included twenty of his drawings.[6] Rackett contributed two views for Sandby's fourth set of aquatints of Welsh views, '*Twelve Views in North and South Wales*' of 1786. As an antiquary and artist, Rackett's sketches of archaeological sites and discoveries were included in papers given to the Society of Antiquaries.[7] At that date such accurate drawings were the only means of documenting and recording British antiquarian and natural monuments.[8] Rackett also produced an early sketch of astronomer William Herschel operating his pioneering telescope in the 1780s.[9]

Rackett and his associates enjoyed examining, discussing, classifying and exchanging their collections. He was an important contributor to conchology, an evolving branch of zoology. Early in the nineteenth-century Rackett collaborated with his close friend William Maton over their catalogue of British Testacea, or shells, for the *Linnean Transactions*.[10] Broad interest areas prevailed and this lack of rigidity meant remarkable connections could be made across diverse branches of natural philosophy.

Less mobile towards the end of his life, Rackett (fig. 39) collected medals, seals and coins.[11] He was still documenting a find of bronze Greek coins discovered around Spetisbury, at the time of his death. As much an antiquary and naturalist as a country parson, and prominent in local antiquarian discoveries, he concentrated on the awakening interest in British culture and antiquities. Rackett's importance is in his network of contacts and focus on Dorset, widely promoting its natural history, archaeology and geology to academic contacts and fellow members of important learned societies.[12]

1 Boys wearing red coats at Rackett's school were deemed of the first rank. Romney might have been alluding to Rackett's father's skill as a tailor (cat. 41).

2 The thrill of discovery and anticipation of new horizons was manifest in Captain Cook's first circumnavigation that year.

3 Kim Sloan *'A Noble Art', Amateur Artists and Drawing* Masters c. 1600–1800, New Haven and London, 2000, pp. 135 and 165. Malchair was succeeded as artist drawing-master at Oxford by Dorset-born William Delamotte (fig. 20).

4 The Tattersall and Racketts were close neighbours. Dorothy was daughter of the wealthy Reverend James Tattersall rector of St Paul's, Covent Garden. On her marriage, Dorothy brought a settlement of £3,000, or £200,000 in today's money.

5 Rackett inherited King Street from his father by 1800. In 1823 the family moved to nearby Upper Gower Street.

6 In the production of the prints Rackett collaborated with Tiberius Cavallo (fig. 48), Leroy de Barde and James Basire.

7 Collection of the Society of Antiquaries of London, R.P.Wilts. 12: The Reverend Thomas Rackett, *Stonehenge before 3 January 1797 from the west*. Rackett's watercolour documented the site before the stones collapsed. It illustrated a paper given at the Society of Antiquaries and featured in W. Maton's 1798 article for *Archaeologia*.

8 Rackett enjoyed a reputation as a South West artist worth visiting. Joseph Farington recorded Dr. Fisher describing Rackett 'as being possessed of much taste in the arts, with some ingenuity in the practice of drawing', ed. K. Garlick and A. Macintyre *The Diary of Joseph Farington,* New Haven and London, 1978–1998, 10, pp. 3771–3772.

9 M. Hoskin, 'Unfinished Business: William Herschel's Sweeps for Nebulae', *History of Science,* 63, 2005, Fig. 3.

10 Dr. Maton and chemist and philosopher, Charles Hatchett, were Rackett's close friends; Hatchett was responsible for Rackett's London affairs.

11 J.G. Milne, *Finds of Greek Coins in the British Isles. The Evidence considered in the light of the Rackett collection from Dorset,* Oxford, 1948. In May 1832 Rackett exhibited some of the bronze Greek coin finds at the Society of Antiquaries of London.

12 There is a nineteenth-century appraisal of Thomas Rackett on a stone trihedron memorial in Spetisbury churchyard.

Poole's Merchant Princes

44. **British School 18th Century**
Benjamin Lester (1724–1802)
oil on canvas, 1780s
70×57.5 cm
Provenance: Sitter, then by descent, presented to Poole Borough Council by the Reverend George Lester-Garland, date unknown.

Poole Museum

45. **British School 18th Century**
George Lester Garland (1753–1825)
oil on canvas, c. 1780
76×62.5 cm
Provenance: Gift from Miss Edith Lester-Garland, 1974.

46. **British School 18th Century**
Amy Garland, neé Lester (1759–1819)
oil on canvas, c. 1780
73.5×60.5 cm
Provenance: Gift from Miss Edith Lester-Garland, 1974.

Dorset Natural History and Archaeological Society

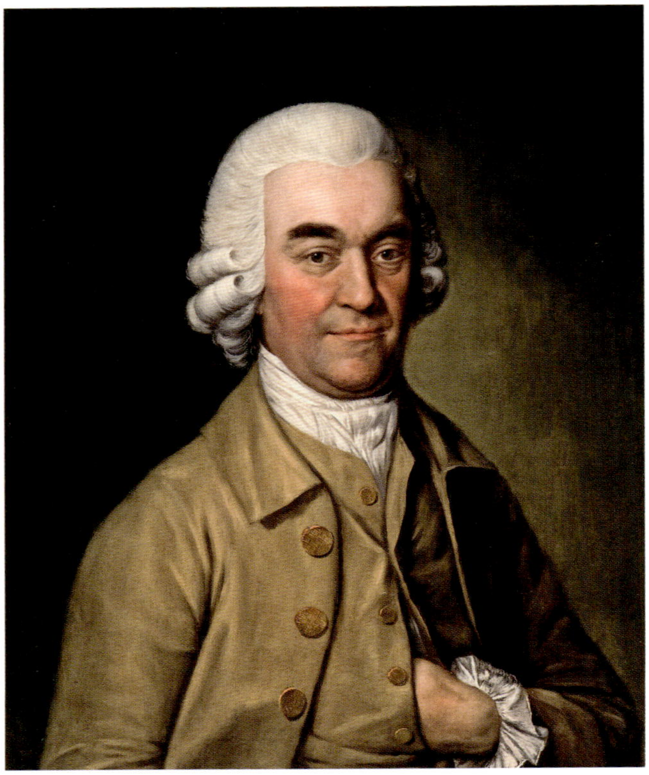

44.

In the early eighteenth century Newfoundland had the most prolific fishing grounds in the world. Poole merchants exploited these and dominated the trade, becoming extremely wealthy as a result. Poole's trade boom started early and lasted for over a century. The ships went out to Newfoundland loaded with salt and provisions, the cod was caught, dried and salted in Newfoundland, see (fig. 41). Laden with salted cod, furs and seal-skins, the Poole ships sailed to Catholic

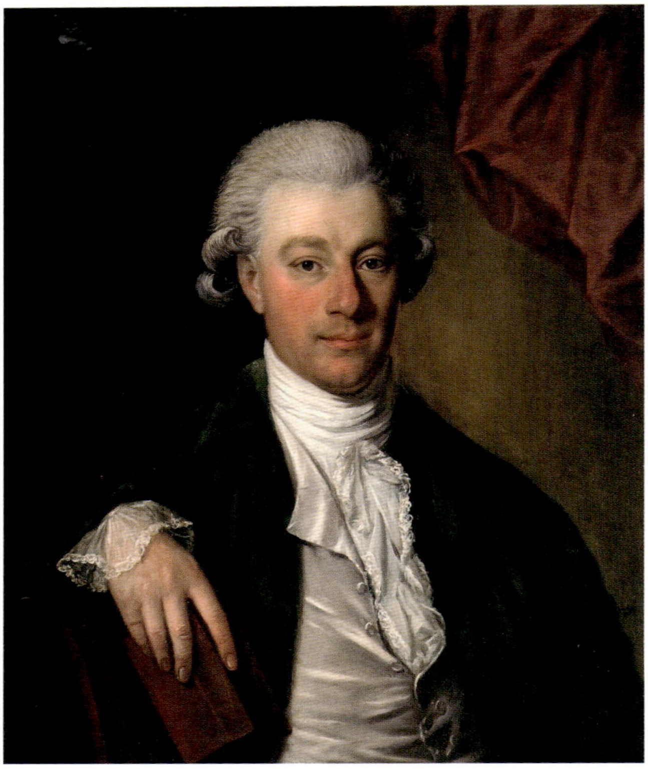

45.

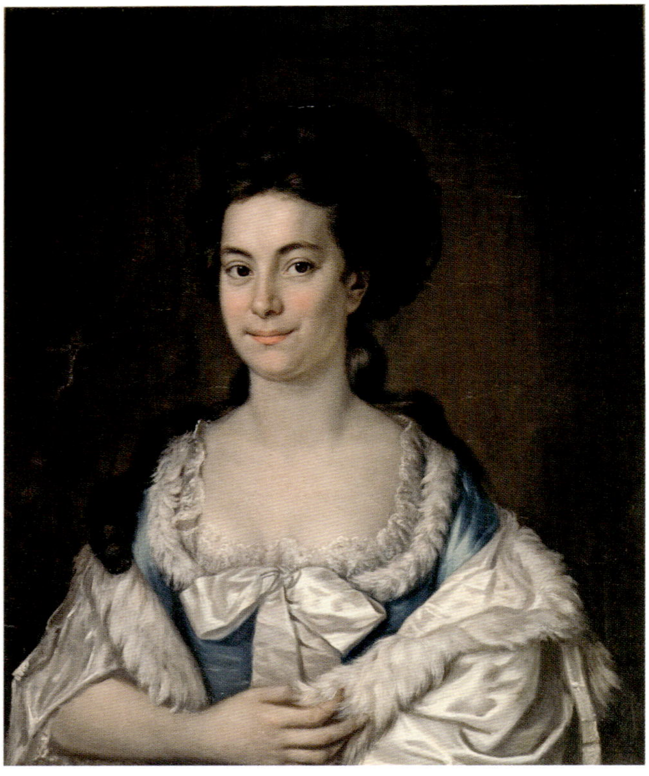

46.

ports in Spain, Portugal and Italy to sell much of the cod. They in turn returned to Poole laden with wine, olive oil, dried fruits and salt, together with the skins brought from Newfoundland. In just one week in December 1779 the *Sherborne Journal* reported nineteen ships returning to Poole from Newfoundland. This business resulted in vast fortunes for Poole families such as the Lesters (cats. 44–46) and Thompsons (cat. 47); their wealth consequently enabled them to build mansion houses in Poole and to engage in local and national politics. The Lesters acknowledged the source of their wealth by commissioning a pair of dried cod to be carved in marble on a fireplace of their Poole house.

Benjamin Lester was born in Poole where his father, Francis, was mayor. Francis traded mainly in cod liver oil from Trinity, Newfoundland where in 1737 Benjamin went to work for another Poole merchant.[1] Benjamin stayed in Trinity after Francis's death and set up in partnership with his elder brother Isaac, who remained in Poole managing the business with their sister Sarah. At Trinity Benjamin engaged in fishing, shipbuilding and the fur trade and was also a magistrate there by 1749. Benjamin strengthened his business links in Newfoundland by marrying his cousin Susannah, daughter of Jacob Taverner of Trinity. The business expanded rapidly to other ports including Labrador, and around 1760 Lester built the first large brick house in Trinity using bricks imported from Dorset. Set against a wooded background, the house is shown with smoke from the chimneys in the contemporary painting by an unknown American artist, *The Old House, Shipyard and Outhouses at Trinity, Newfoundland*. (fig. 40).[2]

Here Lester and his wife raised their family. Lester's headquarters nearby form part of the scene in the painting, *The Old House at Trinity with Wooded Hills, Newfoundland* (fig. 41) complete with warehouses and ships in the bay. Lester's cod business extended along the coast and out to the fishing banks and involved every process from catching to drying the fish, importantly recorded in the painting he commissioned (fig. 41). The ships in the painting are part of his fleet which by 1793 had grown from twelve to thirty vessels, many built at Trinity, resulting in probably the largest fleet owned by a Poole merchant. Both of Lester's paintings showing his business in Newfoundland are on display in the Dorset County Museum.

In 1762 Lester surrendered Trinity to the French during their attack on Newfoundland thus minimizing his losses and those of the community. Though he left Newfoundland in 1776, Lester continued to manage operations from England and his business expanded during the boom years of the 1780s. In Poole his political influence saw him elected mayor in 1779 and from 1781 to 1783, acting as the leading spokesman for Poole merchants. He was also MP for Poole between 1790 and 1796, opposing the extension of civil government in Newfoundland, which he believed would mark the end of the lucrative fishing trade.[3] During the French Revolutionary Wars Lester lost some of his ships after which sales to the European market declined.

Benjamin took on George Garland (cat. 45) as his assistant, later to become his son-in-law through his marriage to Amy Lester (cat. 46). In 1800 Benjamin Lester was assessed at £3,000 value in export and import rates, the greatest amount for any Poole merchant. On Lester's death his Newfoundland business passed to George Garland.

The head and shoulders portrait of Benjamin Lester by an unknown artist shows him facing slightly to right and looking forwards. He wears a white half-wig, buff jacket and waistcoat, both with gold buttons, with his left hand tucked inside his waistcoat. The plain background devoid of any detail and his somewhat austere expression is offset by a ruddy complexion. It may have been painted during the 1780s when Lester was back in Poole.

Born in East Lulworth, the son of yeoman farmer Joseph Garland and his wife Mary, George Garland was

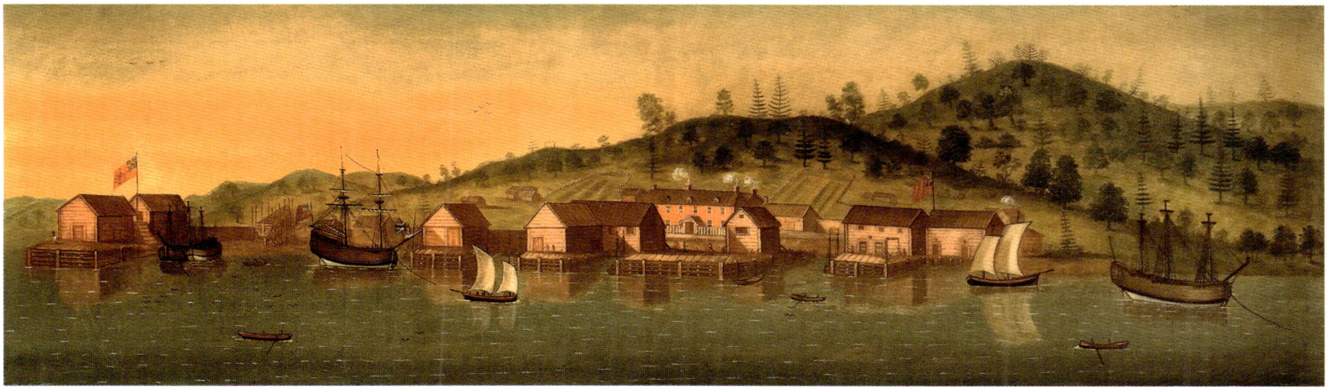

Fig. 40. The *Old House, Shipyard and Outhouses at Trinity, Newfoundland*, oil on panel, American School. c. 1770.

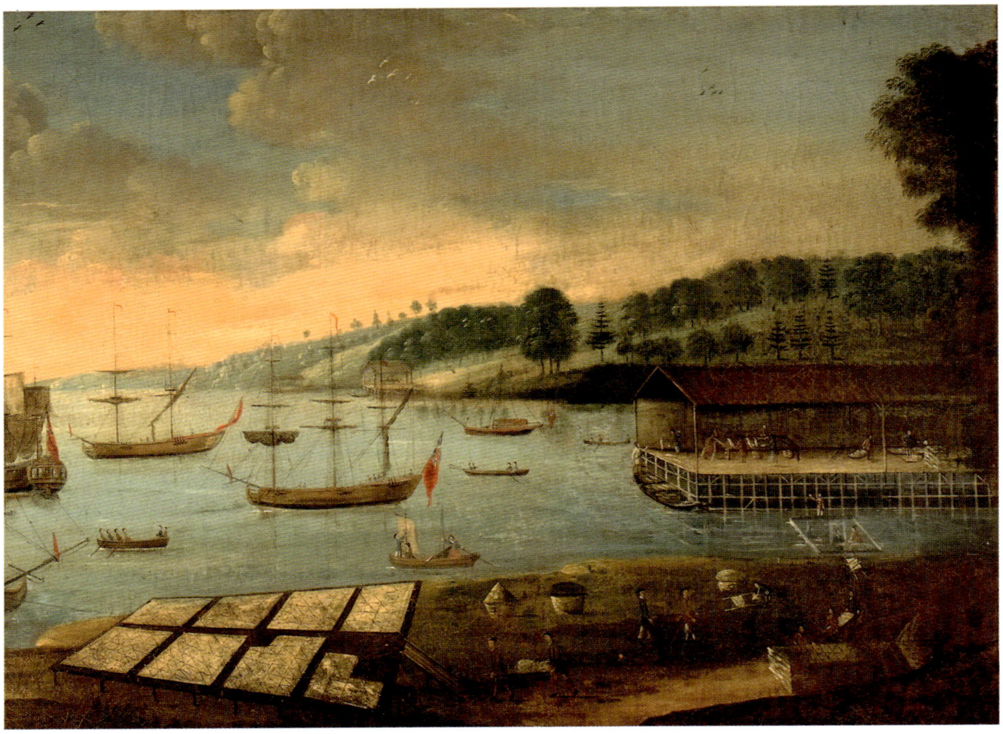

Fig. 41. *The Old House at Trinity with Wooded Hills, Newfoundland,* oil on canvas, 18th century British School.

a merchant and politician involved in Newfoundland fishery. Initially in business in Poole and Southampton with his brother and uncle, in 1779 Garland married Benjamin Lester's daughter Amy, and became manager of Lester's Poole counting-house. The couple raised a large family; meanwhile Garland increasingly managed Lester's Newfoundland trade and served as mayor of Poole in 1788.

Though he never went to Newfoundland, George travelled extensively in England and on the Continent, both buying and selling.[4] He was elected to parliament for Poole in 1801 and, after Benjamin's death in 1802, Garland took over the business following the death of Amy's brother John. From 1805 the firm became George Garland and Sons. Garland seemingly had an exceptional head for business and during the lucrative years of the Newfoundland trade at the time of the Napoleonic Wars, particularly between 1809 and 1815, he made substantial profits and added immensely to his estate. Garland was the MP for Poole from 1801 to 1806 and again in 1810. He passed control of the business to his sons in 1822 but remained involved until his death in 1825.

Benjamin's daughter Amy was born at Trinity, Newfoundland. She married George Garland in Poole where they lived in style and brought up their large family of ten children.

The half-length pair of portraits of George and Amy are probably marriage portraits painted in London by an unknown hand, possibly Gilbert Stuart.[5] George is shown seated and facing forward. He wears a powdered toupée wig, green jacket and white silk waistcoat and cravat tied with lace. There is also lace at his sleeves. His right arm is draped over the back of a chair and he holds a partly opened book in his right hand. On the far right is a draped curtain.

Amy, shown slightly to left, faces forwards. Her brown hair is worn high without adornments with a chignon draped around her shoulders and back of her neck. Her low-cut blue silk dress has a lace collar and is edged with fur secured in front by a large cream silk ribbon. Her cream silk shawl is also edged with white fur. Although Amy wears no jewelry, the considerable amount of white fur undoubtedly bears testimony to her father's and husband's Newfoundland trade and prosperity.

1 For a full account of Lester's activities see his diaries, DHC, D/LEG, F2, F3, F5-10 F2-10, containing many details of Poole and Newfoundland life, as well as national and local politics of the age. D. Beamish, J. Hillier, H. Johnstone, *Mansions and Merchants of Poole and Dorset*, Poole Historical Trust, 1976, contains a detailed account of Lester's business activities. Francess G Halpenny; Jean Hamelin, (1983). Lester entry, D. Beamish, *Dictionary of Canadian Biography*; 5, Toronto, 1801–1820.

2 Possibly the oldest brick-built house in North America, later rebuilt by the Garlands, and now preserved as the Lester-Garland house where it is a museum and learning centre.

3 In 1793 Lester was a member of the House of Commons inquiry into the Newfoundland trade.

4 He later sent his sons John Bingley and George to Trinity to look after the fishery operation. When George Jr and John Bingley were taken into the Newfoundland trade in 1817, their father stated that their investment was £80,000.

5 DNH&AS Library, Lester Garland correspondence reveals that during the twentieth century the family attempted to identify the artist and an attribution of Nathan Cooper Branwhite (1774/5–1857) was tentatively offered, but the dates exclude this. A private conversation with Alex Kidson raises the possibility of Gilbert Stuart and his circle.

47. **Thomas Frye** (1710–1762)

Sir Peter Thompson (1698–1770)
oil on canvas, c. 1745
123×99 cm

Provenance; Sitter, then by descent to Capt. Thomas Thompson, Samuel White, Lt. Col. Peter Francis White who presented the painting to Poole Museum, 1973.
Literature: D. Beamish, J. Hillier, H. Johnstone, *Mansions and Merchants of Poole and Dorset*, Poole Historical Trust, 1976, p. 57.

Poole Museum

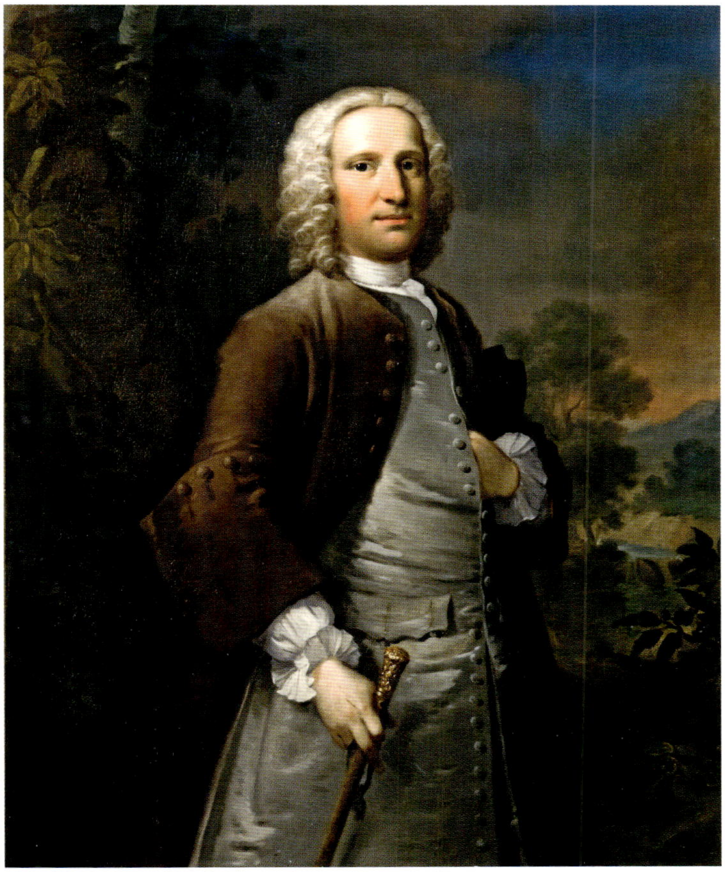

Peter Thompson, third son of Thomas Thompson (1660–1720), belonged to an old mercantile Poole family with business interests in London. At the age of eighteen, Peter sailed to Newfoundland in one of his family's ships. He returned on his father's death in 1720 and joined his older brother James in the family business at Bermondsey. They ran this together until James's death in 1724 when Peter became sole owner. By 1739 Thompson had inherited his family's considerable estates in Poole. He entertained widely.[1] He conducted the Newfoundland interests from Poole and in London traded through Hamburg, a powerful hub for international commerce connecting markets all over Europe. He kept links with a small Poole colony at Bermondsey, including George Lester, and mixed in Johnson's and Boswell's circle. In London Thompson attended natural philosophy lectures, he was elected a Fellow of the Society of Antiquaries in 1743 and became an increasingly important and wealthy figure. From the 1740s Thompson helped Hutchins research his *History,* collate records, and provide information on Poole's history. Antiquarian Browne Willis wrote, 'I hope Mr Hutchins will do Poole justice, but it was not originally Parochial; it savours of being a new Place'.[2] An undated letter from Hutchins to Thompson reveals Thompson loaned his copy of Domesday, and Thomas Coker's manuscript, to Hutchins who returned them to London via Messrs Pitt or Bond.[3] Thompson acquired an important library of antiquarian books, had a valuable collection of ancient glass and recognised Dorset's potential for antiquaries some twenty-five years before the Revd. Thomas Rackett (cat. 43).

Thompson was High Sheriff of Surrey by 1745 and was knighted the next year following his loyal address to George II on the failure of the Jacobite Rebellion. During 1746 Thompson was elected a Fellow of the Royal Society as 'a gentleman of merit, distinction and learning' and commissioned John Bastard (cat. 51) to build his house in Poole.[4] A letter from Bastard to Thompson in July 1752 indicates their relationship was not always smooth. A confirmed Whig, Thompson was MP for St. Albans between 1747–1754, serving on numerous committees and preparing bills.

In addition to Thompson's London parliamentary dealings he was involved with Bubb Dodington (fig. 8) in Dorset politics and actively involved with Poole's affairs. He was a key figure in Poole both with the families involved with Newfoundland trade like the Lesters, (cats. 44–46) and fellow politicians, such as the Gulstons (cat. 49 and fig. 42). By 1754 he retired from business and political life, handing the management of his business to his nephew Peter Thompson. Returning to Dorset by 1762, he threw himself into local antiquarian affairs.

Born in Dublin in 1710, Thomas Frye won acclaim as a painter before coming to London in 1734, gaining early success as a portrait artist. He also worked as a miniature painter, mezzotint engraver and enameller. A keen inventor, Frye experimented with china clay, devising a method for producing soft-paste porcelain using bone ash and resulting in porcelain of brilliant whiteness, luminescence and, most importantly, extraordinary durability. By 1744 Frye and his colleague Edward Heylyn had taken out patents for its manufacture, calling their factory New Canton.[5] By 1749 the Bow china factory was established near Bow Bridge with Frye running the operation. Thompson, at Mill Street, Bermondsey, was living within a couple of miles of the Bow factory. Their proximity, combined with Frye and Thompson's mutual trading interests undoubtedly resulted in the portrait commission, painted to record Thompson's rising success as High Sheriff of Surrey or knighthood in 1746.[6]

The three-quarter length portrait shows Peter Thompson facing to right and looking forwards. He wears a grey full-bottomed wig, brown velvet collarless coat with the powder from his wig clearly visible and large square-cuffed sleeves. He holds a gold-topped cane in his right hand and his left is tucked into his long grey silk waistcoat. The portrait was displayed in Thompson's Poole house in a carved frame, within an oak panelled room with ornamental ceiling and carved oak mantelpiece. Plaster portrait busts of Thompson and his widowed sister Amy stood in the entrance hall.[7] She died on 26 October 1770, followed by Thompson four days later, and they were buried together. His kinsman Captain Peter Thompson inherited Thompson's entire estate.

1 Thompson's London circle included ship's chandler and ironmonger Joseph Ames, George Vertue, engraver, and those antiquaries involved with Hutchins's *History*, William Bowyer, Browne Willis, J Nicholls, Richard Gough and Dr. W. Cummings. See too M. Wynne, 'Thomas Frye (1710–1762),' *The Burlington Magazine*, 114, no. 827, 1972, pp. 78–85 for biographical details.

2 DHC, Sir Peter Thompson archive, D 967. Transcript of a Letter to Sir Peter Thompson from Browne Willis (unsourced) of Whaddon Hall near Penny Stratford, Bucks, 23 August 1749 addressed to Sir Peter at Bermondsey.

3 D. Beamish, J. Hillier, H.F.V. Johnstone, *Mansions and Merchants of Poole and Dorset*, Poole Historical Trust, 1976, p. 61.

4 Royal Society Archive; Ref. EC/1746/08. Thompson's proposers were Joseph Ames; Martin Folkes; Geo Holmes; Wm Jones; Henry Baker; Cromll Mortimer.

5 See E. Adams & D. Redstone, *Bow Porcelain*, Faber & Faber, London, 1981 for a full account of Frye's activities.

6 Thomas Frye also painted the portrait of Peter Thompson's brother-in-law Thomas Hasselden, Master of the Royal Academy at Portsmouth who was married to his sister Amy in 1735. This portrait was turned into a mezzotint in 1740 by J. Faber, see British Museum, 1902, 1011.1514.

7 DHC, Sir Peter Thompson archive, D. 967.

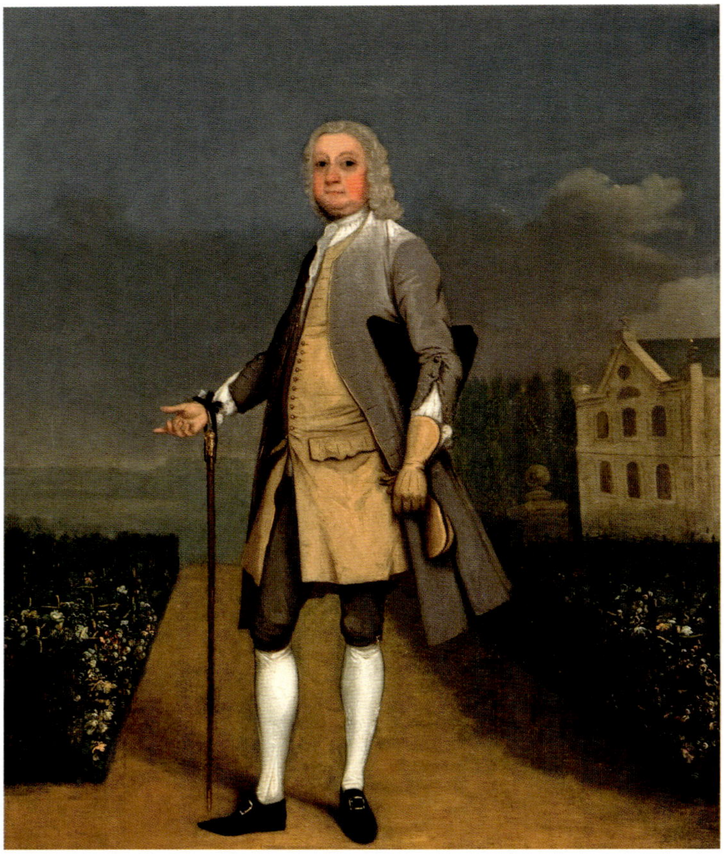

48. **British School 18th Century**

Robert Henning (1697–1757)
oil on canvas, c. 1740
74.5×61 cm
Provenance: presented to Poole Corporation by the Society of Poole Men, 1943.

Poole Museum

Wealthy merchant Robert Henning maintained a powerful position within Poole. An alderman of the corporation, he held a Treasury Commission and was also Receiver General of House Duties for Dorset and Mayor of Poole, from 1739–41.

In 1718 Henning married Margaret Keyn of Church Knowle, they had four sons and one daughter and Margaret died aged 36 in 1736. Henning acquired his wealth during Poole's most prosperous period when fortunes were made and consolidated. During the eighteenth century the town, with its important trade links with North America, was at its peak as one of the busiest ports in Britain. The merchants founded dynasties, and formed an elite group through inter-marriage and alliance, each building houses to outshine the other. The Henning family business was evidently influential since there is a Henning's Wharf in Poole. Henning's circle of contacts included Thomas Hyde (cat. 50), Joseph Gulston (cat. 49) and Sir Peter Thompson (cat. 47).

The full-length portrait, is painted in the manner of Arthur Devis, setting a small figure in a landscape. Robert Henning is shown standing in the formal garden of his Poole mansion. He wears a grey powdered wig, grey velvet coat, buff waistcoat, white shirt, grey breeches and black shoes with silver buckles. He gestures with his right hand towards his estate; his cane attached to his wrist with a black ribbon. He wears a long buff leather glove on his left hand in which he holds his other glove; his black three-cornered hat is tucked under his left arm. The stone fronted house, a merchant prince's mansion, is in the far right with the Dorset countryside in the distance. Intriguingly, the plants in the flower beds in the foreground are recognizable and include bunches of grapes. This rather unusual portrait intentionally demonstrates Henning as a man of substance and possessions and may have been commissioned to commemorate his time as mayor of Poole.

49. **Thomas Hudson** (1701–1779)

Joseph Gulston (c. 1694–1766)
oil on canvas, 1740s
124.5 × 100 cm

Literature: A. Smart, *Allan Ramsay a Complete Catalogue of his Paintings*, Yale, 1999, p. 127, cat. 221; Sotheby's, *Derwydd Mansion sale* 15 September 1998, lot 72.

Poole Museum

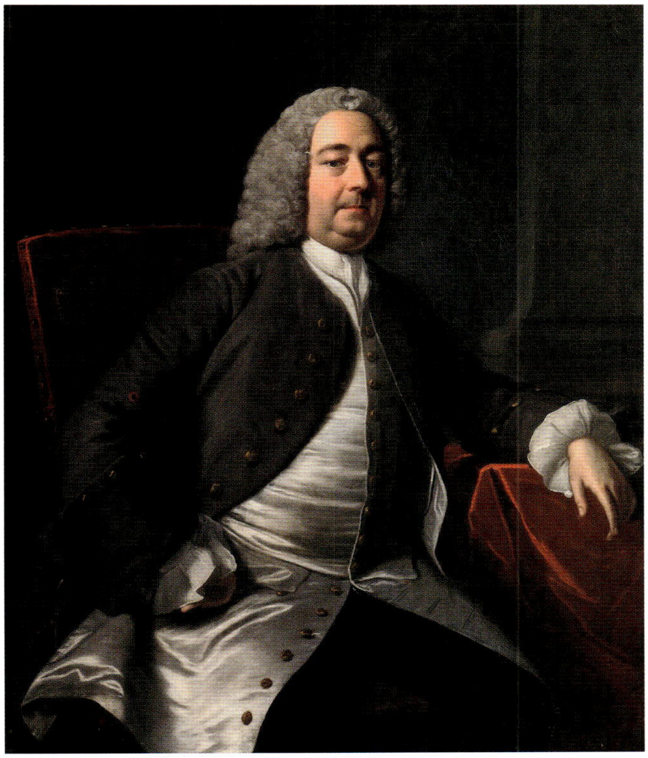

Joseph Gulston was the son of an English merchant and grew up in Lisbon. On returning to England he became a City of London merchant and secretly married the daughter of a Portuguese merchant, Mericas Sylva. Gulston lived in comfort first in London, and later in Poole, where as MP he represented the borough for 40 years. His somewhat irregular marriage apparently meant his four children were raised in secrecy, principally because their mother was Roman Catholic.[1] Gulston's near neighbour at Kew Green was George III, which Gulston found an inconvenience, leading to him building a house at Ealing Grove by 1755. A director of the South Sea Company between 1742–60, Gulston was MP for Tregony from 1737–41 and Poole, 1741–65. He gained a lucrative contract for the Government during the war of Austrian Succession. At his death he left funds of a quarter of a million pounds and his Hertfordshire estate to his son.

Gulston made his fortune through trade with the Americas and army contracts. Another merchant Sir Peter Thompson (cat. 47) sought a coalition in Poole elections between Mr Trenchard, whom he admired, and Gulston, demonstrating how very influential these two men were in town affairs. In 1760 Gulston canvassed Thompson to support him when he stood as MP. Thompson's response was to seek an explanation from Gulston concerning his non-attendance in the House on 21st June 1757 when a Bill was passed to save the Poole road, a matter of interest to every Poole resident. Thompson's point was clear, if Gulston could not support the town of Poole then he saw no reason to support Gulston.

During the 1740s Joseph Gulston sat to three portraits by Allan Ramsay and Thomas Hudson.[2] This three-quarter length is probably the first of the two versions by Hudson. Gulston is shown seated in a red chair facing slightly to right and looking forwards wearing a grey full-bottomed wig, grey velvet coat with gold buttons and large square-shaped cuffs. His white silk waistcoat with matching gilt buttons strains to contain his portly form. Gulston's left hand rests on a table covered in red velvet cloth; in the background on the right is a pilaster. His right arm on his hip lends the portrait self-importance. The drapery was almost certainly painted by Joseph Van Aken for Hudson. A very similar pose by Allan Ramsay may be derived from Van Dyck's *Earl of Carnarvon*.[3]

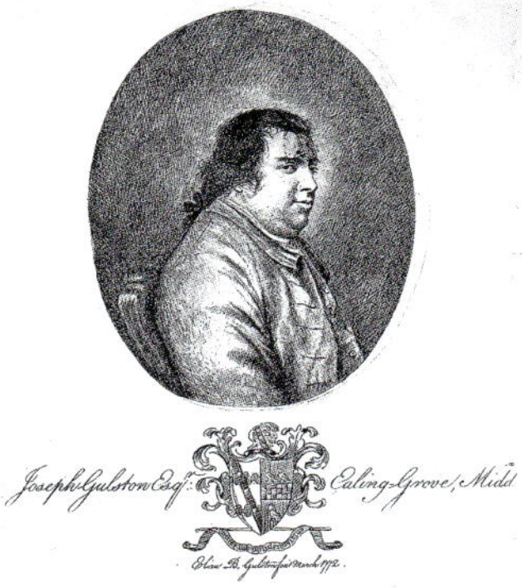

Fig. 42. *Joseph Gulston Esq., Ealing Grove, Middlesex,* after Eliza Gulston 1772.

Gulston's son, another Joseph Gulston (fig. 42) described by Walpole as the 'Algerian hog', attended Eton and spent his short life dissipating his father's fortune. Engaged in a life of connoisseurship, he lived mainly at Ealing Grove, spending vast sums of money developing a massive library and important print collection. He and his wife sat for their close friend the artist Hugh Douglas Hamilton (cats. 2, 3) in 1771. Gulston was also MP for Poole, and when he lost all his money he was forced to sell Ealing Grove and retire to Poole. By 1784 he had also sold all his prints and books. J. Nichols's life of Joseph Gulston, father and son, narrated by their daughter and sister is one of the most revealing and fascinating studies of how fortunes were made and lost in the eighteenth century.[4]

1 Their bizarre youth formed the basis of the novel C. Black, *Mericas*, London, 1880, taken from J. Nichols, *Illustrations of the Eighteenth Century,* 5, pp. 1–59.

2 There are other versions by family descent to Ralph Stepney-Gulston: a) Thomas Hudson, three-quarter length portrait in a red coat, hand resting on papers on a table with panelling and pilasters in the background; b) Allan Ramsay, head and shoulders in a blue coat dated 1746. A decade later Gulston commissioned Francis Cotes to paint portraits of his wife and children. See Sotheby's, *Derwydd Mansion sale* 15 September 1998; Sotheby's 25 November 1998.

3 See A. Smart, *Allan Ramsay a Complete Catalogue of his Paintings*, Yale, 1999, p. 127, cat. 221.

4 J. Nichols, pp. 1–60.

50. **John Hall** (fl. 1762–65)

Thomas Hyde (1731–1795)
oil on canvas, 1765
138.5×98.5 cm
signed and dated: *J. Hall Pinxt 1765.*

Poole Museum

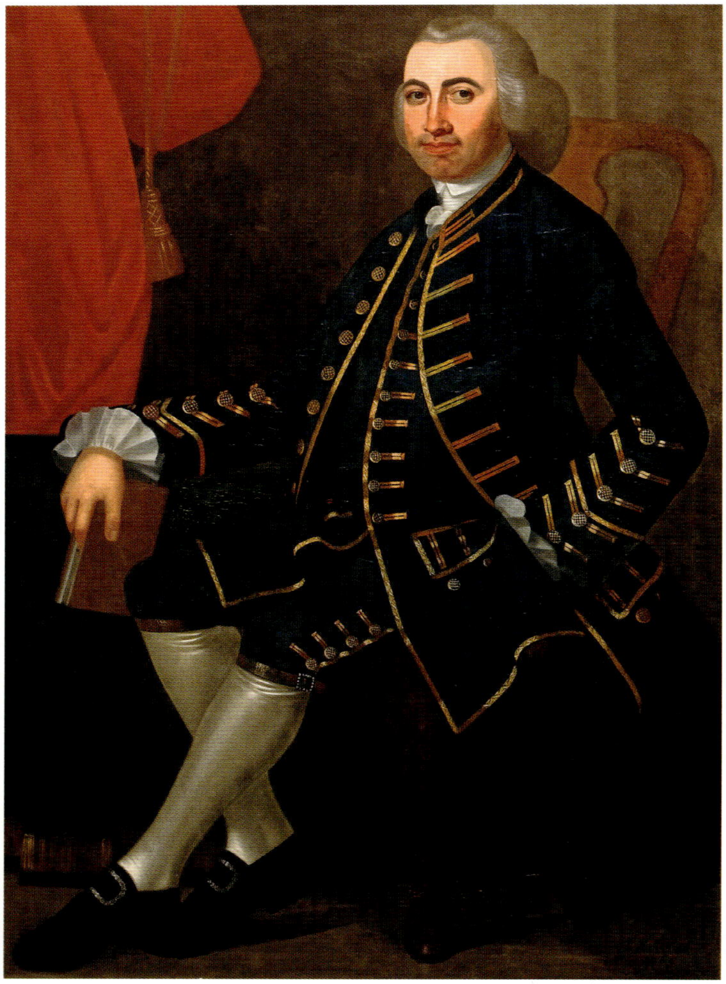

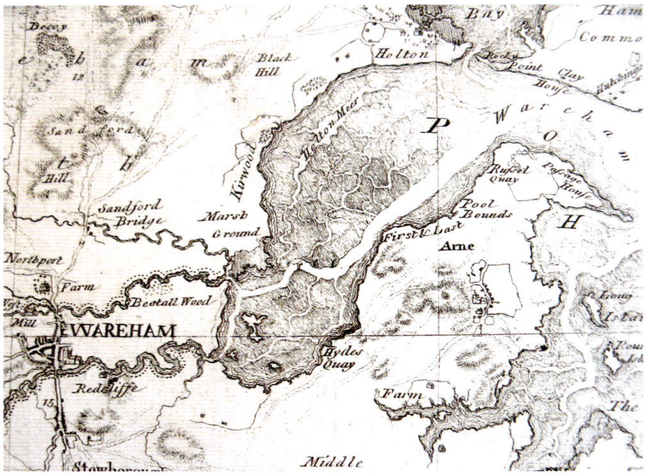

Fig. 43. *Detail showing Thomas Hyde's Quay, Arne, Wareham,* Isaac Taylor, 1765.

Thomas, son of George Hyde, belonged to a well-established Poole family. In 1753 he rented land at Arne, on the Wareham side of Poole Harbour, on an estate owned by Lord Rivers (cats. 26, 27). At the same time he maintained close links with Poole where he was elected mayor in 1764. It was likely that his portrait was painted to celebrate his time in this office. In 1768 Hyde managed the parliamentary election campaign of the younger Joseph Gulston (fig. 42), to the evident dissatisfaction of the electorate (effectively about 100 freemen). Many, like Sir Peter Thompson (cat. 47), were concerned at George III's handling of affairs in America and felt Hyde's autocratic candidate compromised their vital transatlantic commercial interests.

A member of the newly prosperous middle class, during the 1760s Hyde extended his holdings in Arne, becoming increasingly powerful and active in local affairs.[1] By 1772 he was paying for clay mining rights, and enjoying life as a country gentleman in a house with commanding views over Poole Harbour. Hyde had a contract to supply Josiah Wedgwood with 1400 tons of potter's clay. He increased his efficiency by improving trackways over the heath and building a small quay to transport the pipe-clay to Poole (fig. 43). He continued to farm, direct his quarrying and clay mining and trade with Newfoundland, an over-stretch which meant by 1792 he was declared bankrupt.

The full-length portrait shows Hyde seated, in a grey wig, striking blue coat frogged with gold and gold buttons, matching long waistcoat and breeches.[2] The portrait is distinctly signed and dated *John Hall Pinxt. 1765*. Little is known about Hall's activities. He is recorded exhibiting portraits at the Free Society of Artists in 1762 and 1763, living at Henrietta Street off Covent Garden. It is possible that he visited Poole to paint Hyde, who is shown rather awkwardly filling the picture space, a feature of Hall's portraiture, and evident in the portrait of *Ven. William Backhouse, DD, Archdeacon of Canterbury* dated 1762 (Eastbridge Hospital, Canterbury).

1 See B. Kerr, *Bound to the Soil,* London, 1975, p. 34. Kerr argued that Hyde's activities were instrumental in amalgamating numbers of scattered holdings into large farms, affordable only by the well-to-do.

2 A later label on the portrait erroneously names the sitter as William Hyde.

Dorset's Enlightenment
Blandford Forum in the Eighteenth Century

Throughout the country provincial middle-class intellectuals and empiricists were making important discoveries, from the industrial enquiries of the Lunar Society in the Midlands to the intellectuals of the South West. The market town of Blandford Forum, surrounded by large estates, was the locus for a notable group of natural philosophers and antiquarians.[1] From early in the century several scholars resided there including Christopher Pitt, son of the local physician, who translated Virgil's *Ænid*. After the devastating fire of 1731, in which most of Blandford Forum was destroyed, the town was rebuilt, largely by the Bastard brothers (cats. 51, 52), resulting in a town of classical architecture. This contrasted strikingly with the majority of the county's medieval towns and villages. The elegant new town was one of the centres of the county. In July and August races were held on the Downs north of the town. The list of carriages attending in 1786 demonstrates their appeal to the most important figures from across the county. With the races came a series of balls and concerts in the Assembly Rooms which attracted significant London musicians including Johann Christian Bach and his wife Cecilia Grassi, with Antonin Kammel, Giovanni Punto and Johann Christian Fischer.[2] The young Italian musician Muzio Clementi, whom Peter Beckford (cat. 22) brought back from Italy, also contributed to the cultural scene by giving concerts and lessons nearby at Stepleton.

Amongst Blandford Forum's most important residents was Dr. Richard Pulteney (cat. 54) who promulgated Linnaeus's theories. Pulteney had close links with members of the Lunar Society, corresponding and exchanging ideas with the important Midlands scientist Erasmus Darwin. Pulteney lived in a fine house built by the Bastard family; he corresponded regularly with Sir Joseph Banks, Dr Daniel Solander, the Duchess of Portland, Sir James Edward Smith, founder of the Linnean Society, Tiberius Cavallo (cat. 55) and Mary Delany.[3] Within the county Pulteney discussed scientific and antiquarian activities with landowners, fellow physicians, chemists, surgeons and churchmen. The Reverend William Chafin (fig. 9) dispatched plants and birds to Pulteney, Thomas Erle Drax sent his Morden mineral water for analysis and Tregonwell Napier sought Pulteney's advice in identifying and naming his shell collection.

Pulteney demonstrated the growing practice of closely recording local flora and fauna, publishing with Thomas Rackett (cat. 43) their findings of Dorset's natural history in the second edition of Hutchins's *History*. Rackett also collaborated with his protégé and close friend, physician William Maton, on the catalogue of British Testacea.[4] Pulteney and his circle grew exotic specimens and compared notes on horticultural achievements. Rackett received catalogues of seeds from William Salisbury at the Brompton Botanic Garden; Pulteney promoted local natural historians such as John Galpine on the national stage. Galpine was from a family of local nurserymen; he created the small double pink 'Kingston', or 'Blandford Rose' and provided specimen trees for Rackett's remarkable rectory garden at nearby Spetisbury, the Digbys at Sherborne Castle, the Portmans at Bryanston and the second Countess of Ilchester.[5] In 1806 Galpine used the Linnean system in his popular book, *A Synoptical Compend of British Botany,* designed for quick reference and identification in the field.[6] Much as Joseph Wright of Derby painted portraits of members of the Lunar Society, some of the Blandford circle sat to Thomas Beach, including Richard Pulteney and Henry Seymer and his family, with whom Beach was recorded staying at Hanford several times from 1765.

At Spetisbury Rackett and Tiberius Cavallo, inspired by their friends the distinguished astronomer William Herschel and his sister Caroline, studied the skies through a telescope and laid down a meridian line in the pavement of the rectory forecourt two degrees west of Greenwich. Rackett equipped rooms at the parsonage for Cavallo's experiments, perhaps the location in Cavallo's portrait. Herschel famously built the 48-inch telescope which Thomas Rackett painted following the Herschels' move to Datchet in 1782.[7]

Tours of the British Isles were a growing phenomenon during the century; in 1794 Thomas Rackett, William Maton and Charles Hatchett combined talents on a round trip through Dorset to Devon and Cornwall. The intention of '*A Tour into (chiefly the maritime parts of) Dorsetshire, Devonshire and Cornwall*' was to visit and record a lesser known region.[8] The close collaboration between artist, antiquary, mineralogist, physician and empiricist resulted in 1797 in Maton's publication incorporating Rackett's topographical sketches, turned into aquatint prints by Samuel Alken. Imbued with perceptions of the picturesque, Rackett's sketches were indebted to the work of William Gilpin and of Paul Sandby who produced several related books of aquatints of Wales. Sandby commissioned

Rackett to produce two views he had failed to record.[9]

The trio's sense of enquiry is evident in Maton's journal, with acute observations and commentary frequently cross-referenced with Hutchins. Each place was described in terms of history, landscape, geology, vegetation, building, industry, agriculture and antiquities. Rackett wrote home from Plymouth, excited that 'Mr Hatchett's knowledge of mineralogy makes it very entertaining to examine the state of the earth'.[10] Included in the book was an engraved plan representing various rocks and sub-soils.[11] Rackett was not unusual in being both a preacher and a scientist interested in geology, which was viewed as a romantic and spiritual science. Bible teaching revealed that earth and human history started at the same time, tracing both back about 6,000 years. Such assumptions were later challenged as new geological discoveries raised questions about the history of the earth. Rackett knew of the cycles of destruction and renewal and had a pre-Darwinian awareness of linear history.

In Cornwall the trio descended mines then at the peak of production in the county; in the manuscript volume Rackett drew some annotated diagrams of them. The mines and consequent industries were of particular interest since Dorset's lack of coal and minerals meant the industrial revolution largely passed it by. In witnessing the effects of the industrial revolution Maton, Hatchett and Rackett were early witnesses to the human cost.[12] In June 1797 the Racketts and small daughter travelled to Derby and, as industrial tourists, visited a cotton mill and 'Mr Duesbury's china manufactory'.

Thirty-four miles away from Blandford Forum, empirical observation resulted in a Yetminster farmer, Benjamin Jesty, being the first to vaccinate against smallpox in 1774. Aware that his dairymaids who contracted the lesser cow-pox seemed immune from smallpox, the Dorset farmer experimented by successfully vaccinating his wife and two young sons with cow-pox some twenty years before the more celebrated Edward Jenner. Jesty's important achievement was commemorated in 1805 when he sat to Michael Sharp (Wellcome Collection) (fig. 43a) for his portrait.

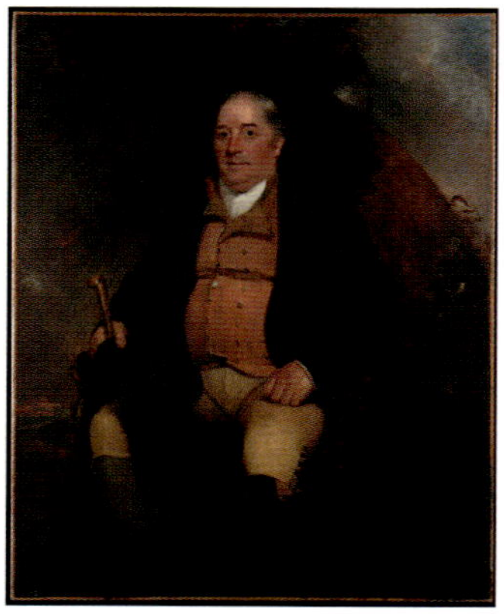

Fig. 43a. *Benjamin Jesty,* oil on canvas, M. W. Sharp, 1805.

Eighteenth century interest areas were not rigidly defined; one discipline invaluably shed light on a totally different subject, enabling intimate connections to be made between various branches of natural philosophy.[13] The circle of south-west intellectuals provided important research for the next generation of scientists in the pre-Darwinian era. Charles Darwin (Erasmus's grandson) took extracted notes from Rackett's article in the Linnean Society's *Transactions* with him on the *Beagle.*[14] By 1829, aware of the effects of rapidly advancing technology, William Maton wrote to Rackett in Blandford about the impact of the railway on Dorset, *'A rail road and a coach travelling 12 miles an hour will convert Dorsetshire into a suburb of London'.*[15]

1 By the end of the century the market town of Blandford Forum had a population of about 2,326. Aside from agriculture its main industry was button making.

2 B. Matthews, 'J. C. Bach in the West Country', *The Musical Times,* 108, no. 1494, 1967, pp. 702–704.

3 Linnean Society, Pulteney correspondence, Mrs. Delany, Anglo-Irish bluestocking and artist, was a favourite of Queen Charlotte and important contributor to natural history. Pulteney also corresponded with bluestockings Hannah More and Catherine Macaulay.

4 'An Historical Account of Testaceological Writers', by William George Maton and the Reverend Thomas Rackett, *Transactions of the Linnean Society,* London, 1804, 7, pp. 119–214, and 'Descriptive Catalogue of British Testacea', William Maton and the Reverend Thomas Rackett, *Transactions of the Linnean Society,* London, 1807, 8, pp. 17–250.

5 Galpine's seed catalogue owned by Thomas Rackett, is in Blandford Museum.

6 E. Slatter, 'From The Archives', *The Linnean,* March 1998, pp. 23–27.

7 Herschel discovered the planet Uranus in March 1781 and dedicated it to George III. For an illustration of Rackett's sketch from a private collection see M. Hoskin, 'Unfinished Business: William Herschel's Sweeps for Nebulae', *History of Science,* vol. 43, pp. 305–320.

8 *Observations relative Chiefly to the Natural History, Picturesque Scenery and Antiquities of the Western Counties of England, made in the years 1794 and 1796,* Salisbury 1797. The draft manuscript in Devon Record Office includes Rackett's original sketches.

9 Sandby's fourth set of Welsh views, '*Twelve Views in North and South Wales',* 1786, included Rackett's submissions of Kidwelly Castle and Abbey on the Wye, indicating the reliance Sandby placed on Rackett's topographical work. See 'Paul Sandby's Tour of Wales with Joseph Banks', Peter Hughes, *The Burlington Magazine,* 117. no. 868, July, 1975, pp. 452–457. Garden theorist and early print historian William Gilpin's picturesque beliefs informed late eighteenth-century theories of landscape architects such as Sir Uvedale Price and Humphry Repton. His accounts of summer journeys through Britain, published at intervals from 1782, were enormously influential.

10 DHC, Rackett archive, D/RAC/81, Thomas Rackett, Plymouth to Dorothea Rackett, 20 August 1794.

11 Though claiming to be the '*first attempt in England to construct a geological map*', it is technically lithological, focusing on the overall physical character of rock formation, description and classification, rather than geological contours.

12 Maton, 1, p. 233, wrote *'Nothing can be more shocking than the appearance which the workmen in the smelting-houses exhibit. So dreadfully deleterious are the fumes of arsenic constantly impregnating the air of these places and so profuse is the perspiration occasioned by the heat of the furnaces, that those who have been employed at them but a few months become most emaciated figures, and in the course of a few years are generally laid in their graves. Some of the poor wretches who were lading[sic] the liquid metal from the furnaces to the moulds, looked more like walking corpses than living beings'.*

13 Michael Faraday, Sir Humphrey Davy, David Garrick, Joseph Banks, Joseph Jekyll and the Herschels all knew the Blandford circle. Devon naturalist George Montagu and Rackett shared interests in conchology, ornithology and zoology, benefiting from each others' visits to London carrying out shared and mutual commissions.

14 T. Rackett, 'Observations on *Cancer salinus*', *Transactions of the Linnean Society,* London, 1815, 11, p. 205.

15 DHC, Rackett archive, D/RAC/34, William Maton to Thomas Rackett, London, 31 December 1829.

51. **Attr. Dietrich Ernst Andreae** (c. 1680–c. 1735)
John Bastard (c. 1688–1770)
oil on canvas, 1728
69×58.5 cm
Provenance: Sitter, then by descent; gift from Thomas Horlock Bastard to the Corporation of Blandford, 1889.[1]
Literature: H. Colvin, 'The Bastards of Blandford, Architects and Master-Builders', *Archaeological Journal*, 104, 1948.

52. **Attr. Dietrich Ernst Andreae** (c. 1680–c. 1735)
William Bastard (c. 1689–1766)
oil on canvas, c. 1728–1735
73×58 cm
Provenance: Sitter, then by descent; gift from Thomas Horlock Bastard to the Corporation of Blandford, 1889.
Literature: H. Colvin, 'The Bastards of Blandford, Architects and Master-Builders', *Archaeological Journal*, 104, 1948.

Blandford Town Council

John and William were two of the six sons of architect and joiner Thomas Bastard (d. 1720) and Bridget, née Creech. They belonged to an important Blandford family of builders. Their wide-ranging business interests included not only architecture, building and surveying, but carpentry, furniture design, clock and barometer making and much else.[2]

The brothers played a large part in the rebuilding of Blandford following the disastrous fire of 4 June 1731, working with master mason and builder Francis Cartwright, local MP Sir James Thornhill, and Nathaniel Ireson.[3] The fire destroyed most of the town's buildings including the Bastards' own house, workshops and possessions; their recorded losses reveal the extent and scope of their cultural interests.[4] The Bastards rebuilt Blandford Town Hall, initially working to a plan by Sir James Thornhill, as well as several surrounding buildings, including the church, apart from the cupola and Greyhound public house.[5] Key figures in Blandford, John and William were intermittently bailiffs there between 1738 and 1759. Together with Francis Cartwright they were key members of the group Oswald has loosely defined as the Blandford School of architects.[6]

Their employment by many of the major landowners in Dorset meant they came into contact with the metropolitan tastes of important designers, architects and artists. They were much in demand from the 1730s to 1760s, building and redesigning many of the county's important houses. During the rebuilding of Blandford in 1735 they also built Spetisbury House, and Crichel House for Sir William Napier following a fire in 1742.[7] Payments are recorded between 1743 and 1747 not only to the Bastard brothers but also to Francis Cartwright.[8] In 1749 John built Sir Peter Thompson's fine mansion house in Poole complete

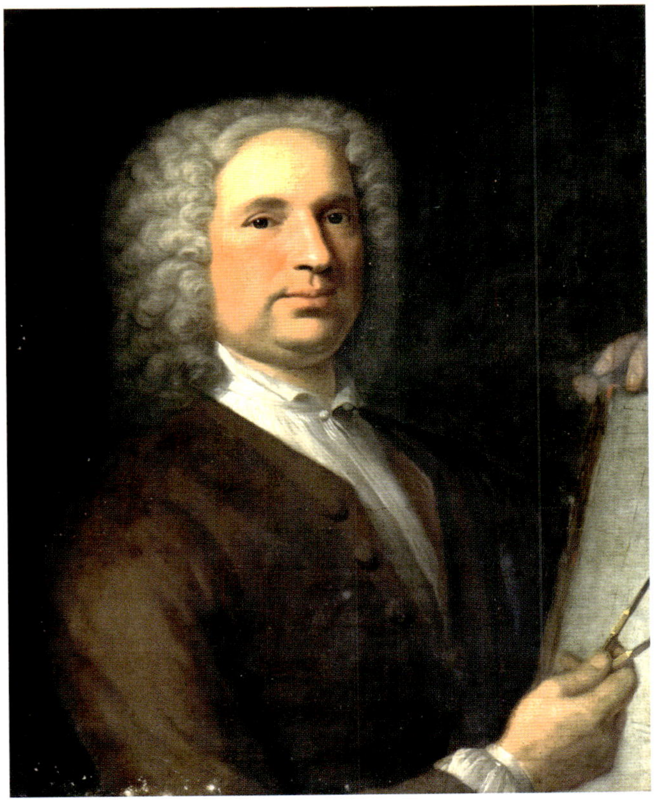
51.

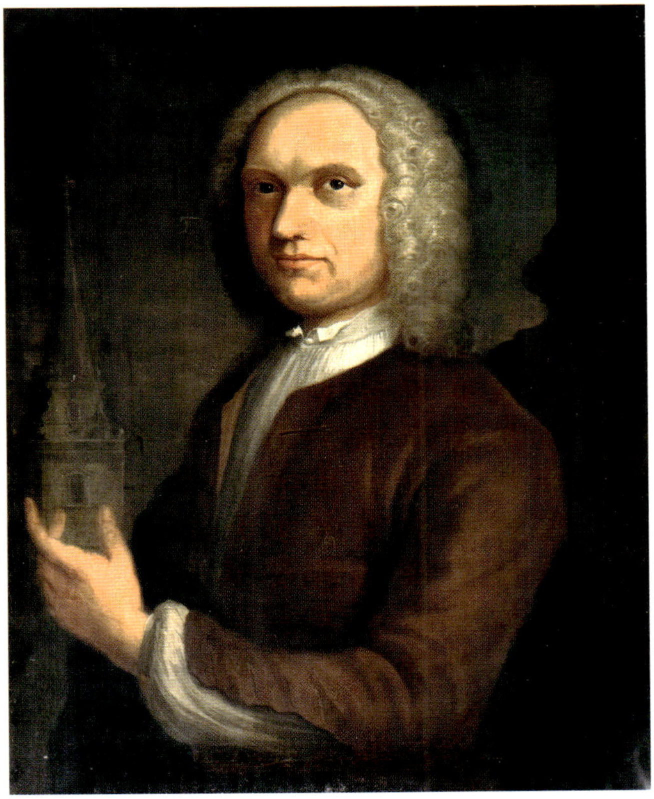
52.

with a large garden and ornamental canal (cat. 47). Though we cannot be wholly certain, the Bastards probably built the west front and staircase at Ranston c. 1750, worked on Whatcombe House 1750, Merly 1752–56, rebuilt the façade of Smedmore 1761, Stepleton c. 1758, Lulworth (from 1727, 1754, 1759, 1761 and 1770–71) as well as additions at Edmondsham, Mapperton and houses in Dorchester such as South Lodge. The Bastards had a hand in various churches such as Charlton Marshall, Almer and Gillingham. Comparatively little is known about their training and contacts, though the brothers consulted with fellow architect John James of Greenwich who stayed with them in Blandford Forum. They also used William Halfpenny's source books.[9] Their hallmark was a capital with inturning volutes from Borromini, also used in the 1720s by Thomas Archer, who lived not far away at Fordingbridge. Other commissions ranged from updating some of the main rooms at Lulworth Castle to providing school desks for Blandford School.[10] Their furniture designs were taken from Gaetano Brunetti's *Sixty Different Sorts of Ornament,* 1731. A monument to John Dirdoe d. 1724 in Gillingham church is signed 'John Bastard & Co.'

The attribution of John's portrait to 'T. Andree,' a protégé of Thornhill's, was made by a great nephew Thomas Horlock Bastard.[11] The timings certainly fit, since the brothers had close contact with Thornhill over a number of years. Another brother Benjamin (1698–1774) worked in Sherborne on the construction of Sherborne House for Henry Portman c. 1720 for which Thornhill painted the staircase hall, and the Bastard brothers worked with Thornhill in the rebuilding of Blandford after the fire. In his portrait John looks forward facing to right. He holds an architectural plan in his left hand and a pair of open dividers/compasses in his right, to demonstrate a distance on the plan. He wears a full grey wig, white shirt closed at the neck and a brown jacket. John Bastard worked as a fire assessor before and after the 1731 fire so was involved with a large number of construction projects. John Bastard drew the plan of Poole for Hutchins's First Edition, 1, p. 1. In 1760 when the rebuilding of Blandford was officially completed, John erected a monument in the form of a portico to the church to commemorate the fire, enclosing a pump. He left money to maintain it as well as £500 to buy South Sea Annuities, the interest of which was to be applied to the education of thirty-five poor children in Blandford.

Perhaps painted several years after his brother's portrait, William looks forward and faces to left, with a column behind on the far right. He wears a full grey wig, white shirt closed at the neck, and brown jacket slashed at the wrists to reveal full sleeves. The business coats in the portraits emphasise their intellectual and artistic position. William was a skilled draughtsman, and Colvin has suggested he points reproachfully at a model, perhaps of the spire he intended for the main church in Blandford.[12] However the spire was never built, Nathaniel Ireson added a cupola instead.

The brothers died unmarried and were buried in a vault in the church they built. Their nephew Thomas Bastard junior, (youngest son of their brother Thomas, d. 1731 soon after the fire, and Mary Horlock) was the last family member to carry on the business, inheriting all the Bastard property and business. He erected an obelisk in the churchyard with his cousin Thomas senior, 'To the Memory of John Bastard aged 82 & of William Bastard aged 77 whose skill in Architecture & Liberal benefactions to this Town well deserves to be Publickly Recorded'.[13]

1 Blandford Forum Borough Council Minutes, 21 October 1890, 'Thomas Horlock Bastard of Charlton Manor presented the Council with portraits of his uncles John and William Bastard'. H. Colvin, 'The Bastards of Blandford Forum, Architects and Master-Builders', *Archaeological Journal*, 104, 1948, p. 191, fn. 50, refers to a MS note by T.H. Bastard in 1881 in the British Museum copy of Hutchins, 'that of John was painted in 1728 and both portraits have lately been restored under the supervision of Mr. T. Armstrong, Director of Art at the Kensington Museum'.

2 The monument to Thomas Bastard d. 1720, in Blandford Forum Church describes him as 'a man useful, and industrious in his generation ... and eminent for his skill in Architecture'.

3 See Isaac Taylor's sketch of Moreton House for what is believed to be an example of Cartwright's work (fig. 5).

4 See P. Legg, 'A Bastard Barometer' *Proceedings of the DNH&AS*, 107, 1985, pp. 1–5. Legg suggests technical details used by the Bastard brothers demonstrated their knowledge of Robert Hooke's *Micrographia*, 1665. See 'The Bastards of Blandford Forum: An Inventory of their Losses in the Fire of 1731', *Furniture History*, 30, 1994.

5 From 1732 until his death in 1734 Thornhill was one of the Commissioners hearing cases resulting from the fire in Blandford Forum, DCRO, B5, Commissioner's Book. Thornhill's design for the new Town Hall is in the Sir John Soane Museum.

6 Oswald, 1935, p. 72.

7 J. Cornforth, 'The Building of Crichel', *Architectural History* vol. 27, 1984, pp. 268–269.

8 Humphrey Sturt (fig. 6) enlarged Crichel after inheriting from his uncle in 1765, employing the Bastard family as builders and James Wyatt as designer between 1772–1780.

9 See transcript of John Bastard's letter to Thompson in D. Beamish, J. Hillier, H. Johnstone, *Mansions and Merchants of Poole and Dorset,* Poole, 1976, pp. 58–62. John James was assistant clerk of works at Greenwich between 1705–1718.

10 DHC, DCRO, B5, Corporation Memorandum Book, 1733–1822, 21/8/57.

11 A later inscription by T.H. Bastard, was added to the painting *painted 1728 by T. Andree of poland, historical painter,* together with J. Bastard's birth details. There is a reference to 'Signior Andrea' in Hutchins's *History*, 3rd edition, vol. 2, p. 463, relating to the sale of Thornhill's art collection purchased by the Duke of Bedford for his Gallery. See 'Sir James Thornhill's Collection : A Postscript', *The Burlington Magazine,* 83, August, 1943, p. 207.

12 See the Bastard drawing *The New Church At Blandford Forum Dorset,* Bodleian Library, M.S Gough Maps 6, f.43v. Spetisbury Rectory was attributed to the Bastard's father Thomas, rebuilt for Dr Sloper in 1716.

13 Thomas Bastard snr. was the son of John and William's brother Samuel and Thomas Bastard jnr., son of their brother Thomas, who died in 1731. He left all the Bastard wealth and possessions to his son Thomas Horlock Bastard who was consequently able to assume the status of a gentleman, residing both at Charlton Marshall and Blandford Forum. He was High Sheriff for Dorset in 1812 and very friendly with his neighbour the Reverend Thomas Rackett (cat. 43), with whom he undertook local antiquarian excavations.

53. **Thomas Beach** (1738–1806)

Henry Seymer (1714–1785)
oil on canvas, c. 1788–1800
75×61 cm
Signed *T Beach p*

Provenance: Donated by Aylmer Bourke Lambert, 1761–1842, to the Linnean Society, 1802.

The Linnean Society of London

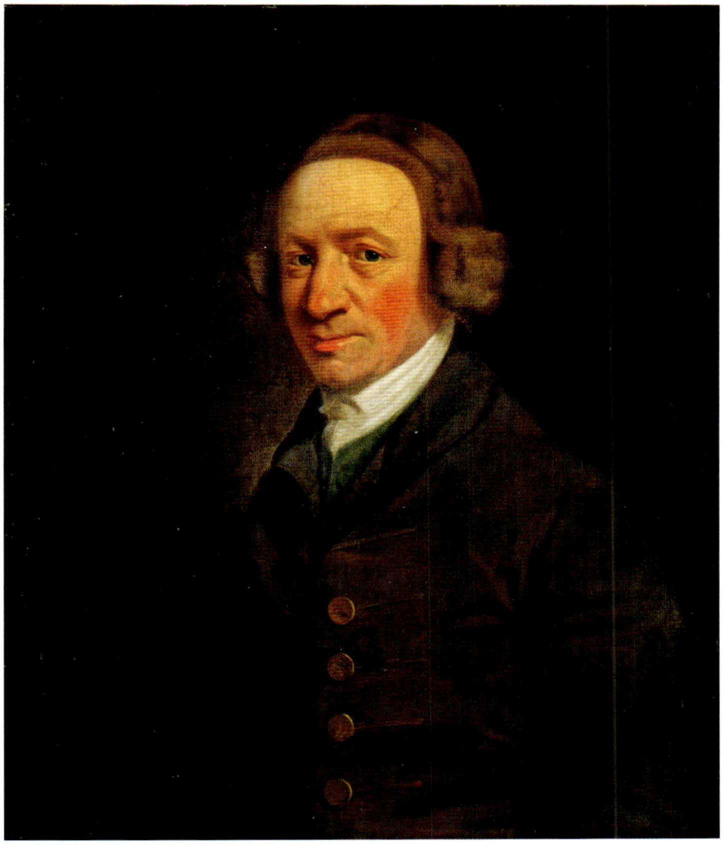

Henry Seymer was a naturalist and amateur butterfly painter with an extensive range of interests, in botany, exotic natural history, mineralogy, fossils, molluscs and entomology. Between 1755 and 1783 he created a remarkable set of butterfly paintings, (fig. 44) many from exotic locations such as India, Jamaica and importantly Java, and was joined in this enterprise by his son Henry Seymer junior (1745–1800) from 1772.[1] These paintings were done for personal interest and many of them remained with the family until the 1990s, when they were sold.[2]

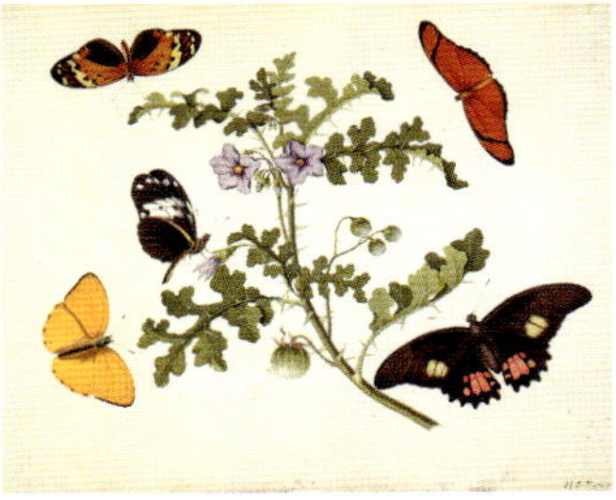

Fig. 44. *Five South American butterflies,* Henry Seymer, 1765.

Although Seymer was never a member of any learned society, he had a wide circle of like-minded friends and maintained an extensive correspondence with fellow naturalists. He also employed agents to send him exotic specimens from overseas. Between 1770–75 he exchanged and purchased insects through the important entomologist Dru Drury. At his country seat of Hanford, near Blandford Forum (fig. 45), Seymer developed a famous and extensive garden of exotic plants. He maintained a close circle of local friends including Peter Beckford (cat. 22) whose daughter Frances married Henry Seymer junior. Seymer was also closely associated with a group of neighbours who all sat to Thomas Beach, including the Reverend William Chafin (fig. 9) with whom he hunted, Henry Portman and Richard Pulteney (cat. 54). The Reverend Thomas Rackett (cat. 43), was also a close friend of his son.

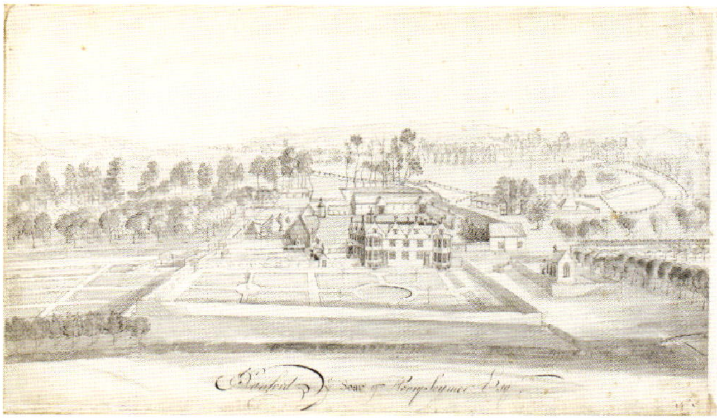

Fig. 45. *Hanford Seat of Henry Seymer Esq,* pen and ink and watercolour on paper, Thomas Robins, 1747–1770.

Beach knew the Seymer family well over a period of thirty years. Henry Seymer's diary for 1765 first mentions Beach in February 1765, with a reference to Beach's colourman Charles Sandys of Long Acre.[3] Beach stayed at Hanford from 16 August 1765 when Henry Seymer junior sat to him. On 31 August 1765 Beach began the portrait of Henry senior, aged 51, and his 18-year old daughter Bridget. The Linnean portrait is probably a copy of Beach's portrait of Henry senior, started on 31 August 1765, copied for Aylmer Bourke Lambert at the end of the century. If this copy was indeed painted by Beach it may date to 1788, the year he was in Blandford painting the portrait of Richard Pulteney. Lambert, a botanist much influenced by Seymer, presented the portrait to the Linnean Society in memory of Seymer who died three years before the Society was formed. The copy has not stood the test of time with thin paint resulting in the bare canvas showing; furthermore since the original is not known a comparison cannot be made.[4]

The half-length portrait, unsigned, shows Henry Seymer looking to left. He stands against a dark background and looks out of the picture space toward the viewer, wearing a brown wig and has a ruddy complexion. His brown coat has indistinctly marked gold buttons over a turquoise waistcoat and white stock.

Beach was at Hanford again in 1798 when his diary records him staying with Seymer junior for the whole of July when Mrs Seymer also sat. At the same time he immediately started work on a second version of Mrs Seymer's portrait for another member of the family, Mr Ker. Beach's diary for January 1798 records Seymer junior sitting for Beach in Bath. It is possible that Beach worked on the second Seymer copy on that visit, but since it is not recorded in his diary it is more likely to have been on another occasion. 1799 was the last year Beach is known to have had any commissions, after which he only produced two self-portraits in 1801 and 1802. So given the date of the presentation to the Linnean Society it is possible this was a late production by Beach.

1 See R.I Vane-Wright & H.W.D. Hughes, *The Seymer Legacy. Henry Seymer and Henry Seymer Junior of Dorset, and their entomological paintings, with a catalogue of Butterflies and Plants* (1755–1783), Ceredigion, 2005.
2 A number of the butterfly paintings were disposed of at a far earlier date.
3 I am indebted to Dr Dick Vane-Wright's assistance using his transcription of the diaries of Henry Seymer senior and junior, which remain with indirect descendants of the family.
4 The portraits are probably in the possession of indirect descendants of the family.

54. **Thomas Beach** (1738–1806)

Richard Pulteney, M.D. (1730–1801)
oil on canvas, 1788
74.5×62 cm
Provenance: Sitter; gift from Mrs Richard Pulteney to the Linnean Society, 1811.

The Linnean Society of London

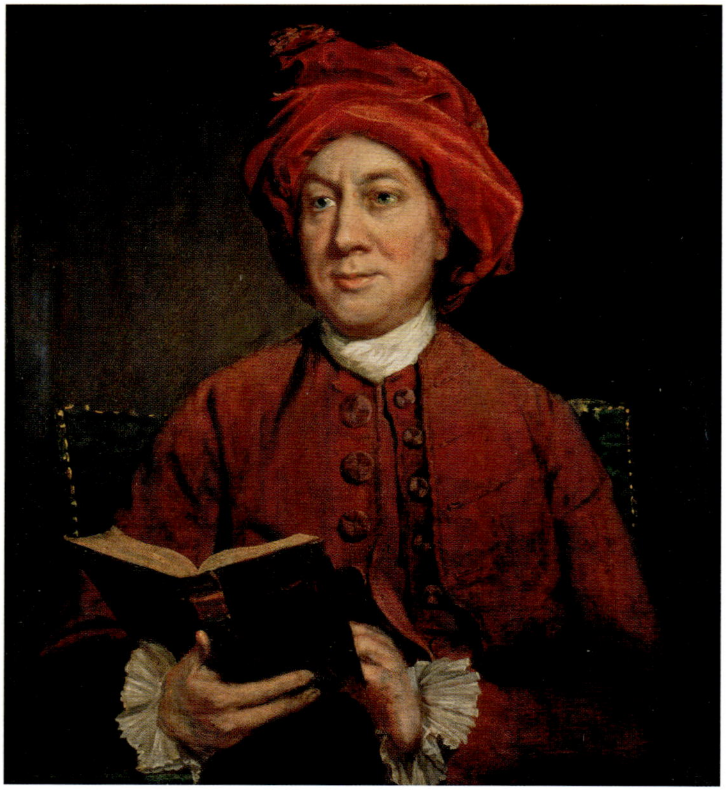

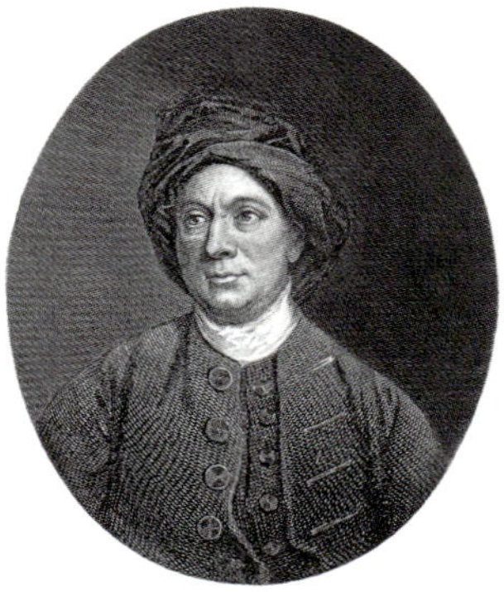

Fig. 46. *Dr Richard Pulteney*, after Thomas Beach, engraved by James Basire,

Son of a Leicestershire dissenter tailor, the botanist and physician Richard Pulteney was a pioneering author of local flora in Leicestershire and Dorset. Qualifying as a doctor in Edinburgh in 1764, he was appointed domestic physician to a relative, William Pulteney, 1st Earl of Bath. The Earl's sudden death forced Pulteney to seek a new position, arriving somewhat reluctantly in Blandford Forum in 1765. Despite an initial struggle for recognition he remained there for the rest of his life, pursuing his deep interest in local botany with the first systematic study of Dorset flora. In 1779 he married bluestocking Elizabeth Galton, from an old Dorset family, who was an artist and extensive correspondent.[1] As Blandford Forum's physician, Pulteney lived first at Coupar House, built by Nathaniel Ireson and the Bastard brothers, and later nearby at Langton Long, Blandford Forum.

Between 1750–1801 Pulteney contributed a number of articles on botany, medicine and archaeology to the *Gentleman's Magazine.*[2] The Reverend Thomas Rackett (cat. 43) and Pulteney collaborated on the important *Catalogue of the Birds, Shells and more rare Plants of Dorsetshire,* for the second edition of Hutchins's *History,* for which a cousin of Pulteney's wife, Mary Foster, provided the plates. Close neighbours, Pulteney was a key influence on Rackett over a number of years, see (fig. 47).

Devoted to the Linnean taxonomic system of natural history, Pulteney wrote *A General View of the Life and Writings of Linnaeus,* in 1781, including Carl Linnaeus's first biography in English and *Historical and Biographical Sketches of the progress of Botany in England,* 2 vols, London, 1790. Through his extensive correspondence with physicians and botanists, Pulteney maintained a network of highly important natural history contacts in Britain and Europe, meriting his description as a true enlightenment figure.[3]

Pulteney advised Daniel Solander on the Duchess of Portland's important collection.[4] He was a contributor and member of a number of learned societies including the Royal Society 1762, Royal Medical Society of Edinburgh 1782, Bath Philosophical Society, and Linnean Society of London from 1790.

Thomas Beach knew Richard Pulteney over a long period and they shared the same circle of associates. In 1788 Beach painted two half-lengths of Pulteney seated and holding a book, in one he is wearing a wig, and

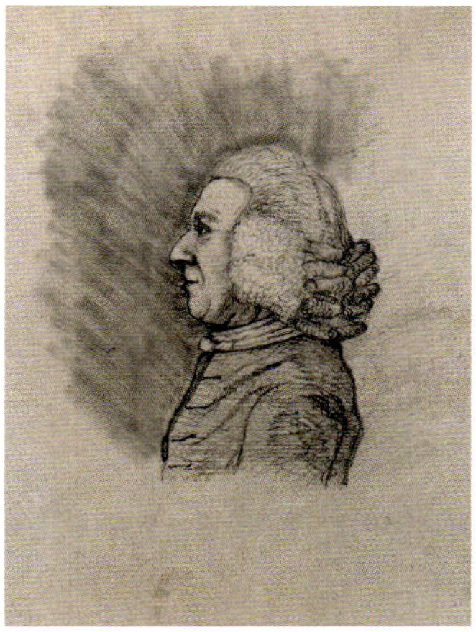

Fig. 47. *Dr Richard Pulteney*, pencil on paper, Thomas Rackett, 1780–1800.

here, a red turban.[5] In this portrait Pulteney is seated in a green patterned chair looking slightly to left, against a dark background. He wears a red coat and waistcoat with matching silk buttons, a white stock, white pleated cuffs. His red velvet turban signifies Pulteney as a man of learning, reinforced by the open book he holds. The portrait differs from many of Beach's works. He has not set the sitter in his more typical feigned oval and it is freer in style than many of his commissions. Both Beach's versions were engraved, (fig. 46).[6]

Pulteney's collections and extensive correspondence were left to the Linnean Society, together with stocks worth £200 in 1802. His wife placed a memorial tablet to him in Blandford Forum church engraved with a sprig of *Pultenaea stipularis*, an Australian shrub named by J. E. Smith in his honour.

1 Related to the Galpines and St. Barbes. Richard Pulteney also knew the bluestocking, Mrs. Montagu.
2 Pulteney contributed some 26 articles mainly on a range of botanical subjects and on the writings of Linnaeus.
3 See Royal Society of Physicians, William George Maton's collection of memorials of Richard Pulteney, MS-MATOW/441, lists likenesses and other material.
4 D. Landry, 'Green Languages? Women Poets as Naturalists in 1653 and 1807', *The Huntington Library Quarterly*, 63, No. 4, Forging Connections: Women's Poetry from the Renaissance to Romanticism, 2000, pp. 467–489
5 Another version: Leicester City Art Gallery, signed and dated 1788; stipple by P. Roberts, engraving (after T. Beach, 1788), 1805. See Waterhouse, 1981, 2, p. 44.
6 Engraving by J. Basire, 1804 (after T. Beach, 1788). See J. Nichols's, 8, p. 196 for Basire's engraving.

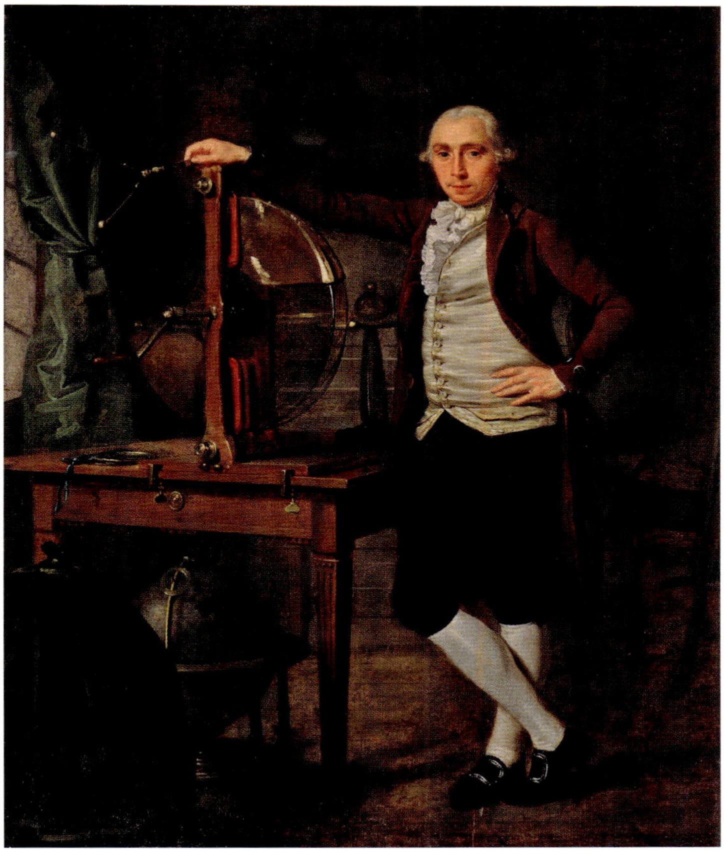

55. **Artist unknown**

Tiberius Maria Francesco Gaetano Vincenzo Cavallo (1749–1809)
oil on oak panel, c. 1785–90
59.1×48.9 cm

Provenance: Christie's sale, 1904, as Humphry Davy; NPG Purchase from George H. Gabb, 1905.

Literature: John Ingamells, *Mid-Georgian Portraits, 1760–1790,* NPG, pp. 95–96
F. Gordon Roe, 'Forgotten Group of Profilists,' *Apollo*, 22, 1935 pp. 287–289.[1]

National Portrait Gallery

Born in Naples the son of a physician, Tiberius Cavallo came to London in 1771.[2] A natural philosopher, chemist, musician and mathematician he associated with fellow scientists, attracting interest through his electrical experiments.[3] By 1779 he was a Fellow of the Royal Society, supported by Dr Daniel Solander, and other distinguished scientists. He pioneered electro-therapeutics, worked on medical uses of electricity and, from 1782, gave the Bakerian lectures at the Royal Society on his research into electricity. With Peter Beckford's (cat. 22) protégé, the virtuoso keyboard player and composer Muzio Clementi, Broadwood employed Cavallo's acoustical expertise to improve piano design.[4]

Cavallo published treatises on electricity and magnetism in 1786 and 1787; he worked on refrigeration; his work on hydrogen resulted in experimenting with flight, influencing pioneer balloonist Jean-Pierre Blanchard; and was the first to use the term 'soda water'.[5] Cavallo spent time at Windsor Castle, collaborating with royal physician, Dr James Lind, producing portraits in silhouette using the print process they invented.[6] A keen astronomer Cavallo appeared in Paul Sandby's image standing on the terrace at Windsor Castle with Lind, Dr Lockman and Thomas Sandby, observing a meteor at night tracking across the sky in August 1783.[7]

Cavallo and the Reverend Thomas Rackett (cat. 43) were close friends for over thirty years; and Cavallo spent prolonged periods at Spetisbury.[8] Inspired by their mutual friend William Herschel, Cavallo and

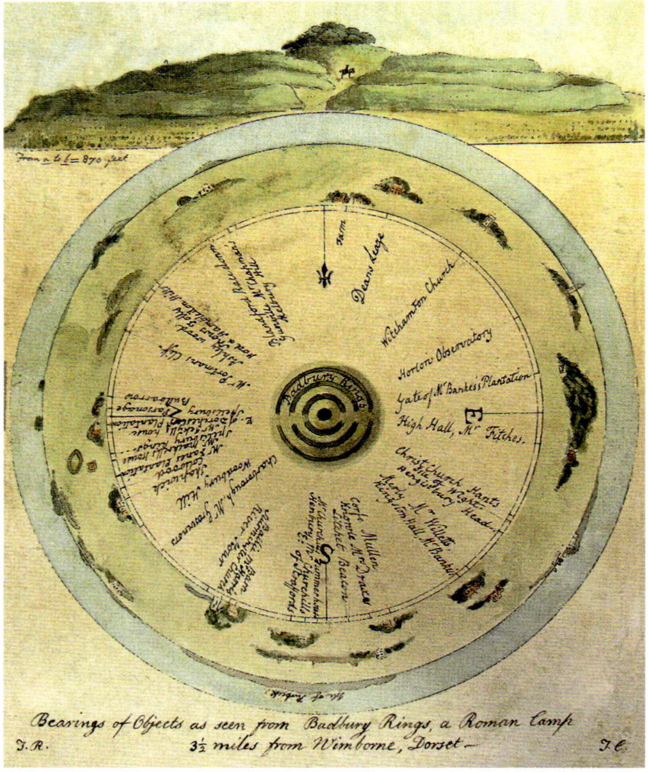

Fig. 48. *Bearings of Objects as seen from Badbury Rings,* later appeared in Hutchins ed. 2, 2, p. 526, Thomas Rackett and Tiberius Cavallo.

Rackett studied the skies through a telescope and laid down a meridian line in the pavement of the rectory forecourt at Spetisbury.[9] They were co-authors of a detailed plan showing churches, houses and land, including the named owners, mainly Rackett's neighbours, as viewed from the top of Badbury Rings (fig. 48), the iron age hill fort on the estate of Rackett's close friend Henry Bankes (cat. 25) at Kingston Lacy.[10]

Cavallo was therefore an important member of the Dorset intellectual circle. Rackett kitted out rooms at Spetisbury parsonage for Cavallo's experiments; perhaps the location of the panelled room in this portrait of Cavallo. Initially thought to show Humphry Davy, it was also wrongly attributed to Zoffany.[11] Cavallo is shown standing and leaning against the twin-plate frictional electrical machine he invented in 1770.[12] This is clamped to a table with an astronomical globe underneath, next to the Leyden jar used to store electricity. Behind him on the far right an artist's easel and palette rest against the chair. The presence of these artist's materials is significant and may be intended to give a clue to the artist. Most of Rackett and Cavallo's circle were amateur artists, and whilst this could be the work of Rackett, it is more likely to be a self-portrait.

Cavallo published numerous works on different branches of physics.[13] At his death Cavallo left Thomas Rackett, as his executor, the unenviable task of finding an inheritor, at a time when contact with the continent was not straightforward due to the Napoleonic wars.

1 See too W. Hackman, *Electricity from Glass; the History of the Frictional Electrical Machine 1600–1850,* Alphen aan den Rijn, 1978.

2 G. Castellano di S. Sergio, 'Tiberius Cavallo', *Rivista Aeronatica,* Rome, July, 1937. In Naples Cavallo studied English with an Irish monk from the Covent of St Augustin.

3 Cavallo and his colleagues, like Abraham Bennet who invented the gold-leaf electroscope, were closely associated with the Lunar Society, exchanged and shared ideas. Alessandro Volta acknowledged Cavallo's influence on his work on electricity.

4 See D. Wainwright, *Broadwood by Appointment: A History,* London, 1982, p. 72. In April 1788 Cavallo read a paper at the Royal Society 'Of the temperament of those musical instruments in which the Tones, Keys or Frets are fixed, as in the Harpsichord, organ, Guitar, &c'.

5 Erasmus Darwin of the Lunar Society referred to Cavallo's book on magnetism and investigated Cavallo's claim that inflammable air caused magnetism using the mangetometer. Cavallo also claimed iron filings increased their magnetic attractions by effervescence with diluted hydrochloride acid and tested the degree to which chemical changes induced by heat could affect electric or magnetic forces.

6 See letters in British Library, Add 22897 – 22898, Cavallo to Lind, 1782–1809. Cavallo was at Windsor with his friend Dr. Lind who was a scientist and physician to the royal family. Cavallo invented the multiplier in 1795, used for the amplification of small electric charges, making them observable and measurable in an electroscope.

7 British Museum, 1904,0819.427, 1865,0610.1253, Thomas and Paul Sandby, drawing and aquatint.

8 DHC, Rackett Archive, D/RAC/140, Dorothea Rackett's diary of 1801 reveals Cavallo's closeness with the family. D/RAC/149, on his death Rackett observed, 'he was in the habit of passing so much time with us both here and at Spetisbury that he appeared like one of the family'.

9 They were inspired by the astronomical work of William Herschel and his sister Caroline. Herschel achieved fame building a 48-inch telescope and discovering the planet Uranus in 1781.

10 The plan was engraved for the second and third editions of Hutchins, see 3rd ed., 3, p. 176.

11 NPG registered packet 1412.

12 The machine is an uninsulated twin plate machine. The prime conductor was made to touch a Leyden jar for medical electricity when necessary. Eight leather cushions supported by the frame put pressure against the plates with a pressure regulating mechanism. Each plate was rubbed by 2 upper and 2 lower cushions. The base is shown clamped to the table.

13 Cavallo contributed to the *Philosophical Transactions* of the Royal Society and wrote a number of treatises including *A Complete Treatise on Electricity* (1777); *History and Practice of Aerostation* (1785); *An Essay on the Theory and Practice of Medical Electricity,* 1781 dedicated to the Earl of Bute. On 20 June 1782 Cavallo also presented a note to the Royal Society describing successful experiments with hydrogen-inflated soap bubbles.

56. **Jonathan Richardson** (c. 1665–1745)

Sir James Thornhill, Kt. (c. 1675–1734)
oil on canvas, c. 1733
76.2×63.5 cm

Provenance: NPG, 1955 purchase from Brig H.D.K. Money of Omagh, by descent from John Douglas (1721–1807), Bishop of Salisbury and Chancellor of the Garter.
Reference: National Portrait Gallery, *Later Stuart Portraits 1685–1714,* John Ingamells, NPG London, 2009, pp. 286–287; David Piper, *Catalogue of 17th century portraits in the National Portrait Gallery,* Cambridge, 1963, pp. 342–43

National Portrait Gallery

Born at Melcombe Regis, Thornhill was apprenticed for seven years to his relation Thomas Highmore, the King's Serjeant-Painter. He worked with the Italian

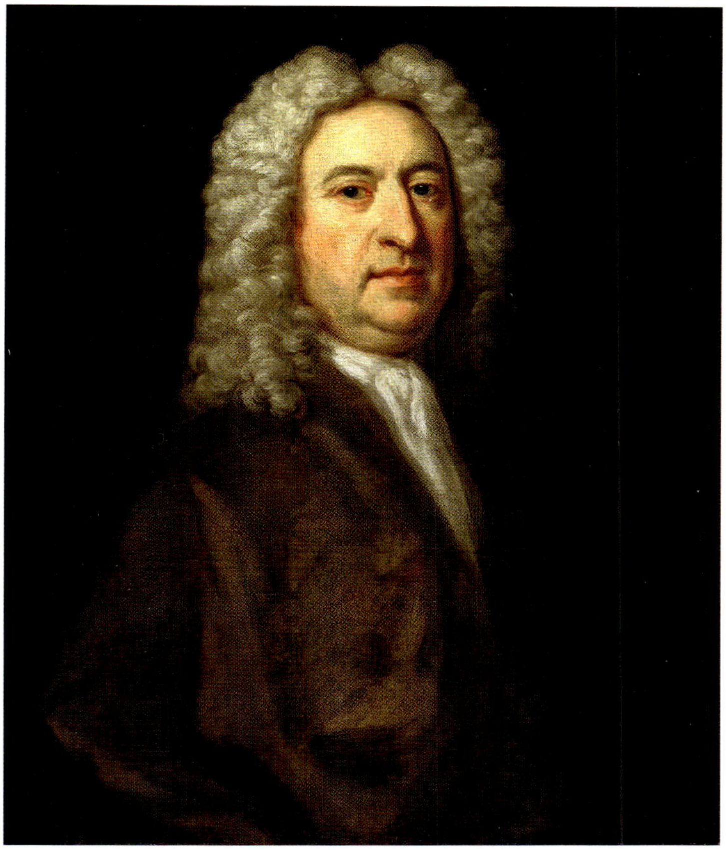

painter Antonio Verrio at Hampton Court and became a freeman of the Worshipful Company of Painter Stainers in 1703. Four years later he began work on the hall at Greenwich Hospital, his principal commission for the next twenty years.[1]

The major British decorative history painter of the early eighteenth century, Thornhill was the first British artist to be knighted. Working during a period of immense political flux, his large-scale commissions of classical, historical and religious subjects were frequently dependant on politicking and positioning, often in the face of foreign competition. Appointed History-Painter-in-Ordinary to the King in 1718, he had the responsibility of overseeing the decoration of royal residences, the Greenwich commission and, between 1716–19, scenes from the life of St Paul in the cupola of St Paul's Cathedral.

In the 1720s the taste for large-scale decorative schemes went into decline and at the end of his career Thornhill had to rely on Dorset patrons. In 1718 he decorated the stairway and ceiling at Charborough Park with the *Judgement of Paris* for Thomas Erle.[2] He also worked at Eastbury for Bubb Dodington, his political sponsor. Dodington was undoubtedly instrumental in encouraging Thornhill to enter Weymouth politics, and in 1721 he was granted the Freedom of the town. In gratitude Thornhill painted the Royal coat of arms (fig. 23) for the town, and an altarpiece, *The Last Supper,* for St Mary's Church, Melcombe Regis. He also built an almshouse for distressed mariners at his expense, a strategy ensuring his election as Whig MP for Melcombe Regis. As his political aspirations increased, his artistic ones seemingly waned. In 1732 he was appointed a Commissioner assessing claims for the rebuilding of Blandford after the disastrous fire and working with the Bastard brothers (cats. 51, 52) he also produced an early design for a new Town Hall there (Sir John Soane Museum).

Thornhill built a house at his family's former estate, Thornhill near Stalbridge, between 1720 and 1725 incorporating a long picture gallery for his collection of Old Master paintings.[3] He spent his last years as a country gentleman, visited by fellow artists such as portrait painter Jonathan Richardson who visited Thornhill between July and August 1733.[4] Friends since 1719, Thornhill and Richardson shared an interest in art theory and the conviction that native English painters could develop an English school of painting.[5] By the time of Richardson's visit to Dorset Thornhill was visibly ailing. Of his death in 1734 Walpole wrote *'affected with the gout and his leg swelling, he set out for his seat at Thornhill near Weymouth, where four days after his arrival he expired in his chair, May 4, 1734, aged fifty-seven.'*[6] Thornhill was buried in nearby Stalbridge church; his widow inherited the Dorset house though she finally lived with her daughter Jane and son-in-law William Hogarth.[7]

By the time Thornhill died his work was out of fashion. Less than fifty years later, when Hutchins was trying to write an account of the artist's life in Dorset he found direct information scarce. In 1767 Hutchins approached Horace Walpole for biographical detail but was informed, 'Sir, in the autumn I turned over Vertue's MSS to see if I could find anything satisfactory for you relating to Sir James Thornhill but indeed I could not. There is nothing, but some few notices relating to his works, the principal of which were the cupola of St. Paul's and his paintings at Greenwich. I believe it would be your best way to apply to his daughter Mrs Hogarth, widow of the famous painter. I believe she still lives at the Golden Head in Leicester Fields. To be sure she would be glad to contribute to the illustration of her father's memory. etc. PS. I shall immediately send and subscribe, Sir, to your work.'[8]. Walpole did indeed subscribe to Hutchins, but his lukewarm view of Thornhill was clear, 'He had some merit, and we have few good painters; but surely Sir James was not one of the first class!'

Richardson's head and shoulders portrait of Thornhill shows him half right looking directly at the viewer. The sitter wears a long curling wig, white stock and brown gown. Painted towards the end of Thornhill's life, the portrait undoubtedly resulted from

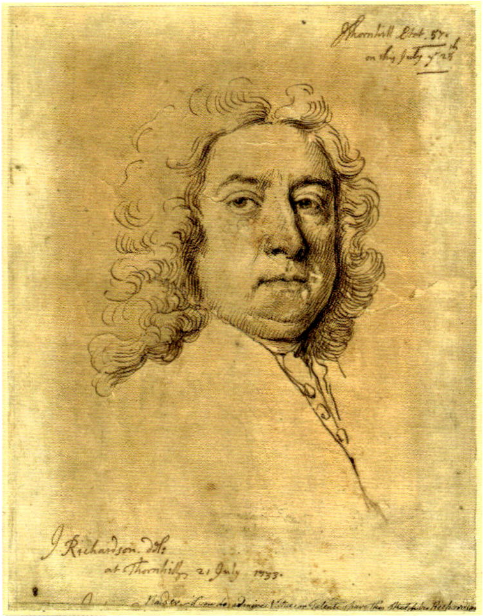

Fig. 49. *Sir James Thornhill,* pen and brown ink on oiled paper, Jonathan Richardson, 1733.

Richardson's Dorset visit. The sketchy treatment of the draperies suggests the portrait was unfinished and that Richardson was working over a previously used canvas since an upside-down image of an unknown face is clearly visible coming through Thornhill's robes on his right. This further confirms the portrait was never finished. Richardson was known to draw portraits of himself and his close friends, an activity he pursued with Thornhill in July 1733 since several of his sketches of Thornhill exist (fig. 49).[9] He gave one of them to Thornhill, which was subsequently owned by Thornhill's son-in-law Hogarth, and two drawings relating to the visit are in the British Museum.[10]

1 See J. Brocklebank, *Sir James Thornhill of Dorset, 1675–1734, Tercentenary Exhibition,* DNHAS, (Dorset County Museum, Dorchester), 1975, for biographical details.

2 Christopher Pitt of Blandford dedicated a poem to Thornhill's Charborough commission, *To Sir James Thornhill, on his excellent Painting the Rape of Helen, at the Seat of General Erle in Dorsetshire',* 1718. Thornhill's other Dorset commissions included Minterne for the Churchills and Sherborne House for Henry Seymour Portman.

3 See Gawen Hamilton's *Sir James Thornhill Showing his Poussin to his Friends,* 1720, Beaverbrook Art Gallery, New Brunswick.

4 George Vertue claimed Hudson 'learnt of' the London artist Jonathan Richardson (Vertue, *Note books,* 3.66) and married Richardson's daughter Mary by 1725. Until Richardson's retirement in 1740, Hudson painted mainly Tory sitter's portraits in Devon and Bath, developing a chain of patronage through connections with Tory politicians. Hudson's success attracted such apprentices as Joshua Reynolds, Joseph Wright of Derby and John Hamilton Mortimer.

5 J. Richardson, *'Essay on the Theory of Painting,* London, 1715, p. 12.

6 H. Walpole, *Anecdotes of Painting in England,* London, 1782, 4, p. 46.

7 It is likely that Hogarth visited Dorset to stay with his brother-in-law John Thornhill where he painted the portrait of *Thomas Coombs,* Dorset boatman (cat. 62).

8 Ed. W. Lewis, *The Correspondence of Horace Walpole,* 1, p. 334, Lewis Walpole Library, Connecticut, Horace Walpole to John Hutchins, from Arlington Street, 17th February 1767. Walpole sent Hutchins a draft of his entry on Thornhill for inclusion in the 4th vol. of his *Anecdotes.* See too Hutchins, ed. 3, 4, pp. 461–463.

9 C. Gibson-Wood, *Jonathan Richardson: Art Theorist of the Enlightenment,* 2000, New Haven and London, pp. 75–76.

10 *Sir James Thornhill,* Jonathan Richardson, 1733, pen and brown ink on oiled paper, inscribed by the artist : *J. Thornhill aetat 57 on this July ye 25th. J. Richardson del: at Thornhill, 21 July 1733.* Another hand has written, apparently repeating an inscription by the artist which has been cut off: *Reader, if you do admire Virtue or Talents spare this sketch by Richardson. Sir James Thornhill,* Jonathan Richardson, 1733, graphite on vellum, wearing night-cap, dressing-gown open in front, and shirt buttoned at the throat, inscribed on the back: *Aug 1, 1733, done at Thornhill in Dorset.* Both sketches were exhibited in the Tercentenary Exhibition *Sir James Thornhill 1675–1743* at the Dorset County Museum, 1975.

57. **Thomas Beach** (1738–1806)

Self-Portrait
oil on canvas, 1801
73.6×60.9 cm
Inscription. Lower left in oval *T Beach. Painted by himself. 1801.*

Provenance: Sitter, then by descent
Exhibition: Royal Academy British Art Exhibition, 1934 (352).
Literature, Beach, 1934, p. 54, No. 8 ; M. Green, *Eighteenth Century Architecture of Bath,* London, 1904, p. 226.

Private Collection

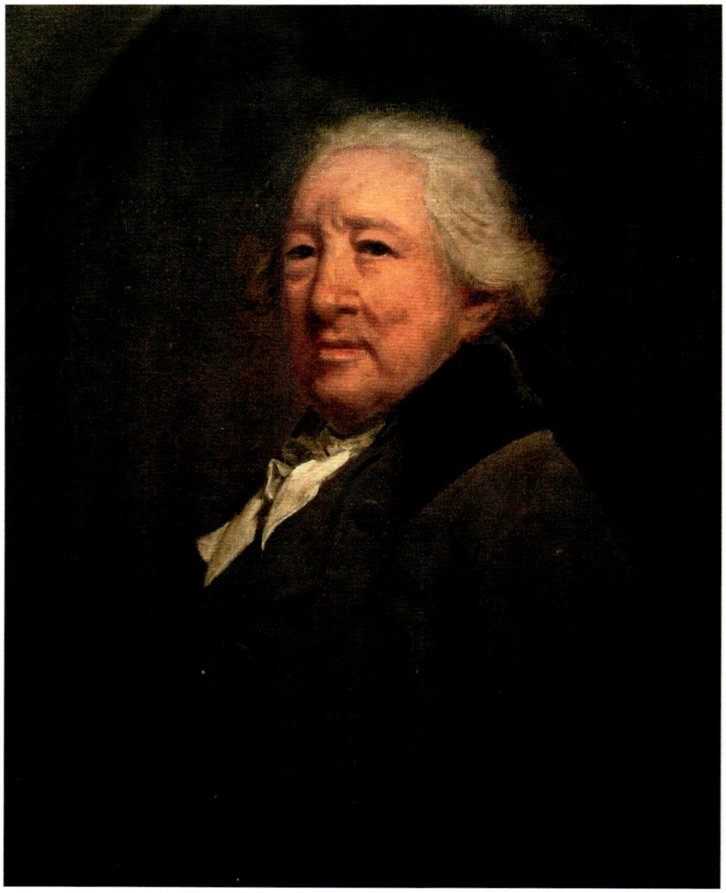

This head and shoulders self-portrait possibly painted in Dorchester, shows Thomas Beach aged 63 years. One of four known self-portraits, it was painted by Beach during the last five years of his life and may be his penultimate portrait. Only his self-portrait of 1802 (NPG) was painted afterwards and it is thought unlikely that he painted at all after 1802. Beach has placed himself in his typical device of a painted oval. He is facing to left and looking to the front to meet the gaze of the viewer. He wears his own white hair, brown everyday coat with brown buttons, velvet collar and a white stock. Though the portrait is relatively simple it is sensitively handled, revealing a man with a kindly, intelligent face. We know from Beach's 1798 diary that he became ill as the year progressed, which is perhaps revealed in the face.

58. **After Giles Hussey** (1710–1788)

Self-Portrait
Stipple engraving, 1773
30×22.5 cm
Inscribed: *Giles Hussey. Esq. ÆTAT LXIII. From a copy of an original drawing by himself in the Possession of T. Weld Esq.*

Private Collection

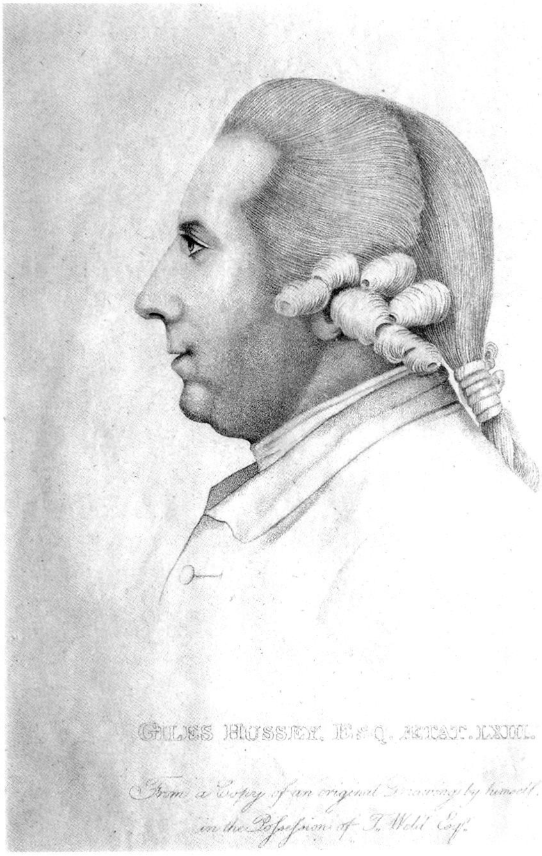

Giles Hussey was the sixth son of John Hussey of Nash Court, Marnhull, from a Roman Catholic Dorset family of landowners and farmers.[1] Educated at Catholic colleges on the continent, on his return to England in 1727 he became apprenticed to the portraitist Jonathan Richardson (cat. 56).[2] Hussey left within a month, to begin work with the Venetian history painter Vincenzo Damini, executing with Damini a fresco of Saints in Lincoln Cathedral. Hussey and Damini then travelled to Italy where in Bologna Hussey studied drawing, composition and design and copied Old Master paintings. In Rome Hussey moved in the Jacobite circle of the exiled James Francis Stuart and his son Charles Edward, then resident in the Palazzo Muti where both sat to Hussey.[3] Over a twelve-year period Hussey repeated their portraits in oils, pencil, red chalk, ink and coloured washes, selling them to British clients.[4] Though this association with the exiled Jacobite court provided Hussey with a steady income it may have compromised his reputation in England.

After his father's death in 1737 Giles returned to Dorset. His main patron during this period was Hugh Smithson, later 1st Duke of Northumberland.[5] Hussey returned to London by 1742, promoting himself in London as a neo-classical history painter. Potentially vulnerable through his Jacobite associations in Rome, Hussey vacated his London studio during the Jacobite Rebellion of 1745, when his movements become unclear. Late in 1745 he was offered membership of the Spalding Gentlemen's Society, confirmed by election to the Society that December. Early in 1746 he was listed there as: *Gyles Hussey History Painter Dorchr,* the last reference to him in the Society's records.[6]
After the failure of the Jacobite rebellion Hussey returned to London in 1748, still maintaining links with Rome through patrons including Matthew Duane.[7] Hussey preferred pursuing his obsession with theories of beauty, rather than painting portraits for his living. He criticised the incorrect proportions of antique statuary, applying his formulas with triangles and trigonometry. This resulted in Hussey being mocked by William Hogarth in his *Analysis of Beauty,* perhaps somewhat unfairly since the engravings supporting Hussey's theories were produced by John Vardy in reverse which wrongly exaggerated his theory. Nonetheless this public act probably destroyed Hussey's London reputation.[8] By 1768 a disappointed Hussey, described by Whitley as 'solitary and mysterious', felt he was the victim of a whispering campaign and finally abandoned London for Dorset.[9]

On inheriting the family estate in 1773, Hussey received local commissions to draw portraits of distinguished, principally Catholic families in the West Country, including the Arundells of Wardour and the Weld family of Lulworth.[10] Between the early 1770s and 1785 Hussey produced a number of profile drawings for Thomas Weld showing his family, relations and friends of which at least twenty-four are still identifiable.[11] Hussey pursued his theory that principles of harmony prevail through nature and therefore in art; that the human face is in harmony with itself, resulting in profile portraits drawn as if on the musical scale (fig. 50).

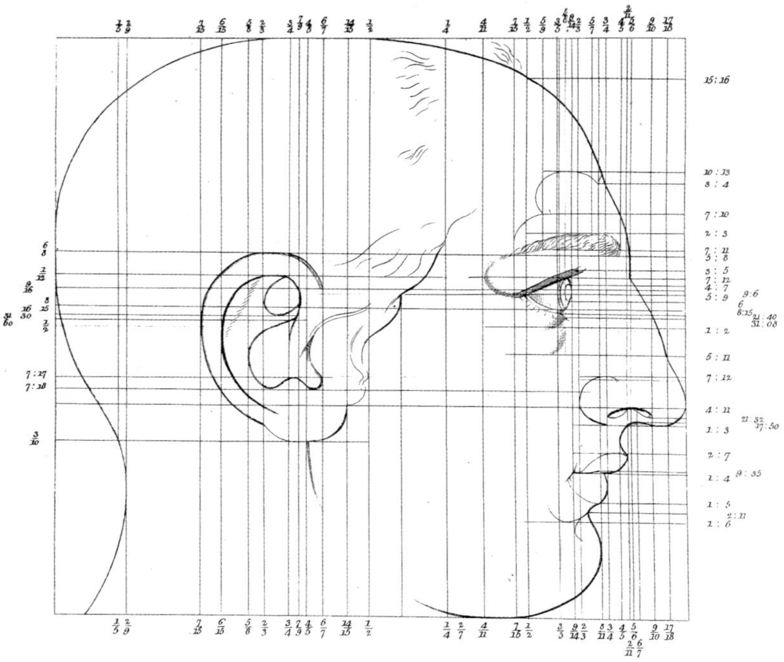

Fig. 50. *Profile head defined using a harmonic scale,* after Giles Hussey, Hutchins, ed. 2, 4, p.157.

In 1779 Hussey wrote to a Dorset neighbour, 'the order of nature in harmonical progression of numbers becomes the rule of art, from which we cannot deviate without error, and consequent reproof'.[12] This led to the distinctive qualities of his instantly recognisable faces as he forced head and shoulder portraits into his tightly conceived formula, described in detail by Hutchins.[13] Thomas Weld also owned drawings by Hussey after the antique and commissioned him to produce a drawing of Lulworth Castle, engraved by James Basire in 1774, for inclusion in Hutchins.[14] This was undoubtedly at the request of local physician Dr William Cuming, whose portrait belonged to Thomas Weld, and who used his role as local physician to encourage landowners to donate plates of their houses to Hutchins.[15] Hussey corresponded with Lord Arundell about the movement for Catholic Emancipation and with Lord Petre, who lobbied for the relief of the Penal Laws against the Catholics.[16] Hussey never married, and from 1782 was managing the estate on his own.

The portrait stipple engraving after Giles Hussey of 1773 is taken from his self-portrait drawing aged 63, from the collection of Thomas Weld. The portrait dates from the year Hussey inherited the family estate, and its inclusion in the Weld portfolio demonstrates his importance to Thomas Weld. Applying his theories of harmony to the portrait, he has adapted the self-portrait to position himself in profile facing left wearing a wig and queue, and coat. In the autumn of 1787 he departed for Devon to be cared for by his nephew and heir John Hussey, where he continued working on the symbolism of numbers, sketching and drawing botanical subjects and calculating equations relating to the science of cultivation. He died there following a stroke in June 1788.

1 There is a comprehensive account of Hussey in the second and third editions of Hutchins. See too John Britton, *The Beauties of Wiltshire,* 1801, 1, pp. 287–303.

2 Jonathan Richardson offers a link between Thornhill and Giles Hussey to whom Richardson was briefly tutor. Thornhill lived only 6 miles from the Hussey home at Marnhull.

3 A letter read to the Society of Antiquaries in London in 1734 by Sir John Evelyn stated '*one Hussey, a Dorsetshire Gentleman was the Most Celebrated Master in Drawing'*.

4 These portraits became iconic images of the exiled leader for British Jacobite supporters. Hussey's final portrait in black lead and a grey wash was made in 1746 before Charles Edward Stuart escaped back to France from Scotland.

5 Smithson was a first-generation Anglican with close Catholic family connections. Hussey's paintings *Bacchus* and an *Ariadne* are still at Syon House. A self-portrait by Hussey wearing a fur-lined blue coat, turban and holding a sketchbook (Courtauld Photographic Survey) also exists. Hussey apparently burnt many of his other works, and some are only known through engravings and mezzotints.

6 Hussey was listed as an honorary member. His name appears in the Minutes for November 1745 when his membership was proposed and later accepted, though by 1747 his name is omitted. I am indebted to Dr. Michael Honeyborne for this information.

7 During which time his mother and several siblings died.

8 History painter and fellow Catholic, James Barry was commissioned to paint six vast murals on the theme of the 'Progress of Human Knowledge and Culture' for the Society of Arts in 1774. Barry assembled 125 identifiable portraits of men and women who he believed had contributed to the progress of civilization. A portrait of Hussey in artist's smock and cap, features in the final mural *Elysium and Tartarus* or *The State of the Final Retribution,* amidst seven painters from the 16th-18th centuries including van Dyck, Rubens and Reynolds; a public, though highly biased endorsement of Hussey.

9 Whitley, 1928, I, pp. 125–129.

10 Amongst Lady Arundell's cabinet rarities were a number of Hussey's pencil sketches and drawings, one of which was a self-portrait coloured with a thin water-colour wash.

11 See *18th and 19th Century British Drawings and Watercolours,* 12 March 1987, Sotheby's, property of the Trustees of Lord Clifford of Chudleigh, from Ugbrooke Park, Devon. The drawings forming the Weld portfolio were uniform sizes, either 17.8×15cm or 30.5×22.9cm.

12 Hutchins, ed. 3, 4, p. 310.

13 Hutchins, ed. 2, 4, pp. 154–160; ed. 3, 4, pp. 307–314.

14 *Centaur ridden by putto*, red chalk sold by Lord Clifford, Sotheby's 1987.

15 Giles Hussey, 1774, *S. W. View of Lulworth Castle taken from the Grove*. A copy of the print was in George III's Topographical Collection, now in the British Library.

16 Lord Petre's portrait by Hussey was in the Weld portfolio. His daughter married Edward Weld, brother of Thomas, in 1763.

59. **Giles Hussey** (1710–1788)

Mary Weld (1753–1823)
pencil on paper, 1770s
27.5×44 cm
Inscribed on mount *Miss Weld (poor Clare)*

Provenance: Thomas Weld by descent to his son Cardinal Thomas Weld and thence to Lord Clifford of Chudleigh, Ugbrooke Park; Sale Sotheby's 18 & 19th Century British Drawings and Watercolours, 12 March 1987, lot 6.

60. **Giles Hussey** (1710–1788)

Sister Euphrasia, a Poor Clare (Mary Weld, 1753–1823)
pencil on paper, 1770s
27.5×44 cm

Provenance: Thomas Weld by descent to his son Cardinal Thomas Weld and thence to Lord Clifford of Chudleigh, Ugbrooke Park, (no 164); Sale Sotheby's 18 & 19th Century British Drawings and Watercolours, 12 March 1987, lot 6.
Literature: *A Portrait of Giles Hussey 1709–1788*, Jonathan Shackleton, 1999, Privately printed.

Private Collection

Two highly contrasting images of Thomas Weld's sister Mary, by Giles Hussey. Hussey made a series of portrait drawings of Thomas Weld and his family and associates. The portraits, all ovals, reveal that Hussey, a neighbour, was a regular visitor to Lulworth.[1] Weld kept them in a portfolio where they were a feature for visitors to view, a self-portrait of Hussey was included. Thomas Rackett's (cat. 43) friend Dr William Maton recorded visiting Lulworth to look at Hussey's drawings, noting the Pythagorian concept that every face was in harmony with itself.[2] Once Hussey had achieved a likeness he then adapted it to comply with his belief that the face represented an octave and adjusted the likeness to fit this.

Mary was the youngest of the five children of Edward and Mary-Teresa Weld of Lulworth and sister of Thomas Weld (cat. 31). She often travelled to the Continent, staying with the Catholic community and seeing her older siblings studying there; her oldest brother Edward was educated abroad and was in Rome in 1761. Mary was in Bruges in 1765–1768, in Douai in 1769–70 and at an English Catholic community, Britwell, in 1774; so from a young age Mary had a strong sense of vocation. Hussey (cat. 59) shows Mary in profile, facing left and looking ahead. Her hair is curled and pinned but the drawing is free of any adornments or jewels.

At twenty-four, in 1777 Mary became a nun of the Bridgettine Order, known as the Poor Clares, at Aire,

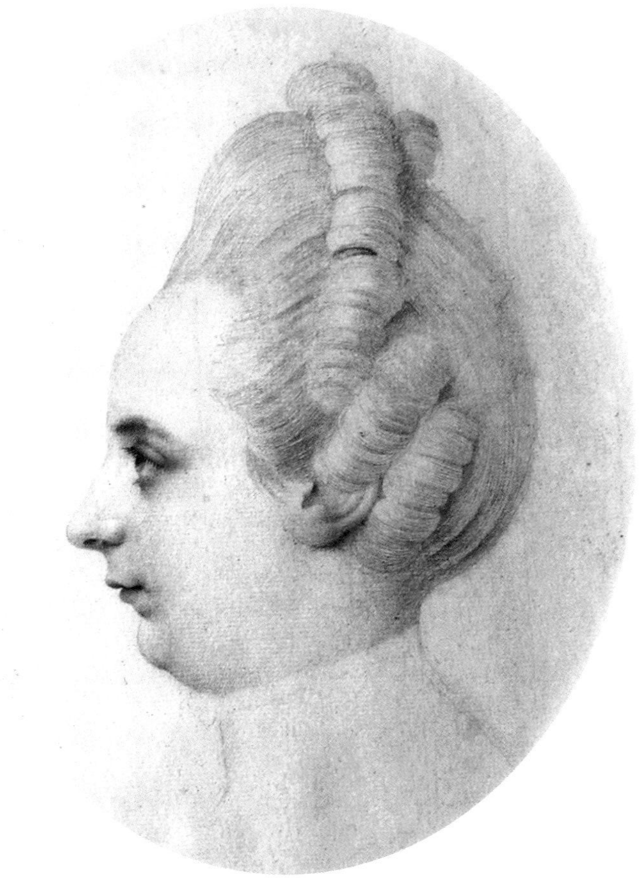

59.

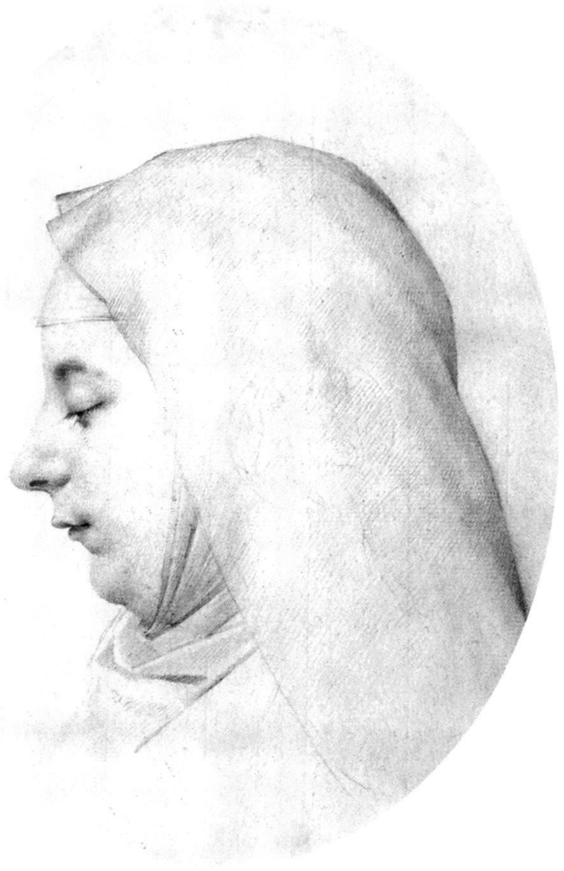

60.

Artois, where she was known as Sister Euphrasia.[3] Her daily life became one of penance, contemplation, work and prayer. Hussey's sensitive drawing of Mary as Sister Euphrasia is in marked contrast to the earlier drawing (cat. 59). Hussey's definition of 'an idea of divine perfection' due to a virtuous mind is implied by her downcast expression and confining nun's headdress.[4] There is another version in the British Museum. Sister Euphrasia died a nun at Clare House near Plymouth Dockyard.

1 Hussey also visited the Arundells of Wardour Castle.
2 *Observations Relative Chiefly to the Natural History, Picturesque Scenery, and Antiquities of the Western Counties of England, Made in the Years 1794 and 1796,* Dr William George Maton, Salisbury, 1797, 1, pp. 35–42.
3 The Poor Clares were established in 1629 as an offshoot of the convent at Gravelines. They comprised several orders of nuns in the Catholic Church and were the second Franciscan order to be established. Founded by Saints Clare of Assisi and Francis of Assisi on Palm Sunday in the year 1212.
4 Whitley, 1928, p. 128, letter from Giles Hussey to seal cutter, Wray, 1756.

61. **Attr. Robert Byng** (fl.1697–1720)

Harry Good, Deer Catcher
oil on canvas, early 18th century
73.5×60.5 cm

Provenance: The Reverend H. Good, 1869; The Hon. Clive Lawrence; Viscountess Hailsham; Sotheby's *British Paintings 1500–1850,* 11 July 1990 lot 117
Engraved: Charles Reuben Ryley, 1782
Literature; Hutchins, 3rd ed., 3, p. 411.

Private Collection

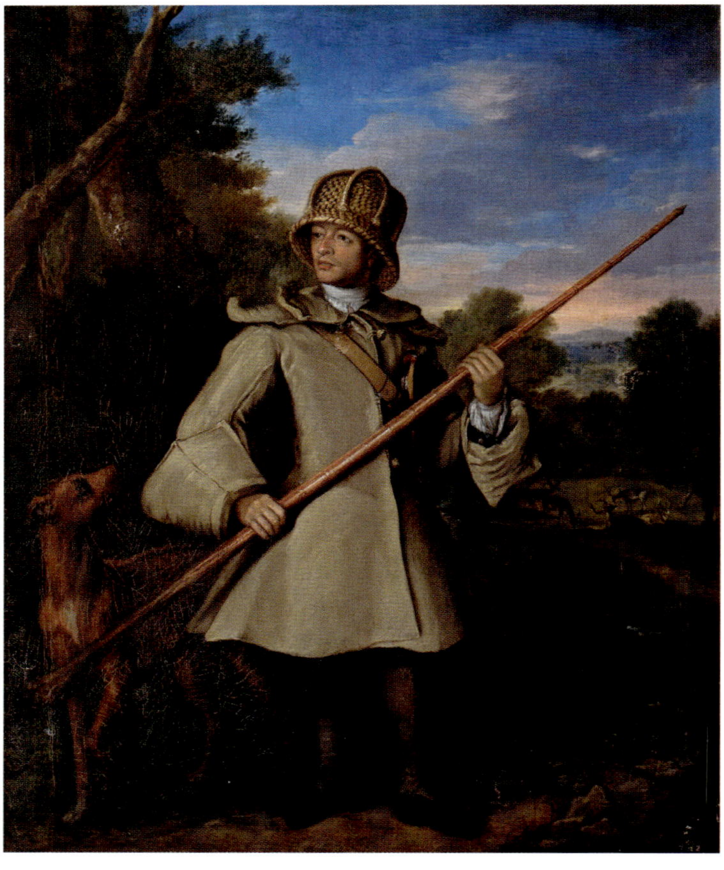

For centuries the economy of Cranborne Chase was based on hunting deer and trading venison. During the Earl of Shaftesbury's tenure of the Chase, from 1671, relations between landowners and tenants were amicable. From about 1700 there was a vogue for deer hunting, which ceased by 1736 when they began to be seen more as deer stealers. The best known was Harry Good of Bower Chalke, Wiltshire who led the hunts, with between four and twenty hunters. They gathered in the evening with their dogs who drove the deer into nets; once entangled the deer were then strangled. Increasingly the emphasis was on the sport, which became progressively more violent and attracted rougher participants, often from the same families. By 1730 the hunting had turned to poaching, leading to ugly incidents between keepers and the deer-stealers as the century progressed.[1] At the time of Byng's portrait deer-hunting on the Chase was practised by 'substantial gentlemen' in the neighbourhood.[2] In this small-scale full-length portrait the canvas has been damaged and subject to substantial restoration, but is certainly the painting engraved by C.R. Ryley in 1782 and formed the frontispiece of William Chafin's *Anecdotes and History of Cranbourn Chase,* London, 1818.[3] Good is shown wearing the distinctive deer hat known as a cap, made of straw and lined with wool for protection against antlers. The coat, known as a jack, was made of quilted canvas. Good carries a quarter-staff pike and small iron bars. Increasingly guns and pistols were used, together with a flail-like weapon called a swingel. The deer catcher is shown standing in a clearing in the woods with Cranborne Chase unfolding on the right. He is accompanied by his hound on the left, with deer visible in the distance. Little other work is known by the artist, who was both a portrait and sporting painter. He worked with his brother Edward, chief assistant to Godfrey Kneller. An important series of drawings survive in the British Museum by Edward and Robert Byng. The portrait may have been commissioned by one of the great landowning families of the Chase.

1 The second half of the century was marked by a controversy between Lord Rivers and a group of landed gentry, including the Earl of Shaftesbury, (cat. 21) and Lord Arundell of Wardour, known as the Proprietors. They sought the disfranchisement of the chase on moral grounds, claiming the chase was conducive to poaching, stealing, and smuggling, leading to idleness and profligacy of the rural population.
2 Hutchins, ed.3, 3, p. 411.
3 The Deer Catcher was turned into two different engravings later in the century. The first was an etching by C.R. Ryley, 1782; the second, unsigned, formed the frontispiece of William Chafin's *Anecdotes and History of Cranbourn Chase,* London, 1818. Chafin claimed this was after a drawing by Byng.

62. **William Hogarth** (1697–1764)

Thomas Coombes, aged 108
oil on canvas, 1742
58×51.7 cm
Inscribed: *'Dorsetshire aged 108'*[1]

Provenance: In Mrs Hogarth's collection 1781–1785; Earl of Charlemont by 1867; Henry White and then by descent to S.F. White, sold Christie's (19 January 1901, lot. 24, as *Portrait of Old Coombes, the boatman at the age of 108*), bought F.M. Nichols and thence by descent to present owner.
Literature: J. Nichols, *Biographical anecdotes of William Hogarth and a catalogue of his works chronologically arranged with occasional remarks* London, 1781, p. 59; 1782, p. 88; 1785, p. 98; J. Nichols & J. Steevens, The Genuine Works of William Hogarth, I, 1808, p. 396; III, 1817, p. 177; Nichols 1833, p. 385; A. Dobson, *Hogarth* London, 1907, p. 209; R. Beckett, *Hogarth,* London, 1949, p. 49; G. Baldini, G. Mandel, Gabriele *L'opera completa di Hogarth pittore* Milan, 1967, p. 106, cat. 141.
Exhibited: British Institution 1867, 145; Dublin Exhibition of Arts, Industries, Manufactures and Loans Museum, 1872, 224; Whitechapel 1906, Upper Gallery, 77.

Private Collection

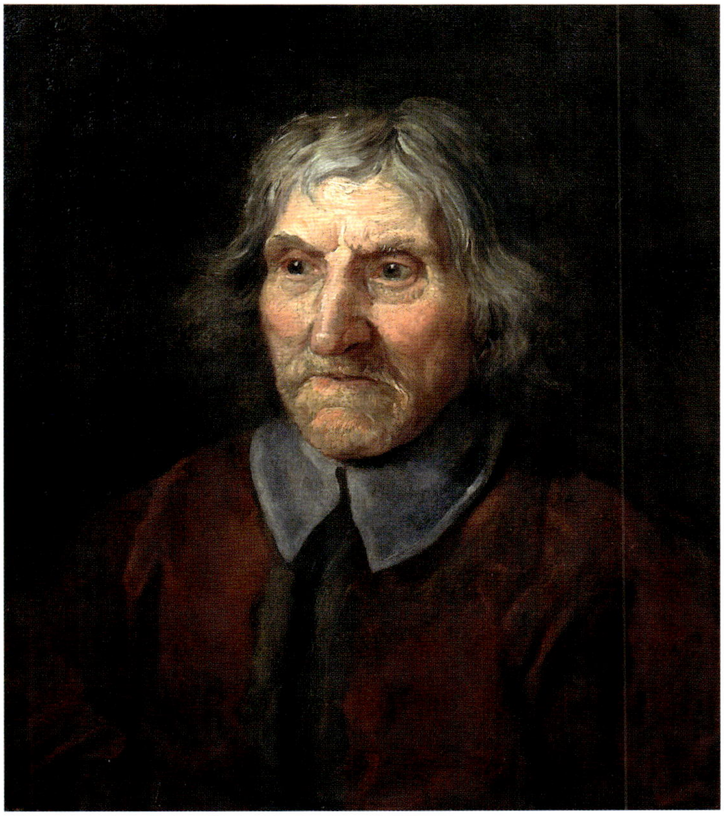

William Hogarth's portrait of Thomas Coombes was probably painted during a visit to his wife Jane's family home Thornhill House, near Stalbridge. Jane Hogarth was Sir James Thornhill's (cat. 56) daughter and despite initial opposition to the union, Thornhill and Hogarth became close, Hogarth presumably visiting his father-in-law and subsequently also his brother-in-law, John Thornhill, in Dorset.

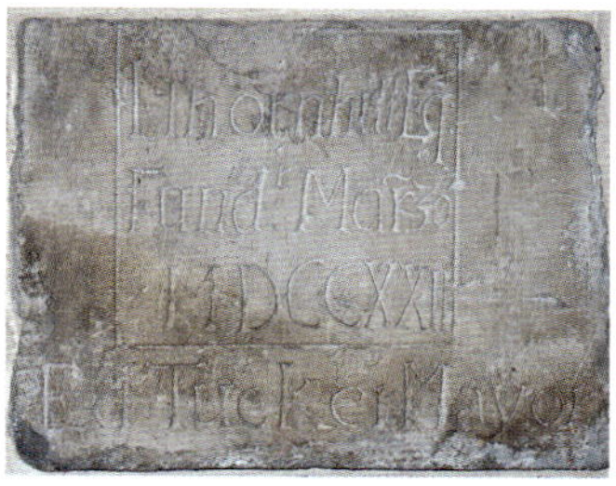

Fig. 51. *Fragment of Almshouse Wall, Weymouth*, Inscribed 'Thornhill Esq. Fundr. Mar 30 MDCCXXII. Ed. Tucker Mayor.

Hogarth's compelling portrait shows Thomas Coombes as a very old man. His eyes are rheumy grey-green, his pursed mouth firmly closed to indicate he is toothless. The strong weathered face, particularly the forehead and chin, has been painted in bold impasto in contrast with the thinner, smoother execution of the clothes. An inscription on an associated drawing made in the Hogarth household in 1782 by Richard Livesay provides the only clue to Coombes's identity. Despite extensive research nothing else is known about the sitter; Coombes being a common Dorset name.[2] He may have been a retired mariner who became an inmate of the almshouse for 'decayed seamen', built by Sir James Thornhill in Melcombe Regis (fig. 51).[3] Elizabeth Einberg has suggested that eighteenth-century interest in centenarians led Hogarth to regard Coombes as not only a suitable painterly subject and an interesting local character, but one with attendant potential for making money through a popular print from the portrait.[4] Perhaps Coombes's age made him a local celebrity, though he does not feature in Hutchins's *History*.[5] He may have been a boatman working on an inland river like the Stour, which ran very close to the Thornhill estate. Working nearby he would have been known to the Thornhill family and may have worked for them.[6] Other boatmen working across Dorset included the licensed boatman on Chesil Beach.

The painting originally showed Coombes wearing a plain drab coat with buttons down the front and white necktie, consistent with his status. Later Hogarth altered the portrait to show him as a seventeenth-century Parliamentarian in a russet coat with fur trim and turned-down white collar. Elizabeth Einberg suggests this may have been in homage to the great pride his wife's family took in its distinguished service on the Parliamentarian side defending Weymouth during the Commonwealth. Hogarth also removed an initial false oval together with its inscription.[7]

The portrait was first recorded by John Nichols as in Mrs Hogarth's possession in 1781, as 'Thomas Coombes of Dorsetshire aged 105', corrected to 108 in subsequent editions, although it was not included in the 1790 sale of her collection.[8]

This catalogue entry is indebted to Elizabeth Einberg and based on the draft for her forthcoming catalogue raisonné, *William Hogarth. Catalogue of Paintings.*

1 'There are remains of an inscription, painted in black cursive lettering, on the upper rim of the original false oval, later overpainted, probably by the artist himself, no longer legible, but concordant with the title.'
2 In 1782 the engraver and painter Richard Livesay, lodged in Mrs Hogarth's house in Leicester Square and made accurate drawings of several pictures in her collection, including Thomas Coombs. Signed R.L. Delin.t 1782.' The inscription on the drawing 'M.r Tho.s Coombes of Dorsetshire/Aged 108/Hogarth Pinx.t 1742', (Burghley House).
3 Samuel Lewis, *Topographical Dictionary of England*, London, 1831, p. 442. Having no endowment, the almshouse did not survive the century.
4 Certainly Thornhill and Hogarth had collaborated on portraits of unconventional individuals. Elizabeth Einberg suggests Hogarth did not pursue making a print from the portrait because the age of the sitter may not have been provable.
5 No mention of Coombes's age has been found in contemporary local or national newspapers. A 'Thomas Combs' was buried without comment on 20 January 1744 in St Mary's Melcombe Regis, Dorset.
6 Bought by Mrs Hogarth's father, Sir James Thornhill, it remained in family possession until sold by Thornhill's grandson in 1774. In 1742 her son John Thornhill mainly lived there, though it was still owned by the widowed Lady Thornhill (d. 1757) who lived mostly with the Hogarths. John Thornhill and Hogarth were on very good terms.
7 Suggested by the remnants, now illegible, of an explanatory inscription, later painted out, along the upper rim of the original false oval, visible during cleaning and restoration in 2008, by Hamish Dewar, London.
8 John Nichols was an important publisher who published Hutchins's *History*, *Literary Anecdotes*, the *Gentleman's Magazine* and Hogarth's first biography, *Biographical Anecdotes of William Hogarth*, London, 1785.

63. **Mary Frampton** (1773–1846)

Phillis Frampton (1736–1829)
Silhouette paper cut-out, undated
10.5×9 cm
Provenance: sitter, then by descent.

Private Collection

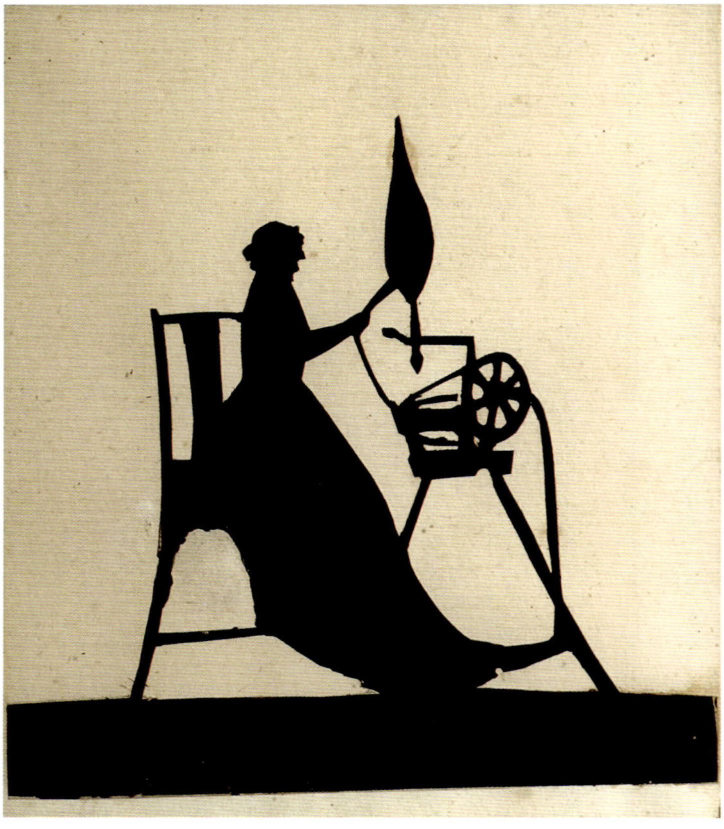

Phillis Frampton was the mother of James and Mary (cats. 65, 66), from her second marriage to James Frampton senior (1711–1784).[1] She is shown at her spinning wheel in this cut-out made by her daughter Mary, amply demonstrating how gentry women occupied their time – by spinning, creating cut-outs and drawing together. According to Mary Frampton's diary, Phillis Frampton was thrown into confusion at her Moreton home whilst sewing with Mrs Drax in 1799, when King George III appeared at the garden gate, followed by four princesses and household.[2] She was required to feed the large gathering with no notice.[3] After the regal visit the family were invited to Weymouth to attend the theatre with the royal party. Thereafter the Framptons kept a plan of the table layout, should the king ever call unexpectedly again, with cold meats, fruit and bread arranged in a symmetrical pattern on the 'long table' (fig. 51a). Phillis Frampton was kind to Mrs Fitzherbert after her widowhood from Edward Weld.

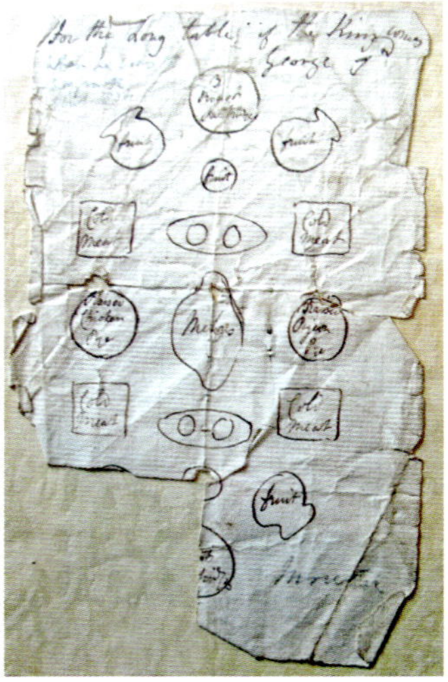

Fig. 51a. *Moreton House Plan For the Long Table if the King Comes*, Phillis Frampton, c. 1799.

1 Her first husband was Dr. Wollaston, physician to King George III. He was elected a Fellow of the Royal Society in 1756 and allegedly died from poisoning after opening a mummy. Their son, Charlton Byam Wollaston, was Recorder for Dorchester. Mrs Frampton was the daughter of Edward Byam, Lt. Gov. of Antigua.
2 Sarah Frances was married to Richard Grosvenor in 1788 who took the name Drax. One of the original officers of the Dorset Yeomanry Rangers, he sat to Thomas Beach in 1795.
3 See Frampton, pp. 106–108 for a lively account by Phillis Frampton in a letter to her sister-in-law Mrs Heberden at Windsor, 12 September 1799.

64. **Mary Frampton** (1773–1846)

Lady Harriot Frampton (1778–1845)
Silhouette, paper cut-out, 1810
10×7.5 cm
Provenance: sitter, then by descent

Private Collection

Lady Harriot Fox-Strangways, daughter of the 2nd Earl of Ilchester (cat. 15), was educated at a boarding school in Weymouth in 1787 in the hopes that the sea would help a congenital knee condition.[1] She

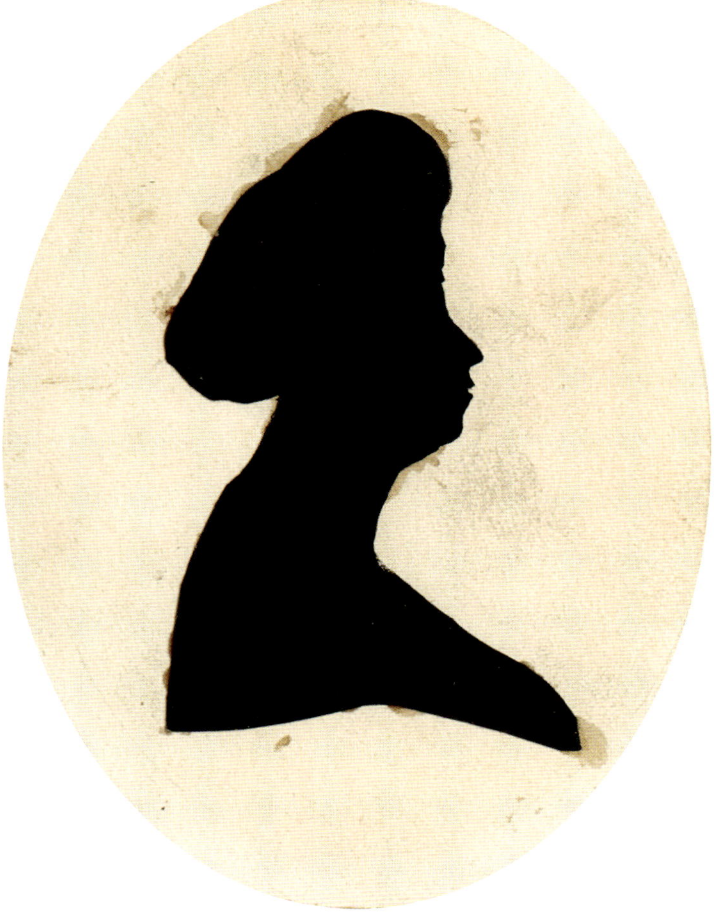

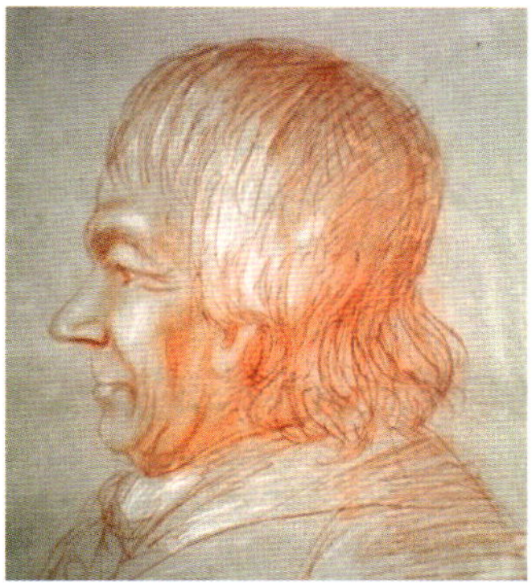

Fig. 52. *Joseph Brownjohn, Gardener at Moreton*, Mary Frampton, red and white chalk, 1789. Private Collection.

The Gamekeeper was given a house, garden and three fields. All the men except the butler and gardener, Joseph Brownjohn (fig. 52), had liveries.[2] From the age of sixteen Mary Frampton was recording family, friends and members of the Moreton household, such as Brownjohn, in head and shoulder sketches.

1 J. Martin, *Wives and Daughters. Women and Children in the Georgian Country House*, London, 2004, p. 202.

2 Private family papers..

65. **John Miers** (1756–1821)
James Frampton (1769–1855)
silhouette painted on plaster, c. 1793
18.9×15.5 cm

66. **John Miers** (1756–1821)
Mary Frampton (1773–1846)
silhouette painted on plaster in oval, 1793
16×15 cm
Miers Trade Label 11[1]
one of 2 versions.

Private Collection

married James Frampton junior (cats. 29,65) in 1799 at her family home Melbury. Her fortune on the day of her marriage was three thousand pounds, just under £100,000 today. Her father stayed with the couple at Moreton and at his death nine years later she was left an annuity of £300 per annum, or £9,600 today, which just covered the wages of their staff. Their establishment at Moreton in 1800 consisted of:

Yearly Wages

Staff	£.	s.	d
Housekeeper and Lady's maid	20	0	0
Cook	21	0	0
Upper Housemaid	7	7	0
Under Housemaid	7	7	0
Laundry maid	7	7	0
Kitchen maid	6	6	0
Butler and valet	42	0	0
Footman	12	12	0
Groom	16	16	0
Gardener	30	0	0
Gamekeeper and assistant	30	0	0
Steward	25	0	0

James and Mary Frampton were the children of James Frampton senior and Phillis (formerly Wollaston née Byam). The Frampton family rented houses in Hill Street and Clarges Street for two to three months for the season, once every two years. On their final visit they rented the house of the bluestocking, author and literary hostess Elizabeth Montagu. Mary Frampton recalls seeing the Gordon Riots in 1780.

The silhouettes were produced after James Frampton returned from France in 1791. There he witnessed at first hand the riots and violence of the French Revolution, recording seeing the French royal family at Versailles and at the First Assembly. James was a founder member of the Dorset Volunteer Rangers (cat. 29) involved in Dorset's defensive preparations against the threat of invasion by Napoleon.

Mary was a diarist, and friend of Princess Elizabeth, third daughter of George III. Like the princess, Mary

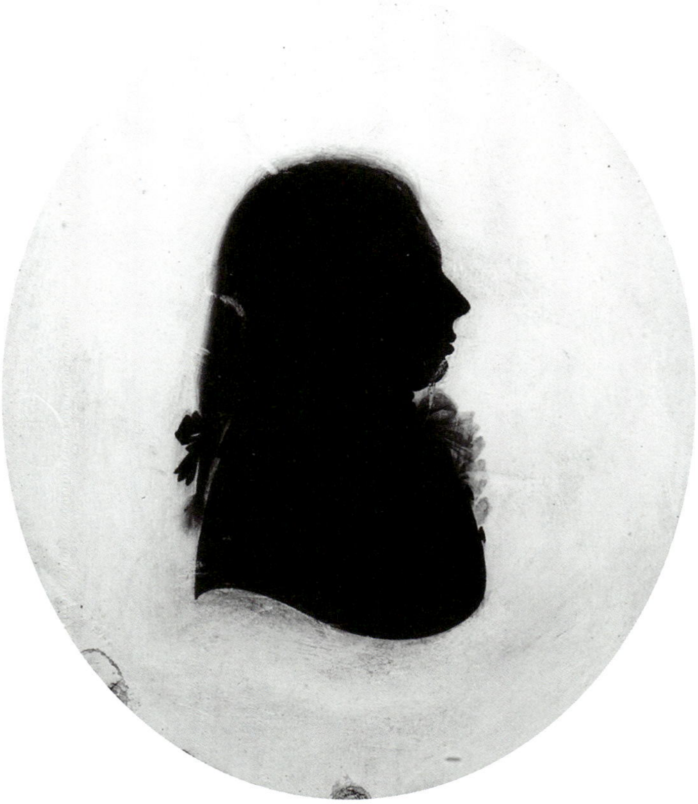

65.

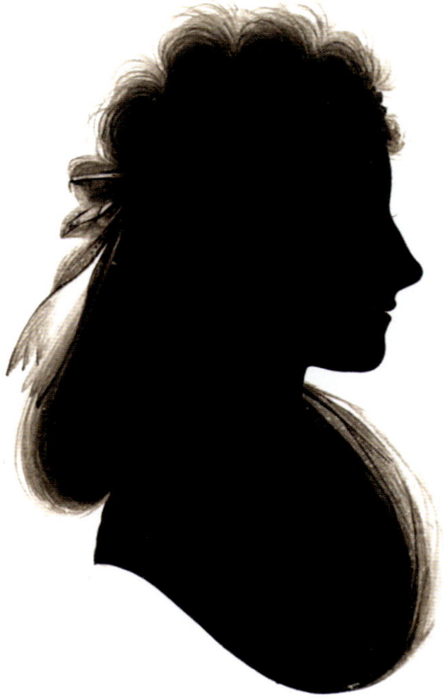

66.

produced cut-outs and also botanical paintings of some distinction, placing her amongst other talented amateurs like Mary Delany. She knew the Pulteneys (cat. 54) in Blandford, and perhaps through them was inspired to record and illustrate the plants of Dorset, later mounted in four large volumes. Of her royal acquaintance Mary wrote, 'The Weymouth visits made me to a certain degree, familiar with the good, the excellent George III, his Queen, and most of the Princesses, but not in their *first* visits there'. The Framptons were probably welcomed at court once James Frampton had married Lady Harriot Fox-Strangways, (cat. 64) the third daughter of the Earl of Ilchester (cat. 15).[2]

The silhouettes were made in London at Miers's fashionable studio in the Strand. Born in Leeds, Miers ran a silhouette business in Edinburgh and the north of England before setting up in the Strand in about 1788. Probably the most famous silhouettist of the day, his successful operation consisted of three-minute sittings to produce silhouettes on ivory or plaster. John Field (1771–1848) was the main artist working for him from perhaps as early as 1791, and it is likely the Framptons sat to him at 111, The Strand.

1 S. McKechnie, *British Silhouette Artists and Their Work 1760–1860*, London, 1978.
2 Frampton, 1885, p. 27.

67. **Princess Elizabeth** (1770–1840)

5 cut paper, stained matt black silhouettes, c. 1800–09
l to r: Winged cherub, 3.6×2 cm; Child with stick and ball, 3.5×2 cm; Seated woman reading and standing child, 3.3×4.5 cm; Baby waving rattle, 2.5×3.2 cm; Winged cherub with torch, 3.4×1.2 cm.

Provenance: artist to Mary Frampton and by descent.
Literature: J. Roberts, *Royal Artists From Mary Queen of Scots to the Present Day*, London, 1987; *George III & Queen Charlotte: Patronage, Collecting and Court Taste*, ed. J. Roberts, London, 2004.

Private Collection

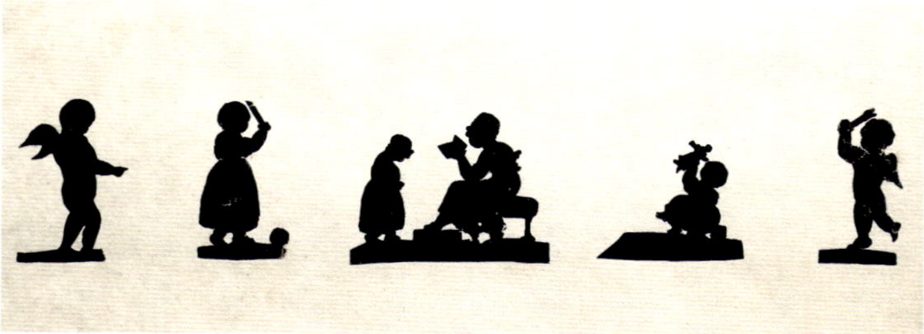

This group of silhouettes consisting of cupids and children, and similar in subject to her work in the Royal Collection, was presented by Princess Elizabeth (the King's third daughter) to Mary Frampton. The two women probably struck up a friendship after the marriage in 1799 of Mary's brother James to the aristocrat Harriot Fox-Strangways (cat. 64) and thereafter corresponded and exchanged news, Princess Elizabeth signed letters to Mary Frampton, 'Yours affectionately'.[1]

From the age of ten Princess Elizabeth joined her sister, the Princess Royal, in making cut-outs. It has been suggested they were shown paper-cutting techniques by Mrs Mary Delany, an associate of Dorset botanist Richard Pulteney (cat. 54). After her death they may have turned to royal family physician James Lind, and another of Pulteney's associates Tiberius Cavallo (cat. 55) since both collaborated on the production of portrait silhouettes at Windsor.

The Princesses' silhouettes were intended for use in domestic decoration, on blotters, fire-screens and friezes. The highly prolific Princess Elizabeth also gave Sarah Sophia Banks, sister of Sir Joseph Banks, twenty-six cut-outs in 1808.

In 1795 a series of Princess Elizabeth's silhouettes of winged cherubs showing *The Birth and Triumph of Cupid* were engraved by P. W. Tomkins and published as a series. The 26 plates were reissued in 1796, 1822 and 1823 and several of the designs also featured on a Berlin porcelain tea service.

In his portrait of Princess Elizabeth (fig. 53) commissioned by George III, Henry Edridge shows her holding a pair of scissors in one hand and a piece of paper in another: she was evidently making cut-out silhouettes. The artist has set his drawing at Frogmore House in the Home Park at Windsor, where Queen Charlotte and the Princesses spent their days, reading and drawing.

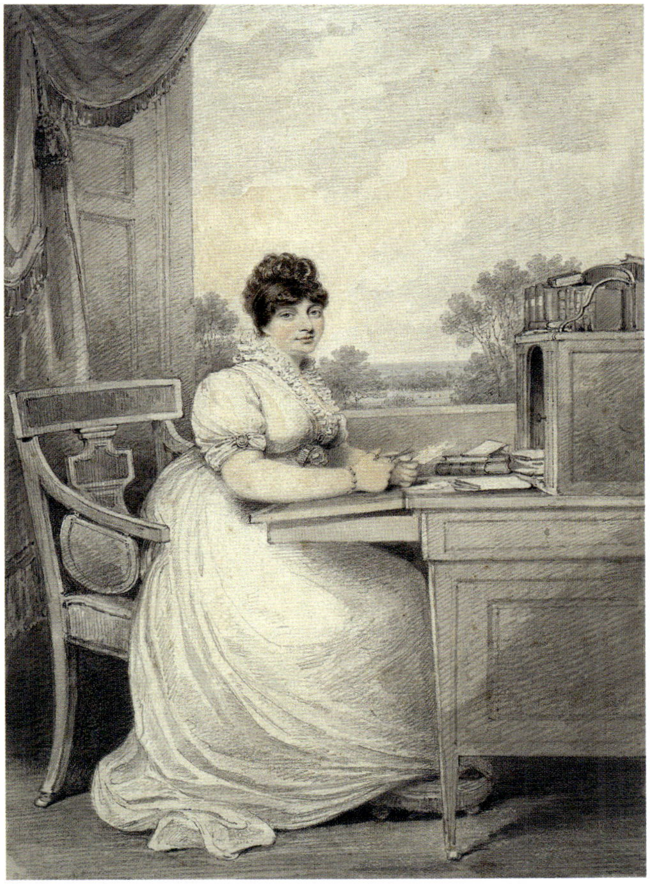

Fig. 53. *Princess Elizabeth*, pencil and grey wash, Henry Edridge, 1804.

1 Frampton, 1885, p. 138.

Picture Credits

Every effort has been made to contact copyright holders: any omissions are inadvertent, and will be corrected in future editions if notification is given in writing. We are grateful to the owners and lenders to the exhibition and the following copyright holders who have kindly agreed to make their images available for this book.

Images reproduced by kind permission of:

fig. 48, Blandford Museum; cats. 51, 52, Blandford Town Council; figs. 19, 28, 49, © Trustees of the British Museum; cats. 20, 21, 36, 38, 39, 41, 42, 43, 45, 46; figs. 1, 2, 3, 8, 10, 11, 12, 13, 14, 15, 16, 22, 24, 26, 27, 29, 30, 32, 34, 35, 40, 41, 42, 43, 46, 50, 51 & inside cover, © DNH&AS; cat. 18. © The Holburne Museum; cat. 27, The Keep Military Museum; Dorchester; cats. 53, 54; fig. 39, By permission of the Linnean Society of London; cat. 37, Long Bredy Parochial Church Council; cats. 1, 55, 56, © National Portrait Gallery, London; cat. 25, © NTPL/Christopher Hurst, National Trust, Kingston Lacy, Dorset; cats. 44, 47, 48, 49, 50, Poole Museum Service; cats. 2, 3, 8, 10, 11, 15, 16, 17, 19, 22, 23, 24, 26, 28, 29, 31, 32, 33, 34, 35, 40, 57, 58, 59, 60, 61, 62, 63, 64, 65, 66, 67; figs. 4, 5, 6, 7, 9, 20, 31, 33, 36, 37, 38, 51a, 52, private collections; fig. 25, The Royal Collection © 2010, Her Majesty Queen Elizabeth II; fig. 53, The Royal Collection © 2008 Her Majesty Queen Elizabeth II; cat. 30, Russell-Cotes Art Gallery and Museum; cats. 4, 5, 6, 7, 9, 12, 13, 14, Sherborne Castle; fig. 44, © R.I. Vane-Wright & H.W.D. Hughes; fig. 45, Photo © Victoria and Albert Museum, London; figs. 43a, 47, Wellcome Library, London; figs. 17, 18, 21, 23, Weymouth Museum.

Index

Bold denotes catalogue entry